MANOPOLY!?

The Persian Affair

JAMES PHILLIP "PHIL" JONES

Best wishes!

[signature]

PJS Publishing

Names: Jones, James Phillip, 1956- author.
Title: Manopoly!? : the Persian affair / James Phillip "Phil" Jones.
Other titles: Persian affair.
Description: Jefferson City, MO : PJS Publishing, [2020]
Identifiers: ISBN: 978-1-7349288-0-8 (print) | 978-1-7349288-1-5 (ebook) | 978-1-7349288-2-2 (audio) | LCCN: 2020908067
Subjects: LCSH: Economic forecasting--Fiction. | Econometric models--Fiction. | Business intelligence--Fiction. | Espionage--Fiction. | Targeted killing--Fiction. | Technological innovations--Fiction. | United States--Politics and government--Fiction. | Middle East--Politics and government --Fiction. | Iran--Politics and government--Fiction. | Self-actualization (Psychology)--Fiction. | GSAFD: Suspense fiction. | LCGFT: Political fiction. | Thrillers (Fiction) | Romance fiction.
Classification: LCC: PS3610.O62564 2020 | DDC: 813/.6--dc23

Print ISBN: 978-1-7349288-0-8

Digital ISBN: 978-1-7349288-1-5

Library of Congress Control Number: 2020908067

Cover Design: Kyle Caraway

Edited by: Roger W. Hatfield, Ph.D.

In memoriam:
Remembering: Jeremy Phillip Jones (1978-2017)
My son.

To my wife: Donna Gail

My children:
Crista Elizabeth Beckhaus & Kurt Beckhaus
Jared Phillip Jones & Ashley Jones

My grandchildren:
Jane Elizabeth, Claire, Graham, Elizabeth Grace, Thomas Frederick,
Jobey Ryan, Corbin James, Wyld, Matthew, Seth, Pierce, & Baby
Merritt

And to my best buddies:
Cam & Jan Lupkey

The kids and faculty of Calvary Lutheran High School

Chapter 1

January 8, 2020

A tall, handsome Persian man wearing a thick, jet-black beard, was seen getting out of a taxi in front of the Imam Khomeini International Airport, Tehran, Iran. He hopped out, looked down at his watch, and sprinted to catch his outbound flight. With only a small carry-on suitcase, he stopped at the Ukraine International Air terminal, had his bag X-rayed, and got his boarding pass. Since he was booked on an international flight, he also had to go through a customs checkpoint. He was directed to take off his jacket and his cotton, button-up, collared shirt. He was patted down, emptied his pockets into a plastic bin, and walked through a metal detector. The old metal detector was about three feet deep, and it honked like an electric goose as he walked through. He wondered what the noises meant but was pleased when they waved him through. He removed his sunglasses from his pocket, put them on, and walked on through the process.

For some strange reason, his bag was selected to be inspected. The man appeared to have an idiosyncratic twitch that was visible while he watched the inspector dump his suitcase. Lying on the table was his twisted pair of slacks, a wadded-up shirt, a couple of pairs of boxers, and three pairs of socks. He was a bit embarrassed when he saw his worn-down toothbrush lying there on the table. It was apparent that he was a light and frequent traveler.

An Iranian Revolutionary Guard Corps soldier stood next to the table with a bomb-sniffing dog, wearing a digital desert camouflage pattern uniform of tan and brown. Hanging on his shoulder was an Iranian-made KL-7.62 assault rifle. The outfit was topped off with a black beret, indicating he was a member of the elite Quds Force. He was an old hand at operating in high-pressure situations and hadn't even broken a sweat during his screening. Putting his shirt back on, he then replaced the items from his pockets. He walked to the counter, validated his boarding pass, and walked into the waiting area. He sat down, finally waiting to board.

The man looked around, making observations about anything that appeared out of place. He was anxious and was ready to be on his way out of Iran. His flight arrived. He watched it taxi to the jetway, its door opening, and passengers deplaning. The flight attendant followed the last passenger and was pushing a cart with trash and debris from the plane. The cart was exchanged with a cart containing soft drinks, bottled water, and juice for the outgoing international flight. After about a fifteen-minute wait for the return of the attendants with a new supply of beverages, the overhead speaker announced, *"Passengers for Ukraine International Airlines Flight 752 may board at this time."* The announcement sounded oddly different in Persian. He boarded the flight and began the first leg of his journey home. The flight was exactly on schedule.

As he waited, he mused about how funny life worked. One minute you were on top of the world, the very next, you found yourself struggling to get out of a rut and back home. It seemed you never knew what came next. Would you be the hero tomorrow, or the villain? It seemed to be the way life was designed. Airline waiting areas were very well known for random thoughts and reflection. This trip was no exception.

He was seated next to the window in aisle seventeen on the left side of the plane. He was relieved to be leaving Tehran, but he seemed to be a bit on edge. Was the man across the aisle looking at him too closely? Did that second look by the attendant mean anything, or was it all in his imagination? The plane began to push back from the terminal as he heard the Rolls Royce engines of the Boeing 737 begin to whine. The plane, under its own power, crept to the designated runway for takeoff. The vibrations of the plane and the bouncing of the wheels had a soothing effect on the man. The flight lifted toward the end of the runway. Suddenly the tire noise stopped, and the plane banked to the east. The man loosened his tie and heaved a visible sigh of relief. He settled back and readied himself for a long flight. From his window seat, he looked out. At the same time, he saw the shrinking city below. Suddenly, he thought he saw a flash that caught his attention. Was it a reflection from the tip of the wing? He saw another; was it the sun peeking through the clouds?

Immediately, there was a much larger flash and a huge noise. The passengers were screaming very quickly. Then, there was total silence. Ukraine International Airlines Flight 752 exploded, with all 176 souls killed. It was the last thing he ever saw.

What had gone so terribly wrong?

Chapter 2

Present Day

In the White House, President Donald Trump was discussing a new tax cut to counteract the drag that Boeing's 737 MAX debacle had put on America's GPD. Most of his financial experts were telling him that Boeing's issues were negatively affecting GPD by a full fifty basis points. The first tax cut stimulated the economy, but the tax cut was not permanent. Trump needed a BIG win to assure re-election in the upcoming November elections after multiple failed impeachment attempts.

Additionally, the recent coronavirus pandemic (Covid-19) had driven the stock market down to levels not seen since 2008. Then, all three indices again experienced the largest percentage drops dating back to the Great Depression. In a handful of instances in March the markets were stopped automatically after selling off in excess of 10 percent of the aggregate market value. Most all of the American states had been forced to issue stay-at-home orders in response to the global pandemic. New York City had become the epicenter of the pandemic. Trump had mobilized the Department of Defense to help increase hospital capacity and was doing daily press conferences to update the American public. Businesses were closing due to fear of spreading the virus. Congress had passed numerous stimulus packages designed to keep the citizens afloat financially. The global medical and pharmaceutical industries had shifted into high gear to race toward a vaccine or remedy. It appeared that the world might be coming to an end.

Additionally, due to a Saudi and Russian oil price war, and fear caused by the coronavirus, gas prices fell. This was exacerbated by the cessation of consumer driving and the shutdown of the airline industry on a global scale. Trucks and railroads were the only transport being used to carry supplies to a hunkered down citizenry. The reduction in oil prices threatened to break the entire energy sector. The economy seemed to go from boom to near the brink in a matter of a couple of weeks. The global economy seemed to be slowing drastically as supply chains were collapsing due to industrial plant closures in China, continuing to ripple across Europe to America.

Medical equipment and supply shortages caused the president to invoke the Defense Production Act, thereby forcing entire manufacturing sectors to retool and begin manufacturing medical supplies. Surgical masks were no longer available, nor were hospital gowns. Rubber gloves were in short supply, and ventilators, required to keep the infected alive, were in short supply. The auto industry retooled to make ventilators and now America had shifted to a wartime footing.

The Federal Reserve was forced to add liquidity to the United States economy and reduced the funds rate to zero percent. There were also discussions in the financial sector regarding the viability of utilizing a negative funds rate. The discussion of negative rates was squelched due to negative experiences with the policy in Europe. Each week as businesses closed, unemployment surged. Between the month of

March and April over seven million workers suddenly became unemployed. The Federal Reserve received seven hundred and fifty billion dollars to create loan programs to keep business from failing. The IRS sent out stimulus checks to taxpayers to keep the economy from free falling. Something was desperately needed to help find the bottom, then to help re-inflate a once vibrant economy.

Locating the perfect type and amount of tax cut, aid, and stimulus package to propose to the House and Senate had never been as crucial. The president had a love/hate relationship with the Federal Reserve, as most presidents did, but this tax and aid bill had to be perfect. Trump was very keenly aware of what was at stake with this bill.

GDP had fallen from almost 3 percent to an anticipated rate of possibly negative 25 percent from the first quarter to the second. The president would have to be looking toward the brightest minds and the best thinkers to bring the best financial advice forward.

This is the story of how a brilliant think tank came into existence.

Chapter 3

2006

Jackson Reynolds's office at Northwestern University, Kellogg School of Business, Evanston, Illinois, was dimly lit by a couple of bankers' lamps. There was an eight-foot folding table centered under a hanging fluorescent light fixture. The ballast was humming annoyingly. On the table were several boxes of the classic family game made by Parker Brothers, Monopoly. Several boards were positioned all around the office. Monopoly money was scattered everywhere.

Jackson was sitting directly across from his economics teaching assistant, Brooke Benoit. Brooke was a striking, beautiful young lady. She had long blonde hair that looked like golden silk flowing over her shoulders, hitting her about halfway down her back. Her eyes were a very striking shade of brown that made it difficult even to see her pupils. Her makeup was classic yet understated and flawless. She was wearing a sharp business suit with a white blouse with a scooping turtleneck collar. Her business suit was a very rich brown and tan tweed with dark brown leather patches sewn over the elbows. She exuded confidence and intelligence.

Brooke appeared to be in her middle to late twenties. She had a hint of a southern accent that screamed generational wealth from the Deep South.

Jackson Reynolds was a striking figure of a man. Had he been a statue, he would have been an ancient Greek Olympian. He was a former college athlete, standing six-feet, six-inches tall. His hair was a sandy blonde. His eyes were hazel; a hazel that made you stop and look at the beauty in his sockets. The pupil was framed by a beautiful dark honey brown that suddenly turned to a striking green with brilliant flecks of color radiating from the center. His hair had a bit of a wave and was unbelievably thick and shiny. His shoulders appeared to be twice the width of his waist, although that seemed very unlikely. One would guess his weight to be two hundred twenty pounds; as we all know, his massive muscle mass would weigh more substantially than he looked. He was wearing a pair of tan-colored Dockers, a white Oxford shirt with a neatly buttoned-down collar, a deep red silk power tie, and a classic navy-blue blazer. He appeared to be in his late twenties to early thirties. His accent was nondescript, and he was very well-spoken and exuded confidence. In every way, he looked successful.

Brooke had a bachelor's degree in economics from Louisiana State University and had been working in the field of economics for some time. However, she desperately aspired to continue her education to at least an MBA. Her employer was an alumnus of Northwestern University and pulled some strings to get her an economics residency in the Kellogg School of Business at Northwestern.

Jackson was possibly one of the brightest economic minds in the country working in academia. An issue that he had struggled to overcome kept him from being at Harvard or another Ivy League college. He was the youngest Department Director at any university in the Midwest, and Brooke regarded having received the opportunity to work with him as a coup! Brooke and Jackson looked as though they had been born and bred to be married, have children, and rule the world together. In the seven months that they had worked together, their chemistry had almost ignited several times. One would be shocked if these two beautiful people did not end up together in a retirement home in fifty years.

Brooke had a brother, Beauregard Benoit, who was also an LSU alum, working in Manhattan among the power brokers of the world. Currently, Beau was an executive V.P. of a Manhattan CPA firm with very close affiliations to the Federal Reserve. He was in the thick of the machine that made and influenced fiscal policy in the United States and the democracies of Western civilization.

Jackson and Brooke were cleaning up the Pizza Hut box on the table. They began to discuss the status of the data that had been collected that day at a campus-wide Monopoly tournament they had organized. Potential graduate students in the School of Economics were the intended participants in the match. The competition had been designed to select the smartest and the best students for their new research project.

They were modifying a household game. It was being altered in a manner so that the components of the game captured true cause-and-effects on the outcome of the entire economy within each board. The components design had been changed from a game with pieces representing business transactions for fun to a set of tools used to collect and record situational economic data. The data was recorded electronically. As their research progressed, the components were also developing into programmable parts that calculated an infinite number of variables. When all of the operational games were wired together to collect a global snapshot of the data, minute details in any economy could be calculated with ever-increasing accuracy. Eventually, one could measure real-life economic policies in a real economy. Their goal thus far was to see if the components of the game could be adjusted to measure actual financial adjustments. Could they reap real, measurable, and repeatable data that could accurately predict outcomes from changes in policies and parameters?

It was a bold idea that harkened back to ideas that were explored in the 1975 book and film *Rollerball*. In *Rollerball*, each county had a rollerball team that played a roller derby like game. World wars and international disputes were decided by who won a sanctioned Rollerball match. The 1983 movie *War Games* was a movie that explored having a computer that seized control of the nuclear trigger and surrendered the power of atomic warfare to that computer. The WOPR (War Operation Plan Response) is hacked into by a young computer genius. He starts a game of "Global Thermonuclear War." He believed he was on a video game developer's computer. However, before the network launched the warheads, it learned from the childhood game Tic-Tac-Toe that the first strike was a no-win scenario.

These were the childhood movie favorites of Jackson as a boy. Jackson, who was now in college, had discovered a deep passion for economics and teaching. His Midwest family life might have appeared to be much like that in *Leave It to Beaver*. When Jackson was a child, very close family and friends from a nearby convent often played board games in the Reynolds' home. Monopoly was always his favorite, and he *always* won.

Jackson's ability to make fast decisions had served him well from kindergarten through post-graduate school. He was considered a phenom among his university peers. As an undergrad at the University of Arkansas in Fayetteville, attending on a full-ride baseball scholarship, Jackson was a key player during the NCAA Division 1 World Series Tournament. He also won the national batting title that year with a phenomenal .487 batting average. He was contacted by scouts from the St. Louis Cardinal organization and destined for a career in the Major Leagues. Tragically, during a random drug screening at the College World Series Game, he tested positive for performance-enhancing drugs. This event had branded him as a cheater. In return, he lost his last year of eligibility and any chance at a professional baseball contract.

Furthermore, his university scholarship at the University of Arkansas at Fayetteville was gone. They all considered him untouchable. So, despite his grades and incredible test results, Ivy League universities viewed him as a pariah. As a result, Jackson had to go to a less prominent grad school, so he ended up at Northwestern University in Evanston, Illinois.

Brooke Benoit grew up in a wealthy family in Baton Rouge, Louisiana, where she completed her high school career at the acclaimed Baton Rouge Magnet High School. She was also a legacy Gamma Phi Beta at Louisiana State University. She grew up in the affluent suburbs of Baton Rouge, and her momma was from ancient money—oil money from the Louisiana swamps. Their family home was an immaculate nineteenth-century plantation that sat in the middle of a twenty-four-hundred-acre, family-run crop farm and cattle ranch.

Beauregard Benoit was four years older than his sister Brooke. He had been an all-conference strong safety at LSU. After graduating summa cum laude at LSU and with his family connections, it was easy for him to get into grad school at Harvard. He completed his master's degree in Accounting and Finance in less than two years. He also sat for and passed his Certified Public Accountant exam within a month of graduating from Harvard. So, Wall Street loved the idea of getting a newly minted Harvard CPA from a family with pockets of depth to rival most "wealthy families." His rise on Wall Street was quick, moving to the Securities and Exchange Commission within five years, then to the Federal Reserve. These moves placed him in the ideal spot to launch Jackson's idea into place to be a global game-changer.

Chapter 4

2008

Jackson and Brooke were back on campus at Northwestern University. Jackson was now chair of his Department of Economics in the School of Business. Brooke had finished her MBA with an emphasis in Economics. She used their grand Monopoly idea as a disguised basis for her master's thesis. She received her MBA at the neighboring Missouri University campus in Columbia, Missouri. Her additional education served several important purposes: First, it allowed Jackson to elevate Brooke to Assistant Chair in the Department of Economics. It also gave them valuable input from other notable economists relevant to their research. Additionally, it generated positive peer review exposure within academia. Finally, the presentation and subsequent validation of the concept occurred without a hint of the PED scandal associated with Jackson's name.

As the chair and assistant chair of the Department of Economics, they were doing very well financially. They dutifully worked the necessary hours required to teach, while also doing administrative paper shuffling. However, these hours were challenging to do because their mutual love was their research project, which was coming along very well. Alterations to the original game of Monopoly were now strikingly apparent.

Justin Walker was a mechanical engineer in the Department of Computer Sciences. He had become friends with Jackson during undergrad school as a player from an interconference university. Justin had struggled with hitting the curveball. He always swung way too early and well ahead of the break in the pitch. Jackson had jokingly nicknamed him "The Whiffer." As luck would have it, his teammates and family members picked up the nickname, and it stuck! Jackson and Whiffer had maintained their friendship throughout the entirety of the steroid ordeal. Jackson admired his loyalty, and Whiffer had earned his trust. Jackson trusted him almost as much as he did Brooke, but he only trusted him with small components of the grand idea. He kept assignments for programming and engineering aspects of the game out of context and obscure so that they appeared to be innovations that could have utility across many applications.

Jackson was very faithful and respectful of Whiffer's friendship and his abilities. He faithfully named him on the ensuing patents, copyright, and trademark applications filed with the United States Patent and Trademark Office. Even though Whiffer had no clue what, nor to the extent that he was assisting Jackson, he was set to hit a financial windfall when the Grand Idea came to fruition. Jackson and Whiffer had amassed quite an extensive intellectual property portfolio. Some of the innovations that Whiffer had assisted in programming, developing, and patenting included:

• Programmable currency that could be adjusted to reflect inflation, devaluation, or dilution. This innovation made dollar outcomes adjustable for either deflation or inflation and to any percentage in the same game.

• Programmable Community Chest and Chance cards.

These cards, when landed upon, could add details such as inheritance and stock gains without insurance offset, etc.

• And most impressive in his list of programming and engineering achievements for 2007 was his completely impenetrable random generator. It would never repeat a sequence of dice rolls in at least ten raised to the twelfth power of rolls. It had remained the industry standard in the field.

Just as Whiffer came on board to advance the Grand Idea, Brooke had improved the playing board with the aid of a collective group of great minds in the School of Business. Brooke had a sorority sister from LSU that had also attended the University of Missouri in Columbia. She, like Brooke, had gotten her MBA in Economics. Now both were in the School of Business. Libby Ross was a whiz in real estate and a master at real estate appraisals. Libby had given Brooke numerous algorithms and formulas that had been funneled directly to Whiffer. Whiffer used the algorithms to engineer a program to adjust the price of houses, hotels, property purchase prices, and rents. Additionally, the program accommodated any level of appreciation or depreciation, property tax increases/decreases, insurance increases, and resulting losses from naturally occurring events dealt by the Community Chest and Chance cards within a single or an array of game boards/games.

Whiffer's most significant contribution was a programmed interface that read results from the gameboards in real-time. It also captured statistical data on how the events that occurred on the board were immediately calculated. It also extrapolated in hundreds of ways how to predict the outcomes as any single variable or group. Additionally, all selected inputs were adjusted, and the data was tabulated in real-time.

Chapter 5

2009

The stock market crashed at the end of 2008 from unsecured mortgage loans bundled together and sold to Fannie Mae and Freddie Mac. The selloff was steep and sharp; the economy was now in deep recession. This event indicated to Jackson that further adjustments were necessary for the game. It needed to capture more global macroeconomic data, so incidents like this could be foreseen in the future. So, as Jackson was working out new ways to introduce more factors, Whiffer designed the hardware to implement it.

Meanwhile, at the Federal Reserve, Beau was feeling the heat for not having read the tea leaves correctly in the U.S. mortgage industry meltdown. He was looking for nontraditional and innovative places to find answers and sound advice on how to steer the economy toward a badly needed recovery. A trip home to Baton Rouge at Christmas made for a monumental discussion regarding the Grand Idea. A shared visit with Beau would sow the seeds for moving the completed research model into an entity with the capability to read the entire United States economy. It could become the predictor to prevent or mitigate such calamities in the future. The stage was now ripe to interject the game into a position to capture massive amounts of economic data.

The Christmas visit in Baton Rouge and the opportunity to move the game into action had put an enormous amount of pressure and urgency on Jackson and Brooke. Complete final testing would be required, and probably many final adjustments. The need to launch a large-scale test scenario they had always thought might be years away might, in fact, be sooner rather than later. Now, with their dreams so close, they had to work hard and move very quickly. Nobody liked a recession, and even less so the longer they lingered.

With the new urgency came the need to further evaluate and identify all aspects of an economy the size of the United States of America. All captured data must be tied together to generate reports that could be broken down by categories and sectors. As they began to go through financial publications for additional research, they noticed that the stock market crash had created large numbers of unemployed and underemployed individuals. They also discovered that anticipated returns from the stock market were reeling, sending many retired people into bankruptcy as their retirement funds failed. Most all of the previous year's financial projections were utterly wrong due to the catastrophic event in the mortgage sector, which nobody had seen coming.

It was a time of great need, and it would require great sacrifice by Jackson, Brooke, Whiffer, and Libby. It would require them to put their heads together and stretch the boundaries of conventional economic theory and data collection. It would require all they collectively had to give to get the Grand Idea into a workable version. The time had come for Jackson and Brooke to reveal the real purpose of the project. Whiffer and Libby needed to know the real meaning of the research. Making them full stakeholders in the entirety of the dream they shared was the only practical way to get the project completed and functional. They needed partners, not just friends and employees. Now, they all had skin in this game.

In a judicial review of the losses and economic changes in the U.S. economy after the 2008 crash, Jackson discovered that there were much larger segments of the population that were now on unemployment, food stamps, and Medicaid. Entitlement programs were throwing the entire economy out of balance, yet people really needed these social nets. There were incredibly large numbers of foreclosures, and the resulting oversupply of homes was massive. Mortgage interest rates were very high, and bankers were very skittish about making new mortgage loans. Many homes sat vacant and fell into disrepair; lenders held properties with liens two to three times greater than the new appraisal values. Many people were retired, and many had incomes tied to returns from investment accounts.

Moreover, rental properties and stock market investments indexed to mutual funds went broke. Mutual funds were now bankrupt. Fixed income employees and retirees lost their entire investment portfolio. This required Jackson and Whiffer to discover an adjustment to the data collection method that generated a computer program to patch into the property/house/hotel buying aspect of the game. Further, they had found that not all areas were affected equally; some had been hit harder than others. Hence, they discovered the need to incorporate these adjustments tied to zip codes so that scenarios could run specific to any given U.S. location for accuracy.

In addition to the aftereffects of the 2008 crash, new industrial segments had risen out of the ashes. These new market segments were led by Apple, Google, Facebook, and that new sector known as "The Tech Sector." This new sector promised as much growth as the loss that the economy had suffered, perhaps even more. The market gains that this sector had made showed real hope that the losses incurred by the 2008 crash might be recouped. One could almost see the "Invisible Hand" at work lifting one portion of the economy, while another had failed. This phenomenon was placing the economy back on a solid footing sooner than expected.

Jackson and Whiffer recognized that a significant gap existed in data, and an adjustment was necessary for the gameboard. The need to have a portal to include new market sectors, new energy sources, and new technologies were suddenly required.

After looking at the board carefully, they identified the four railroads (B. & O., Reading, Short Line, and Pennsylvania). Railroads were no longer big investment stocks, but more likely considered an infrastructure item. These railroads seemed an appropriate place to segue new market segments into the game. Additionally, the Electric Company and Water Works seemed a great place to include the crude oil and energy segment, and the manufacturing sector. Both of these segments were significant indicators and capital contributors to the economy. The changes in the gameboard and the programs and algorithms incorporated current market information. New parameters programmed into the board at the start of each new game resulted in the culmination of the data to be factored into the game.

It appeared that now was time for an acid test of the system. With these enhancements, the board barely resembled the old Monopoly board where this entire idea had begun. There was an incredible resemblance to the transformation of Anakin Skywalker into Darth Vader from the *Star Wars* movie series. The game may have once resembled a handsome young boy but was now a robot with its life sustained by machines. Such was the metamorphosis of a small, square, cardboard gameboard into a robust juggernaut of raw computing power. It was time to test the new, evolved, and repurposed game.

Chapter 6

2010

On December 30, 2008, the most significant point drop in history occurred in the private mortgage industry. Many investment brokerage firms on Wall Street had also failed. The federal government now had to consider bailouts for many privately held companies. A brand-new term was coined: "TOO LARGE TO FAIL." It became a concept that took hold. The idea considered the number of employees that would become unemployed and the loss to the investors if the company failed. It required that it would be determined if it was economically favorable for the government to make loans to keep them solvent. Had the government allowed these large companies to fail, it would have had to have paid out billions in unemployment. Even more would have gone to welfare and food stamps. It would have had to absorb the loss of payroll taxes and business taxes. Further, as each sector failed, ancillary industries would fall. It would resemble an enormous high-stakes game of falling dominoes. A good example would be that if a factory closed, truckers lost jobs as well. Then mechanics had no trucks on which to work. It seemed that each failure represented billions of dollars of additional repercussive consequences. It seemed as though the only way back up was with the aid of the government. Giving these businesses the chance to rebuild their business seemed the best way forward.

The domino effect was cascading through the U.S. economy, and the Grand Idea was going to be required to find a way back to the top. Beau was under pressure to find a solution. He had directed Jackson and Brooke to get the Grand Idea online. After six months of racing to make final inclusions, today was the big day. Today was a HUGE day. The first live test was going online with the very first global readout.

NORTHWESTERN UNIVERSITY GYMNASIUM

Jackson, Brooke, Whiffer, and Libby were sitting high above a basketball floor; Northwestern University had allowed the Economics Department to acquire an old gymnasium on the edge of the older, original campus on a parcel of the original plot of land. Old as it was, it had a freshly painted sign above the door that said, "ECON LAB 1." The bleachers were removed, and an elevated loft surrounded by glass had been built around the structure. In the front of the loft were banks of video monitors. The A/V room behind them was humming from the fans of numerous servers. They were poised to collect and synthesize the data collected from the fifty gameboards on tables on the gym floor. Fifty games were all collecting and consolidating data for the first time. The components had been programmed to exacting standards to correctly reflect the real-life economic conditions in each sector of the economy.

Whiffer was wiping sweat from his brow as he madly programmed in all the data values, factors, and variables for each table. Each board represented a micro-economy, and the totality of the data collected would constitute a macro-economy. On the table was a folder marked TOP SECRET. Beau had provided them with a test case scenario. All of the inputs were only pieces of data to be entered. Only Beau knew where the data came from and what the real reasons for running that specific data would genuinely find. The lights in the stands dimmed as the floor glowed. Two hundred of the very brightest graduate school students and doctoral candidates sat down to play a game of Monopoly. Fifty boards, four graduate school students per table, they were the best and the brightest.

Whiffer finished the final data entry and looked at the radiant floor. He was exhausted but so excited to see the years of hard work taking wing to fly. Suddenly he looked at Jackson and whispered, "*MAN-opoly.* It no longer looks like Monopoly, and it should solve the problems of mankind! Let's name this MANOPOLY!"

Jackson, who was sweating bullets, looked at Whiffer, looked back at Brooke, and grinned. After a short yet pregnant pause, he smiled and said quietly, "Manopoly it is! But let's make it a question *and* a statement; let's make it MANOPOLY!?"

Brooke picked up a Freon can with a horn mounted on top and with a very loud *HONK!!!* the test went live!

━━━

AS THE GAME went live on the university basketball floor, the servers on the fifth floor of the Federal Reserve building on Wall Street started to hum. Lights began to flash, and raw data from the game came into the mainframe that directed the data into the appropriate sheets and rows, tuples and attributes, zeroes and ones. After almost three hours of listening to computers whirl and watching lights flash, the wide carriage tractor feed dot-matrix printer started to spit out page after page of data. Finally, after about twenty minutes, the printer stopped; Beau walked over and tore out the last page. He thumbed through the print-outs and sauntered over to his credenza, pulled on the bottom of a painting, an original Monet worth over five million dollars. A secret door opened on a piano hinge, revealing a safe. He dialed right and left, and back to the right on a combination lock and opened the safe's door. He reached into the safe and pulled out a file with a single name written on the front. That name was HALLIBURTON.

The Federal Reserve was running a forensic review of a significant Defense Contractor. The data was sent to Whiffer for programming. A complete profile of all known financial data regarding global activities and federal expenditures for Halliburton was in the file. The information was faxed to the Internal Revenue Service and the Joint Chiefs of Staff in the Pentagon. Also, unbeknownst to anyone else, a copy was routed to Beau's personal computer.

Meanwhile, back at the university, the gym floor was now empty. Jackson, Brooke, and Whiffer sat, exhausted but thrilled by the performance of their brainchild! Little did they know that the product of their work was already making its way around the known world. It was a personal mission of value for Jackson and Brooke. It never occurred to them to ask Beau whose data was running, or why he had selected this particular set of data. Was this a question they should have asked?

———

THE FOLLOWING morning the alarm went off with an annoying squeal. Brooke rolled into Jackson's arms and kissed him deeply. She raised her head and smiled as big as the crescent moon the night before. She whispered into his ear, "Now will you make an honest woman out of me?"

During the time that passed while implementing improvements, Jackson and Brooke had given into the chemistry that they shared. They had been dating for quite some time, and Brooke frequently stayed over at Jackson's home. It was a starter home, and it was Jackson's first home. It always felt more like home with Brooke there. Had Brooke not been there, he would, most likely, just have crashed on a cot in the Econ Lab 1 building.

Brooke had always been attracted to Jackson, but she had dreams and goals as well, and she had been faithful to her aspirations. Jackson had obviously noticed how beautiful Brooke was as well. He also always admired her intelligence and wit. When he interviewed her for her residency at Northwestern University, even though she had a powerful recommendation, he really found her very charming. Jackson held his cards pretty close to his vest. Whiffer knew the most about Jackson because they played college ball together. Jackson never really talked about his childhood or his family; nobody really knew much about his past. The close proximity to Jackson that Whiffer shared over time had built a relationship of trust between the two of them. They were very comfortable together. Jackson often visited Baton Rouge with Brooke and knew her mom and dad, as well as Beau. The entire Benoit family considered Jackson as a family member. The transition into a romantic relationship was very easy for them both.

He smiled and rolled her over onto her back, "We go immediately back to the gymnasium when we are finished!" he said. She giggled. They made love.

———

WHIFFER HAD an odd premonition that he needed to check out something that he could not put his finger on. Whiffer had always been a massive believer in science, but for some odd reason, the premonition just kept hounding him this morning. He walked into the gymnasium and heard a voice whispering on a cell phone, "*I gotta go, someone is here!*" The man ran; Whiffer followed, but his athletic days were far behind him. The man bolted out of the panic door and jumped into a running car and disappeared. Whiffer muttered to himself, "*What the heck?*" He quickly did a walkthrough and did not notice any damage or anything missing, but he could not help wondering what had just happened.

THE TELEPHONE RANG in an executive office at the CIA Langley, Virginia Headquarters. Ali Assad picked up the phone and said, "Middle East desk."

Chapter 7

2011

The annual meeting of all the deans and directors of the university was gaveled to order. As the discussions regarding the budget slowly came to the school business, Department of Economics, Jackson was nervous. However, he was also excited to get an opportunity to explain the added expenses, while explaining the potential financial boom that his research could generate for the university. As he began to discuss the expenditures that had been used for the initial test, and the hardware costs, an astonishing voice of dissension became very vocal. The Dean of Foreign Studies, Salomon Agassi, cleared his throat very loudly and began in a very thick Middle Eastern accent: "As the faculty advisor on the finance committee, I am very concerned by the amount of money going toward a research program that we know so little about." But before he went any further, his cell phone rang; the person on the other end was speaking very loudly in Persian. Neither of the gentlemen was happy.

Salomon Agassi's blood seemed to drain from his face suddenly, and he sheepishly raced from the room while still on his cell phone. Jackson had a dazed look of confusion on his face, and his excitement suddenly turned to dismay. It appeared that Agassi was about to cause a stink about his budget items. Why would he do such a thing? Jackson barely knew him. The comptroller looked around, and in the absence of the gentleman who had been speaking, resumed the budgetary discussion. Jackson looked at Brooke and Whiffer and simply answered the question, offering no detail or insight to the promise of their research. None of them could understand what had just happened. Salomon Agassi had never been so rude or had spoken thus far out of turn. They were all in disbelief. This was exactly why Jackson hated these meetings.

⊏⊐

IN THE LOBBY of the administration building at the university, Salomon Agassi stood whispering into his cell phone, speaking Persian, and looking as though his life could well be in danger, or a truck was about to hit him. What had Agassi gotten into?

Chapter 8

2011

Back at the Federal Reserve on Wall Street, Beau was taking his seat at a large oval board table with a top made of beautiful American walnut. The meeting had a feeling of tension and the presence of high authority. The Federal Reserve Chairman Ben Bernanke and the United States Senator Darrell Issa, in charge of the Senate Oversight Committee and the Federal Emergency Management Agency (FEMA), were poised precariously at the far end of the table. Beau felt the gravity of the situation but wondered what position he would be managing next. The word of the success of the Halliburton Report had reached the highest levels of the United States government, but access to the project was highly secretive. It was seldom mentioned unless at a top-secret meeting, and strictly on a need-to-know basis. This meeting could be about anything, so he straightened his tie and walked in and closed the door behind him.

The Federal Reserve chairman walked over to the credenza at the end of the room and initiated the signal jamming device sitting on the surface. It would prevent signals from leaving or penetrating the meeting and would ensure absolute privacy. Beau was now very keenly aware that this meeting was not without consequence and would be very weighty. After Chairman Bernanke came back and sat down, he introduced the senator and informed them of his duties in the oversight of FEMA. The senator stood up, cleared his throat, and began to lay out the scenario on the ground as a result of a massive earthquake in Haiti. The senator completed his briefing and immediately turned to Beau and said, "We are going to require your expertise and your project to figure out how to put the economy of Haiti back together." It was exhilarating to Beau; this was just the opportunity the Grand Idea was designed to solve.

He was suddenly excited and could not wait to call his sister and her fiancé and give them the news! Other than the Halliburton Project, the Grand Idea had only been utilized in a handful of small situations and was still a closely held secret. Now was the big chance to make his move!

Back at the university, Jackson and Brooke were sitting in their office. Jackson seated at his desk and Brooke on the sofa on the opposite wall. All classes had been taught for the day. Her shoes were off, and her feet were propped on the arm of the sofa. Her head was comfortably on a throw pillow. She suddenly looked very pleased with herself, smiled, and joyfully interjected aloud, "DAISIES!" The topic was wedding details, and they were having fun planning their special day.

The phone rang; he wrinkled his forehead, looked at the clock, and answered the phone. He heard Beau's voice and immediately hit the speakerphone button so they could all talk about wedding plans together. They all exchanged pleasantries, and Jackson noticed how quickly the siblings slipped back into their Louisiana southern drawls; he smiled a delighted smile. Life was perfect. After the highlights of the wedding plans had been shared, Beau asked them if they were seated. The couple's eyes met, their eyebrows raised together, and in absolute unison, they said, "Yes?"

Beau quickly briefed his sister and brother-in-law-to-be about the FEMA meeting, and the request to utilize their now greatly improved MANOPOLY Project. An earthquake of this severity was a near-extinction event. The economy would be entirely in shambles, infrastructure destroyed, monetary and banking systems devastated. This was the break for which they had been waiting.

Since the initial Halliburton run, the Senate Appropriations Committee had diverted funds to Northwestern University to support the MANOPOLY Project. A substantial budget increase had made the Department of Economics a new booming project on campus. The old gymnasium in the original section of the college had been remodeled. Additionally, the old building was engineered as the home of the MANOPOLY Project.

Bars were built covering the windows, security systems had been installed, and door locks requiring secure identification cards and utilizing biometrics to open had been added. Closed-circuit television monitoring, motion sensors, magnetic door and window sensors, and microphones had been deployed as part of the security system. The electric service to the building had been completely renovated and outfitted with massive diesel backup generators as well.

The folding tables had been replaced with fifty square pedestals built into the wooden floor. In the center of the pedestal platforms were large, hollow, square-shaped tubes with large, thick, black wires having various plugs and ends that connected to the playing boards. There was also a computer terminal at each table, making it easier to program each board locally. The crow's nest that held the master control panels was encased in glass and had four air conditioning units mounted in the back, outside the wall. There was an intercom system that allowed global announcements and speakers/transmitters at each table to communicate easily throughout the building. The locker rooms in the lower level were remodeled into offices. Many of the resident graduate students and doctoral candidates in the Department of Economics maintained offices there.

The handful of small assignments that Beau had given the MANOPOLY Project had allowed the time necessary to establish a routine and checklist of how to prepare and execute a live scenario. Driving up to the Economics Lab 1 Building, one was keenly aware that there was a high demand for power and communications lines into and out of the lab. This university lab was hardwired into the United States economic and government establishment as well as the electric power grid. The rise of the lab had been rapid and substantial. The two doctors running the Department of Economics had become critical players in the national security landscape.

2011

In the basement of the United States Capitol, in Washington, D.C., in the Sensitive Compartmented Information Facility (SCIF), a top-secret meeting was convened to discuss the rebuilding of Haiti. Global humanitarian agencies and foundations had been collecting funds to assist with the successful rebuild of the devastated country, but the lack of a centralized controlling agency to direct the effort was resulting in enormous waste. Money was falling through the cracks. The MANOPOLY Project had been designed for a situation such as this.

Present at the meeting were the vice president, chairman of the Joint Chiefs of Staff, Senator Issa from FEMA, the senator in charge of foreign aid, and Beauregard Benoit.

FEMA Senator Issa opened the meeting. He cued each member present to insert their secure badge into the console in the center of the table. The device confirmed their appropriate security clearance to receive the briefing on the existence of the **MANOPOLY** Project. All four lights switched from red to green, indicating that each had passed the security requirement. The presentation went well, and another meeting for the next day was scheduled with the members of the Senate Finance and Budget Committee chairs to obtain the data required at the university to run the scenario. The meeting was set at the same spot, for ten a.m. the following day!

On January 11, 2010, a massive earthquake hit Haiti measuring 7.0 on the Richter scale. The devastation displaced about 1.5 million Haitians into tent camps and 230,000 people had died that day on the small island nation. In the months immediately following, over thirteen billion dollars lovingly came in from around the world. This country was a third-world country, and their construction standards were not uniform nor designed to withstand the shock of an earthquake. Housing and buildings in Haiti were almost exclusively concrete block and mortar. Concrete block construction lacks any ability to absorb or flex to allow the building to give a small amount and remain intact.

Simply put, concrete has no tensile strength. It cannot give at all; it only breaks. The lack of steel rebar running through the voids in the block means that when the mortar gives, the walls fall.

So, this country had a legacy of an entire country built of buildings that would fall if shaken. This created a problem that compounded the damage. No building in Haiti was sound after the 2010 quake. Therefore, the entire country of Haiti needed to be rebuilt, with modern building codes that would prevent a repeat. This scenario compounded and multiplied the real cost of Haitian recovery.

In the days, weeks, and months immediately following the quake, NGOs (Non-Government Organizations), governments, individuals, the United Nations, and many other entities opened their wallets. They contributed over thirteen billion dollars toward Haitian aid.

As each day passed, more money was given. However, over time, no measurable results were seen. It would appear that very little money to assist the Haitian people arrived on the ground in Haiti. Much was needed to change the plight of Haitian people substantially.

In the SCIF, government officials expressed their frustration with the failing effort to rebuild Haiti. The money kept flowing, and nothing seemed to change. The press narrative was beginning to sour on the undertaking. The administration needed to sway positive public opinion on the financial investments made by the taxpayers. The members present asked Beau if he could evaluate the inputs and find a route to successful management of this enterprise. Beau remained very skeptical about a successful outcome based generally on the fact that there was no one primary entity in charge of coordinating the funds' distribution. Beau did, however, feel the immense pressure from the government to extricate a positive result from the enormous investment in the MANOPOLY Project. He asked that the data be collected as quickly as possible to focus on solving the problem.

Beau shook the hands of his fellow conferees, forced a smile, and walked out of the SCIF. There, he opened his assigned locker from a secured area, retrieved his cell phone, and turned it on. As Beau walked out of the Capitol, he finally had a signal and dialed Jackson. He caught Jackson walking out of a class, and Jackson sensed the urgency in Beau's voice. He walked into a janitor's closet for quiet and privacy. Beau expressed his exasperation with the situation and his displeasure with the pressure being exerted by the government.

After all, this program had not been designed to work out differing opinions between politicians and NGO executives. Beau was concerned about the MANOPOLY Project's ability to accommodate this scenario. Jackson understood Beau's concerns and realized that he needed to speak to Brooke and Whiffer to discuss the necessary adjustments. The work required was successful manipulation of the data to achieve an acceptable solution. Libby's expertise in real estate would bring a value-added asset in trying to find a solution to the sliding real estate values in Haiti.

Jackson, Brooke, and Whiffer walked into the control booth of the Econ Lab 1. As they walked in and sat down to begin discussing the required changes, the fax machine started humming. Sheets of data began flowing from the Senate Oversight Committee on Government Assistance. The phone rang as Beau was checking in from his cab headed to the Econ Lab 1 from the local airport. The entire team was now on the home court to work through this technical challenge. The clock was running, and the starting team was all in the game.

It had been a while since Beau had been back to Evanston, and the changes to the Econ Lab 1 were impressive for him to behold. He was surprised to realize how proud he was of his baby sister, her relationship with Jackson, and the amazing accomplishments that they were achieving together. It occurred to him how truly blessed he was to have the family with whom he was sharing time!

Beau didn't let on much, but he became a born-again Christian shortly after college, and only his closest friends and family members knew how vital his faith indeed was to him. During college, Beau had become a bit too familiar with the party life in his LSU fraternity. The party life had taken hold of his ability to control his alcohol intake. Shortly after he graduated from LSU, the summer before he went to Harvard for grad school, he had run into a young lady jogging around a high school track near where he lived in Baton Rouge. They spent a great deal of time together that summer. She was a strong Christian, and Beau had confessed that he was concerned about his feeling the need to drink.

She would be the person that changed Beau's life, and in doing so, they became life-long friends. Her name was Imogene St. John, a tall, athletic runner who could have passed as an Olympic swimmer. Her hair was bright red and cut into a very stylish mohawk. She was athletic enough to rock the look. Beau thought her an intimidating young lady when he first met her on the track. They spent a great deal of time training together that summer, and they talked about almost everything in their lives. Imogene was a solid Christian from an influential church-going family. After about six weeks, they were going to the Baptist church in the neighborhood. A week before Beau left for Harvard, Beau was baptized, and the change in his life was evident for all who knew him. That summer would prove to be a very formative time in Beau's life. He found the change needed in his life to set him on a path of success.

The void of alcohol in the brain and a newfound moral compass proved a formidable combination when partnered with his good breeding, education, and enthusiasm for life. Imogene ended up as a foreign missionary and tried to drop in to see Beau every time she was stateside. Even though thousands of miles usually separated them, they always remained very close.

After they all caught up, Jackson walked over to the fax machine and began synthesizing the data on the assignment sheet. Jackson, Brooke, Whiffer, and Beau were all but confident that the prospect of recreating an entire national economy after a natural disaster of biblical proportions would surely be the breakthrough that the MANOPOLY Project was destined to repair. It would most certainly send them into the stratosphere of success, but as Jackson read further, he was perplexed by the scope and breadth of the data on the pages.

The four old friends were stoically sitting at the conference table in the Econ Lab 1 with sheets of data scattered across the top of the table in semi-organized stacks. Each stack was representative of an aspect of the game that had been adapted to achieve an acceptable conclusion. While charitable contributions and their relationship to taxes and income had been addressed in many contexts, never had they dealt with philanthropic resources from so many sources, from so many countries, all having different tax and accounting systems. They even had to address the conversion of different currencies and how they exchanged against the U.S. dollar.

To make a very long night, and a very long story short, the adjustments required to incorporate all this data were too extensive to be done in time to remedy the situation. They were able to recommend consolidating all of the donations into an interest-bearing United Nations account. This would assist the Interagency and International Services (IIS) and the U.S. Army Corps of Engineers in working out a system of replacing structures with new dwellings to maximize the number of occupancies per structure. Still, the task was just too large to accommodate. It seemed a very hollow and empty outcome to Jackson and the company, but that net effect was a considerable contribution to an enormous disaster. But more importantly, the government agencies funding the MANOPOLY Project were pleased with the outcome. Additionally, many more critical players in the international government were now aware of the positive benefits coming from the project.

Chapter 9

2012

Salomon Agassi used his position as Dean of the School of Foreign Studies at Northwestern University to write off a trip each summer back to his country of birth, Old Persia, or modern-day Iran. The planning each year for the next journey began as soon as he returned home. Every year, the first person Agassi always saw was Ghassim Kalani, Agassi's first cousin on his mother's side. He also was the last person he would see in Iran every year. Kalani dutifully picked his cousin up and delivered him back to Imam Khomeini International Airport.

Kalani also served the Iranian government as Minister of Energy. Every year, their routine was the same: Kalani picked up Agassi at the airport and drove straight to the Doshan Tappeh Air Base near Tehran. This was also the headquarters of the Islamic Republic of Iran Air Force (IRIAF). This might have seemed contradictory to some because the Doshan Tappeh Air Base from the air appeared to be the same airfield. However, getting to the IRIAF headquarters was a bit of a drive around the city that took you through several very-protected checkpoints and security choke points.

Each year, Agassi and Kalani pulled up to a very secure aircraft hangar, swiped secure identification cards, and a large aircraft door slid open about eight feet, allowing room for his Mercedes Benz to drive in. Within a minute, the door closed, and they were no longer even visible by radar. Once inside the secure door, the two jumped out of the car, speaking fluent Persian. Once they were by two Russian fighter jets, they would pass by a maintenance crew wearing the uniform of the Quds Force, whose members reported directly to the Supreme Leader. They walked into an air-conditioned office, saluted, and began talking to their old friends.

Agassi was sweating profusely. The temperature in the desert was much hotter than he was used to; Evanston was much more temperate. He found himself wondering why he didn't work his annual trip into the winter and miss the snow in Illinois. However, Agassi knew that any radical change like this would interfere with his teaching and advising time for students on campus. Nonetheless, it was an interesting exercise in thought! He chuckled to himself since he thought the very same thing every year in almost the same spot! Surely Pavlov would have a heyday evaluating the programmed stimuli that produced this thought like clockwork. Pavlov and his famous experiment with dogs had always fascinated Agassi. Mental manipulation was a lifelong hobby, and he was very proficient with psychological manipulation. Agassi always seemed to enjoy admiring his mind; he honestly thought he was a legend in his own mind.

As he was walking into the office, amused by his thoughts, Agassi suddenly stopped and stood at attention. His thoughts stopped cold as well. His idol was walking by right in front of him—General Qassem Soleimani. Soleimani was the Commander of the Quds Force and second-in-command only to the Supreme Leader. His heart beat with great pride when Soleimani nodded his head at Agassi and acknowledged his pleasure at seeing him again. Soleimani walked on out, without stopping. Agassi and Kalani walked into the office Soleimani had just exited, saluted, and sat down at attention.

Chapter 10

Back in Evanston, meanwhile, Jackson, Brooke, Whiffer, and Beau sat down at the oval conference table in the Econ Lab 1 Office. Beau slid his briefcase onto the table, manipulated the combination lock, took his keys from his pocket, and selected a non-descript key to open the third lock. Inside the brown leather briefcase was a yellow manila envelope with a red and white label on the face. The warning read TOP SECRET. Beau reached into the case, lifted the envelope onto the desktop, and announced that he had the report from their input on the Haitian economic situation. They all took a deep breath, and Beau tore the envelope open. They paused and began to read.

Inside the envelope was something seldom seen by an American citizen: the outline of a daily briefing given to the President of the United States of America. When Jackson and Brooke saw this outline, they looked up, and their eyes quickly met. This was very surreal. At that moment, they both took a quick trip down memory lane. There they were for the first time together with pizza on the eight-foot folding table, as quickly back into the exact moment where they were! What a fantastic journey their thoughts had made! It merely wasn't ubiquitous for an approach to rise as far; or as quickly! This would be a moment to freeze in time and to remember forever!

Brought back to the present, the group turned their attention to the attached Presidential Briefing Outline, a report that is about one-inch thick. The report contained very detailed data that was a real snapshot of their progress. This was the government's evaluation of the Haitian earthquake scenario they had run. There was some trepidation as they picked it up to review its contents. They were quietly disappointed that the project was too vast in scope for them to process a more comprehensive solution. But there had been so many different variables that were not economical. It was just not the ideal set of circumstances to be evaluated through the entire economic prism utilized by the MANOPOLY Project. After all, it was designed to assess economies. The disaster created far too many non-economic factors that simply did not work in their evaluation. But the economic assessment was sound and followed sound economic theory and practices. It had been outstanding work. Was he just rationalizing and preparing for the worst?

Whiffer was the programmer at the meeting. He began reading way ahead of the others. Jackson and Brooke were very used to Whiffer's attention to detail. Years of experience had taught them that waiting about two minutes was, by far, the quickest way to know what was in the report. So, they watched his face and impatiently waited.

The contents of the report addressed the inputs that the MANOPOLY Project provided. Although they had been unable to pick up the entire country's economy and fix it like a brand-new watch, the report was very favorable, if not almost flattering. The input on how to sort out much of the confusion and better organize the recovery effort had been very beneficial. Even though Jackson, Brooke, Whiffer, and Beau had dreamed that their project would fix the entire tragedy, that outcome was not realistic. It was, however, a great test that resulted in many new changes made to improve the game. The bottom line of the report was: JOB WELL DONE! Just what a government contractor needed to know when the funding came from the American taxpayer.

Chapter 11

Back in Tehran, Agassi and Kalani had finished their meeting, returned to their jet-black Mercedes, and pulled out of the hangar. The building next door housed Quds Force enlisted soldiers; Agassi told Kalani that he needed to stop here for a minute. He walked into the secured Quonset hut barracks and walked about halfway back to a bunk. He turned the corner, and there stood a young soldier wearing a white T-shirt, the front reading NORTHWESTERN UNIVERSITY. That soldier was Muhammed Faruq, the person who had run from the Northwestern University gym the day after the first test run of the MANOPOLY Project. The man who Whiffer had accidentally run across was a Quds Force enlisted man and foreign national in Agassi's School of Foreign Studies.

Chapter 12

2013

Beau was sitting in his loft in the upper west side of Manhattan. He was at a very nice, solid oak desk that overlooked a breathtaking view of the Manhattan skyline from the sixty-eighth-floor dwelling. Beau was single and had way too much going on in his life to consider making time for a woman. The Day-Timer indicated that his schedule was full. But Beau did have an ember that always burned in his mind when it stopped spinning. It was a pain that he had only shared with Imogene, his missionary friend.

While it may seem very random that the first test case that the MANOPOLY Project ran was a careful analysis of Halliburton, Beau knew, quite well, that it was anything but random. While Beau's life had seemed, on its face, to be perfect, there was one thing that he could never entirely move past. This was a secret that only Beau, his mom, and his dad shared; not even Brooke knew about this skeleton in his closet. But he had trusted Imogene with the burden. And tonight, Beau sat at his desk, alone, with the Halliburton data.

He logged onto his computer, opened the middle drawer,

and pulled out a jump drive. He plugged it into the USB port and opened a spreadsheet on the left side of the split-screen. On the right was the report done by the MANOPOLY Project on Halliburton. He seemed particularly interested in the personnel matters and the personal expense account reports of the Halliburton employees. For what, or for whom, was he looking? He combed the files for hours, seemingly on a critical mission.

Beau was the oldest child of Brightwell "Bright" and Patsy (Wilson) Benoit. As mentioned, Pasty was from old oil money in Baton Rouge. As a Wilson, she had been raised Catholic and brought up in local schools in the south. The schools she attended were all-girl Catholic schools taught by nuns. Growing up Catholic in the middle of the Bible Belt in the middle of the Deep South in the 1960s and 1970s wasn't everyone's cup of tea. Patsy, actually Patricia, was a tall, lanky girl that loved music and who played the guitar in her spare time. She was a good student, but she was a free spirit who fell under the influence of a rock band of hippies called The Driftwood.

The Driftwood traveled around the area in an old Volkswagen bus playing local gigs. Virgil William Bagley was a guitar player and songwriter that had a voice that sounded as smooth as silk. Patsy fell madly in love with Virgil, and after about six months, Patsy found herself pregnant. A pregnant seventeen-year old girl in a school full of nuns would undoubtedly stick out! Virgil was five years her senior, and when he learned he had impregnated a rich, young girl in a Bible Belt town in the Deep South, Virgil drove to New Orleans, joined the Marines, and headed to Parris Island for boot camp.

After boot camp, he shipped out to Vietnam. Patsy had kept track of him through a mutual friend. So, in the middle of the Deep South, in the middle of the Bible Belt, in the middle of a wealthy family, in the middle of a Catholic school, a young seventeen-year old was an unwed, expecting mother. This situation was not socially acceptable, especially in the late 1960s in the Bible Belt! Patsy would wear the brand of a harlot, and her family would feel absolute scorn. Abortion was not even a consideration in the Deep South by Christian folk. It would have been a shame for the world to have missed out on the man that she was carrying. Beau Benoit would become a great man.

Brightwell Benoit was a young man from the same neighborhood as the Wilson family. His parents had married very late in life and were well into their late fifties at this time. Brightwell was a very industrious young man who was the neighborhood newspaper boy. He was tall, handsome, very polite, and the Wilsons loved him. He was a year older than Patsy, and they were best friends. Bright went to the boys' Catholic school about six blocks from St. Mary's, where Patsy attended. Bright and Patsy shared all their dreams and stories. Bright was mild-mannered and very easy going; Patsy was a handful, and Bright was the only person she trusted with her secret. Bright had for years secretly loved Patsy and had always wished she could love him back.

With Virgil gone, Patsy found herself in a very untenable position. She knew she would be stuck between the devil and the deep blue sea. She only had one friend in whom she could confide. Bright sat and listened. Now, Patsy needed him, so Bright volunteered to assume responsibility for Patsy and her coming baby. Not even their parents knew the truth. Bright sat in the Wilson living room when they told her parents and took a terrible verbal beating. But eventually, they came around and accepted Patsy and Bright. So, Brightwell and Patricia Benoit started together with a big secret in common. The secret drew them closer together, and when Beauregard was born, they were delighted. Their parents set them up in schools, with childcare, and a life that was fitting for a well-to-do family in the Deep South. Had it not been for the Rh-negative blood type that Patsy carried, nobody would have ever known their secret.

After the baby was born, because of Patsy's O-negative blood type, a blood test was triggered to type the blood of the baby Beauregard Benoit. This practice was commonly done when the mother had an Rh-negative blood type. If the baby's blood type was positive, the mother would be given a shot of an immune globulin that would protect subsequent babies from the mother's antibodies, building up and attacking later babies from additional pregnancies. The mother's antibodies primarily attack a baby bearing an Rh-positive blood type. In the past, the second or third pregnancy of Rh-negative mother having Rh-positive children resulted in what was called "blue babies." The antibodies that the mother built up often killed subsequent children. The treatment for a blue baby was a complete blood transfusion at birth.

So, Beau's blood type was A-positive. Bright's blood type was O-positive. Therefore, the doctor knew that the baby was not Bright's biological child. Two parents having type O blood cannot biologically have a child with type A blood. This was a secret that had to be kept. It could have devastated the entire family and Beauregard's entire future.

Four years later, Brooke was born. Bright had just finished college at Our Lady of the Lake College, a hand up from their priest. He now had a bachelor's degree in agriculture. The Wilson family dipped into their trust fund to buy the young family a farm outside Baton Rouge. He began farming food crops and bought his first horse. This would be a great place to raise their family. Beau was delighted on the farm.

Fast forward twelve years, to when Beau was almost seventeen years old. He was the starting safety for the St. Joseph's Academy High School. St. Joseph's was a very upper-class high school. LSU was already scouting Beau as Patsy was an LSU alum. In the last game in his junior year, Beau was speared in the side with a helmet, resulting in severe blood loss. Later, he was rushed to the hospital in an ambulance. At the ER, an X-ray and examination indicated a kidney injury that required surgery. The bloodwork forced Bright and Patsy to share their secret with their son. Bright and Patsy sat Beau down and told him that Virgil William Bagley was his biological father and that Bright and Patsy had started their lives together bound by a secret. Patsy had kept track of Virgil, who was now in Houston, Texas where he worked for Halliburton, through an old mutual friend. She never said to Beau who her friend was that kept her informed through the years, but he was sure glad.

Back in upper Manhattan, Beau was sitting, staring at the split computer screen, deep in thoughts, wondering if he would ever find or meet his biological father. Was the clue in the data compiled from the MANOPOLY scenario? He was feeling lonely. He reached onto his pocket and pulled out his cell phone. He needed to hear Imogene's voice. Now in Mexico City, she answered and said, "*Hola!*"

Chapter 13

2014

Back at Econ Lab 1, Jackson was working through a list of program enhancements that the MANOPOLY Project had undergone since the report on the Haiti scenario. They were meticulously working over the hardware on the floor and comparing the required data to the physical enhancements completed to each board. Additionally, Whiffer was running all the cables, terminals, fittings, plugs, and junction boxes. The wires all merged into one eventual snake of wires approximately nine inches in diameter, all running back to the banks of servers in the glass crow's nest. After running the cables back to the servers, the methodical Whiffer reversed his direction and headed back toward the gameboards on the floor.

At the central junction box coming down from the crow's nest, there seemed to be a screw missing from the cover plate. Whiffer *never* missed a detail like this! Whiffer had severe obsessive-compulsive tendencies; this missing screw was a flashing red light in his eye. He ran to the crow's nest, grabbed his tool pouch, and ran down to the junction box on the gym floor. Whiffer took out his Phillips head screwdriver and removed the other three screws. As he lifted off the cover plate, his eyes bulged from his face. His face turned suddenly pale, and he screamed out, "*SON OF A BITCH*"!

There, inside the box, in his hand, was a small flashing electronic transmitter. Data was being hacked on the way to the computer. Whiffer grabbed his needle-nose pliers and pulled the component out of the junction box. As he held it up to the light and looked at it carefully, he saw small writing on the circuitry. He jumped up and ran up the steps, two at a time, to his workbench in the crow's nest. There was a circular light with a magnifying glass in the middle, mounted on an adjustable arm. The arm was secured to the benchtop. He turned on the light and carefully inspected the tiny writing on the custom circuitry in his hand. He simply could not believe his eyes; the etching was in Farsi.

Iran, he suspected, had infiltrated the top-secret facility on the Northwestern University campus. He looked up, and his face turned pale as he remembered the man who had run from the building in the early morning after the initial trial run of the MANOPOLY Project. In that instant, Whiffer was keenly aware that the group's data, and the subsequent research that they had done, was now suspect. What information had been compromised, and where had it gone? Who now had access to their data, and where might it show up? He now had to consider that since there was a transmitter, there certainly would be a receiver that he could track. The next question was a very frightening consideration: Was the data being corrupted from an outside source?

Whiffer grabbed the phone and called Jackson. *Ring, ring.*

"*Hello, you have reached Jackson Reynolds. I am either on the phone or in a meeting right now. Please leave a message and I'll get right back with you.*"

He was beyond frustrated and immediately dialed Brooke. *Ring, ring, ring.*

"You have reached Brooke Benoit. Please leave a message; I'll call you right back."

He immediately dialed back to Brooke and again to voice-mail. *Damnation,* he thought. *How can they both be unreachable?*

Whiffer could not reach Jackson or Brooke, so he dialed Beau instead. Beau was beside himself. He was angry because a security breach of this magnitude could shut the program down. It could also have a detrimental effect on Beau's employment and security clearance. Beau called his contact in the Joint Chiefs of Staff and informed them of the breach. These calls triggered a chain of calls throughout the intelligence community. This began a search throughout the government for the trail of the leaked information. This was the beginning of a journey to find who was hacking their data and why.

Whiffer had been exposed to some hacker types in college and was very keenly aware that they might be dealing with some characters of questionable reputation. He was quietly wondering how low the status of the suspicious characters receiving the transmitter signal might have descended. In his heart, he did not have a good feeling about this discovery. It deeply troubled Whiffer's soul.

Chapter 14

Just outside of Tehran in a nondescript Quds Force monitoring station, an operator was frantically working on a computer system. Standing quietly behind him with a scowl on his face, Qassem Soleimani looked at a computer monitor. The system speaker had gone eerily quiet. About seven minutes ago, information was streaming across the monitor. Suddenly there was dead silence. The Quds Force and the IRIAF had been actively monitoring the feed coming directly from Evanston, Illinois. There were vast arrays of servers that were storing the data as it streamed into the Iranian system. The Quds Force had an intelligence officer go through the data and pulled useful nuggets out to pass them up the chain of command. This bug had been a gold mine of data for the Iranians. However, nobody knew that the data was out in the open. It had been a stroke of genius. But it appeared to have just ended.

Soleimani pulled his cell phone from his shirt pocket and dialed a number. "Get here, *NOW!*" He hung up and replaced the phone in his pocket. The operator's face got red, sweat pouring from his brow.

Chapter 15

The next twelve minutes passed very slowly in the monitoring station. Finally, the silence and tension were broken by the door swinging open suddenly. In walked Muhammed Faruq, his Quds Force uniform shirt soaked in sweat. He had obviously run as fast as he was able, to get to the general when he was called. Faruq spun around to attention and saluted his general. Soleimani looked through Faruq and, without uttering a sound, pointed to the computer monitor on the desk.

The monitor was dark. No data could be seen streaming into the servers. The operator stopped in his tracks, took two steps toward the wall, and stood silently at attention. The general walked toward Faruq, stepped to within an inch of his face, their noses almost touching. Soleimani raised his right arm. He pointed to the monitor and started to yell but subdued his voice to say, "Fix this now!"

The quiet of his voice was a sound that Faruq knew well. It was the sound of subdued rage. If Faruq knew anything, he knew that Soleimani's subdued anger would soon come spilling out. He did not want it aimed at him. Faruq turned, sweating profusely, and took a seat at the monitor and began typing at a feverish pace. After about three minutes for diag-nostics, Faruq turned and reported, "The bug is dead. I cannot ping it and get a return ping. We must assume the device has been discovered."

Soleimani was noticeably furious. He turned and stormed out of the small monitoring station. Faruq's head dropped, and he sobbed. He simply could not believe that he had taken a semester off to complete his active duty obligation. What terrible luck!

This development would necessitate a drastic change in the harvesting of **MANOPOLY** information. Soleimani had to plot a new strategy.

Chapter 16

Back in the Econ Lab 1, Whiffer had immediately taken very detailed photos of the device at numerous angles. The transmitter was then submerged into a bell jar of isopropyl alcohol. The alcohol guaranteed that the signal stopped sending, and the receiver stopped receiving instructions. The rubbing alcohol would not allow oxidation to occur on the circuitry. Additionally, the solvent would quickly evaporate completely when Whiffer was ready to perform his forensic examination of the electronics. Whiffer had a friend, Jeff Jones, in the Department of Computer Sciences right there at Northwestern that was a crackerjack hardware specialist. Jeff was a world-renowned expert in computer circuitry. Whiffer would pull Jeff into this project; he was the best in the field, and Whiffer trusted him completely. Trust was critical right now.

Whiffer was very anxious to disassemble and reverse engineer the transmitter/receiver and try to follow a pingback to the receiver where the data was being collected. This task now felt a bit like a detective assignment, and Whiffer liked this kind of challenge. Whiffer had worked extensively with Jeff in the Department of Computer Sciences. Before the MANOPOLY Project had consumed all of Whiffer's time, he enjoyed working on projects with Jeff. Jeff was a hardware kind of guy, but not just hardware per se; he loved taking components apart and finding out how and why they worked together to perform a common task. He also enjoyed following the path that information followed and tried to understand how the software interacted the way it did with the hardware. Whiffer was more of a software kind of guy that could take any finished component and put them together to build an excellent computing machine. Knitting the pieces together with software in a symphony of commands to perform any prescribed task was what Whiffer loved.

Jeff liked the intimate detail. That was why he would be such a great complement to Whiffer. Whiffer also loved working with Jeff and was looking very forward to collaborating. Whiffer was typing furiously on a report for the Joint Chiefs of Staff to update them on the forensic analysis of the spyware that he had discovered located in the junction box in the Econ Lab 1.

This report would travel very quickly up the intelligence community chain of agencies. These agencies would promptly put together a rapid response team for the express purpose of shutting the leak down. After the hole was plugged, the operation would quickly transition into the recovery of any lost information. The United States government directly assigned most of the scenarios run by the MANOPOLY Project. A breach of this magnitude was a dangerous development. At this very moment, all of the intelligence agencies at the disposal of the United States government were instantly revving up at full steam! Within a matter of moments, an inter-agency communication sent through a secure communication system landed on each secure server across the federal government.

Chapter 17

In Langley, Virginia, at the CIA Headquarters, the terminal at the Middle Eastern desk suddenly dinged. Ali Assad quickly moved to the keyboard and clicked on the message; the time and login information were instantly captured by top-secret servers at the National Security Agency in Maryland. As each of these alerts was opened, the list of intelligence agencies and assets coming to bear against this threat grew. This was quickly becoming a national emergency. The cumulative effect of each new agency entering the operation increased the speed and depth of the response. A formidable force was rapidly mounting against the unknown entity at the other end of the transmitter in Whiffer's lab.

Ali Assad quickly scanned the notice and reached for his secure satellite phone, and he dialed a number that he only had committed to memory; nowhere could this number be found written down on paper. The sat phone rang a secure number, at the IRIAF Headquarters deep inside the Doshan Tappeh Air Base outside of Tehran, Iran. A phone vibrated in the pocket of Colonel Muhammed Arman. Arman looked around and hurried into a nearby restroom. He answered in a whispering voice, "*Arman, go.*"

Assad quickly informed Arman that espionage had entered the American university data collection project. He secretly suspected the Iranians when he saw the inter-agency notification. This was the kind of operation he had seen over and over again from Iran. They were notorious for doing long and deep operations. They were thrilled to spend months, or even years, working an asset into a position of trust, and they had the patience to sit seemingly *forever* and just wait until a door opened. Then suddenly, there they sat, in the exact right spot at the precise time. He had to reach out to his Iranian asset and set him on task to search from that perch. This feeling was precisely the reason why he had called Arman first. Intuition—it was Arman's forte!

Further, the entire United States intelligence community had been scrambled to find the leak and run it to ground. He quickly informed Arman to contact his personal assets and find out what alarms their activities could possibly have raised. The call had been swift and precisely to the point, without a wasted syllable. The call ended with Assad saying to Arman, "Call home when all is well." And the connection was terminated, and the phone was dropped into the toilet. The coded message simply meant to contact Assad when any information became available.

Ali Assad sat quietly in his office in Langley and wondered what Arman's assets were doing and where they were. Were any of their operations crossing an intersection point with the ongoing data collection and manipulation processes that were currently running at Northwestern University? He thoroughly combed through each byte of data in his mind on all of the current operations in Tehran. He sat in silence, staring at the wall behind his desk. He shook his head with a vacant look on his face. He could think of nothing. So, the question that any intelligence manager *always* must wonder, deep inside his heart, remained: *What could be happening of which I am unaware?* This question was giving him thoughts of fear and panic.

Arman was now back in the office of Brigadier General Aziz Nasirzdeh, Commander of the IRIAF; he was shaken to his core. Ali Assad *never* broke radio silence, and to have contacted him outside of customarily scheduled contact times, and agreed-upon methods, were totally unheard of. Arman sat with his face in his hands and searched his mind for any intersection between his people and his active operations that could possibly touch an American research project. He could think of nothing. He felt a deep-seated fear, and a foreboding of something very ominous coming his way. This feeling was the exact feeling that a spy never wanted to experience.

Chapter 18

Whiffer was sitting at his preferred desk. When he was thinking intensely about the process, he would be in the crow's nest, at the workbench. In Econ Lab 1, only the exit lights on the game floor of the lab were on. He sat in his captain's chair at the controls of the MANOPOLY Project. Only his magnifying lamp was on, casting a warm glow in the crow's nest. He had to get his mind around how to address this breach. He also felt an incredibly heavy weight of responsibility on his soul to protect the intellectual property that he commanded. But it went much deeper than a sense of professional duty for Whiffer. Jackson and Brooke were his best friends and his family. He decided at that moment that he must go on offense to protect the MANOPOLY Project. He tried calling Jackson and Brooke again. Both went directly to voicemail.

One of Whiffer's less visible duties as the network administrator for the MANOPOLY Project was that of doing data backups of all projects that were contracted by and for the United States government. One of the in-depth details of maintaining this task involved working hand in glove with the NSA's network administrator. This additional level of oversight seemed quite an annoying bit of detail that Jackson and

Brooke considered deep in the minutia of the daily geek work. Neither Jackson nor Brooke paid any attention to this process, leaving it up to Whiffer. The NSA's network administrator was Russell Emming. Russell and Whiffer had long ago become steadfast friends. Later that day, Whiffer and Russell had a data backup appointment to accomplish. In the absence of Jackson and Brooke, Whiffer decided to speak to Russell about how to proceed in better securing the project. He called and posed a hypothetical question to him about how he would go about finding any leaks in his network. Russell knew that Whiffer did not waste many words. There had to have been a reason he was asking this very pointed question. He looked and Whiffer and asked, point blank, "Do you have a leak?" Whiffer melted like an M&M in the hot sun.

⊂⊃

RUSSELL WAS ALREADY in the server room running some diagnostics, waiting for Whiffer to arrive, his tool kit/briefcase was out on the floor next to him, and he was replacing a backup tape that was being systematically switched out of the RAID stack. Whiffer walked in, and instead of sitting down and helping Russell out, he sat down and very shyly cleared his throat. Russell stopped what he had been doing, laid down his tools, and looked deep into Whiffer's eyes. He knew this was a weighty moment; he felt it deep in his soul.

Whiffer proceeded to tell Russell about what he had found in a junction box on the game floor and the processes he had gone through to ping the receiving station for the transmitter. Russell was a tech geek just as much as Whiffer, and he was fascinated as well. They got up and, for a few minutes, forgot the case at hand. Now they were walking quickly toward the crow's nest to have a look at the circuitry in the bell jar filled with isopropyl alcohol. The bell jar was moved under the circular lighted lamp with a magnifying lens in the center.

Russell leaned down, took his magnifying glasses from his shirt pocket, and squinted for a long, close look. Seeing the unique architecture of the circuitry and the Farsi lettering on the board, he simply said, "*Hmmm...*"

There were a couple moments of weighty silence between the two friends. This situation superseded their friendship to a question of their fiduciary responsibilities to their respective employers. Both were keenly aware that national security was paramount in their occupation. Russell sat down in a nearby chair, stared straight ahead, and simply said, "*Holy* shit! You need some help! Let me take you to my boss." Whiffer again tried to call Jackson and Brooke and only got voicemail. He was at a loss and had no guidance. Whiffer trusted Russell and knew he had the proper security clearances. He had to have good advice. This was why they collaborated regularly.

Russell and Whiffer took the elevator from the crow's nest down to the ground floor. Quickly, they moved to the exit next to the parking lot. They engaged the security alarm and exited the building and secured the building. It was about a fifteen-minute drive to a private airport, where the NSA had a Gulfstream G650 twin tail engine jet that had delivered Russell to Evansville. When the pilot saw Russell, he fired up the engines. From Evansville to Andrews Air Force Base was about a thirty-two-minute flight. Russell made a call as they lifted off, and when they landed, Russell's boss was sitting on the tarmac, with a gentleman sitting quietly in the driver's seat. His driver, Whiffer, assumed. Russell and Whiffer got into the car, and the car drove into a nearby hangar out of sight. Whiffer again tried to call Jackson and Brooke, yet they both went directly to voicemail.

In the hangar, Russell introduced Whiffer to his boss. Whiffer knew it was a very solemn meeting when Russell introduced him as Justin Walker, a name he only heard at his parents' home! Ronald Burnett did not remind Whiffer of a professional government executive. Instead, in his blue jeans and T-shirt, he looked much more like an adjunct art professor at Northwestern University. Nonetheless, Russell began the story of intrigue and espionage that was unfolding at Econ Lab 1 in Evansville. Whiffer filled in all of the blanks and details. Burnett listened very quietly, and after about fifty minutes of listening, he looked at Russell, then to Whiffer, and said quite stoically, "Darian, what do you think?"

Whiffer had all but forgotten that there was anyone in the driver's seat. To discover that he was listening and now had an opinion shocked him. It just about made Whiffer lose his mind! Whiffer had walked *way* out on a limb in disclosing the security breach to Russell and leaving the facility and flying to Andrews. Additionally, his decision to speak with the NSA had him quite stressed. He was perhaps a bit angry as well. He needed Jackson and Brooke, and they were absent and unreachable. Burnett was very adept at reading people and was able to settle Whiffer down quite effectively. He assured him that everything he had disclosed was currently being discussed between agencies due to an interagency alert. So, Whiffer's beating heart slowed to an average pace, and the driver began to respond.

Darian Amir was a Persian-American and spoke impeccable English; oddly, almost with a Brooklyn accent. Amir was a confidential human asset for the NSA, and his specialty was the Middle East. Burnett was suggesting that Darian go to work with Whiffer as an investigator-in-residence to observe events at Northwestern University. He would blend in and be unseen. He would be there to watch and just be present as the eyes of the United States intelligence community. Jackson and Brooke were nowhere to be found. Whiffer had to make a decision.

He was impressed by the fact that the NSA was already aware of the leak—and that they were on the case, and were planning on putting an asset in a position to collect information in real-time. He agreed that this would be a prudent plan. But suddenly Whiffer remembered that all of this had happened without saying a word to Jackson or Brooke. How would this disclosure go down, and what would they both think of him working alone, outside the confidence of the MANOPOLY Project, to try to mitigate this breach? Would they be angry? Again, Burnett was an absolute pro at reading people and knew exactly where Whiffer's mind had gone. Burnett smiled and said, "Whiffer, I will call Jackson and set up this placement." Whiffer was noticeably relieved and smiled. He got out of the car and, as instructed, returned to the waiting plane for his return to Evanston, Illinois.

As soon as Whiffer was in his seat and buckled into the Gulfstream, he once again dialed Jackson. To his surprise and relief, Jackson answered the phone, and you could hear the grin on his face when he said, "Holy cow, Whiff! Where is the fire? Don't you have anything else to do but call and leave voicemails for Brooke and me?"

Whiffer was a bit peeved by the cavalier attitude that was spouting from his phone, *Geeze,* he thought, *I have been crapping myself, flying off with the NSA, handling all of this, and Jack is giving me shit?* He took a breath and *just* about gave Jackson a piece of his mind. But Whiffer was nothing if not even-tempered, and he *never* snapped at Jackson. It had always been Whiffer's philosophy that giving someone a piece of his mind was just plain crazy. He figured he needed all of his thoughts, so he never gave any of them away. His policy had always served him well. Besides, Jackson was his best friend, so, he gaffed the tone off and waited for him to finish feeding him a rash of crap. He was familiar with this side of Jackson, and it usually made him laugh. After about another thirty to forty-five seconds of Jackson dishing out nonsense to Whiffer, he had to push out his words. His mind was utilizing the time to carefully craft his exact soliloquy to inform Jackson of the events that had happened this extraordinary day! Jackson finished up the line of bullshit, and Whiffer took a deep breath and delivered.

Jackson and Brooke were *now* on the way into Econ Lab 1.

Whiffer returned to the safety of the Econ Lab 1 and was now sitting in his particular spot in the crow's nest, staring through the transparent glass wall of the bell jar at the mysterious electronic circuitry. This small device had set the entire United States intelligence community on its haunches and had it poised to strike. He was exhausted, and he needed some sleep, but first, he had a call to make; he needed to make an early morning appointment. So, he called his buddy from the Department of Computer Sciences; he was the best circuitry architecture engineer available anywhere, and he was on the same university payroll.

With the rise of the morning sun and a new day, Whiffer started the day clear-eyed and ready for his meeting with Jeff Jones. Jeff was a computer engineer in Whiffer's department who completed undergraduate school at the Massachusetts Institute of Technology (MIT) and earned a master's degree at Washington University in St. Louis, Missouri. He held several patents, including CPU's and video card memory modules that were commonly used by major computer manufacturers throughout the United States. Jeff was a certified genius in computer circuitry. He had seen just about everything in the way of computer hardware on the market. He had served an internship after his completion of his master's degree at INTEL. Jeff had assisted in developing INTEL's last generation of processors. Heck, he was even cited in their patent applications that were submitted during his internship. To put it very bluntly—there was nobody more qualified to do a forensic examination of this mystery circuitry. Whiffer was chomping at the bit to work with Jeff again. The clock seemed to be moving slowly toward their 8:15 a.m. appointment.

Whiffer was at his workbench with all of the tools and equipment that he anticipated being required for the task before them. At 8:14 a.m., Jeff was escorted into the crow's nest by one of the graduate students who played the game and attended classes. Whiffer and Jeff shook hands and exchanged pleasantries. Whiffer closed the door and began to spin the yarn that had been his life the past twenty-four to thirty-six hours. After he finished, Jeff was standing there with his mouth hanging open in disbelief. Whiffer walked over to the workbench and lifted a towel from the bell jar. He watched Jeff's eyes catch sight of the component, and his pupils dilated into a tight focus on the piece of computer spyware in the bell jar. Watching Jeff's face when he saw something new was just the bonus to his day. Jeff immediately stepped over and knelt to where the component was precisely at his eye level. Whiffer reached over and turned on the circular lamp with the magnifying lens. Jeff began to murmur to himself as his eyes traced the outer surface of the component. "Beige base color…Farsi characters…orange printing…printed circuit board—NO! The circuit board is *not* printed; it is custom, and *that* is our first clue."

What Jeff discovered was that this circuit board had not been printed by a circuit copying machine. Instead, it had been hand-etched with acid to remove the silver creating contiguous pathways from one component to the next. Called a breadboard circuit, this device could be used to design a custom, single-use circuit board. This indicated that this device was hand-built, not mass-produced. It also drastically narrowed the field of suspects with that level of talent. This was a very complicated circuit; the level of skill was admirable indeed!

Jeff continued to examine, and almost admire, the circuitry through the bell jar. Whiffer brought in a set of tongs and a can of computer air, and they gently lifted the piece out of the alcohol and laid it on a sterile towel. They gently rolled it over and admired the quality of the soldering of the components onto the custom circuit board. They pulled the lid off of the canned air and gently blew the alcohol away. As the canned air blasted against the edges of the components, the alcohol quickly evaporated, leaving no residue. Whiffer opened a cabinet and removed a very high-end digital camera, and they went to great lengths to meticulously photograph the subject from every angle.

Then, Jeff reached across the workbench and picked up the soldering iron and a solder sucker. He gently placed the tip of the soldering iron on the first solder joint they encountered and waited patiently for the solder to shine and turn to liquid. They were utilizing an infrared thermal scanner to record the exact temperature at which the solder melted. This temperature would be the precise temperature indicating the content and origin of the solder. Jeff gently positioned the solder sucker over the pool of solder and began pushing the button on the end repeatedly. As he did so, the pool of silver solder began to reveal the components' bases. After the solder was finally melted and removed, the individual, smaller segments of the compound device could be gently pulled apart with tweezers. As each piece was removed, it was gently positioned on a glass plate in the order of removal. Then each piece was meticulously cleaned, photographed, and cataloged.

Next in this process was uploading the photographs of the individual components and setting up a computer search to scan the websites showing the known manufacturers of computer electronic components. Each was studied and used to compare the catalog photos in search of an exact match. As each piece was identified, the location of its manufacture and the origin of the critical components were captured. After the parts had all been identified and data collected from the computer search, assimilating the information would indicate where the circuitry was most likely made and assembled. This would tell, with a high degree of certainty, the origin of the hardware. At the end of this process, a computer search of the customer files on the manufacturer's website would give the number of pieces and the customer who purchased this hardware. In the event that serial numbers were located on a component, those could be traced as well.

After an entire day of exhaustive computer forensics, hardware disassembly, and database searches, the computer results identified a small electronics retailer in suburban Tehran.

Chapter 19

Simultaneously at the Quds Force headquarters in Tehran, Soleimani was sitting at his desk on the secure phone line speaking to Salomon Agassi in very heated Persian.

"The stream of data that we were receiving has stopped. What has happened?" Soleimani demanded.

Agassi was shocked by the revelation and replied, "When did it stop? Have you pinged the device back?"

"Do you think I am stupid? Of course, I have done everything possible to reactivate the device from this end! You must find out what has happened and what the Americans know." Soleimani continued, "This is your life at risk here. I demand an immediate response! I also require to know who the most valuable person is on this team, and I need him followed. We may well have to take him for more information and possibly for leverage." Soleimani finished in the deadly quiet voice that everyone around him understood: "Do you *understand?*"

Agassi hung up the phone and was visibly shaken. Was the general really considering kidnapping a teacher from Northwestern? He dropped his face into his hands and cursed in Persian.

Chapter 20

Early the next day, Jackson, Brooke, and Whiffer were all together in the crow's nest, finally able to fill each other in on all of the facts and events that had occurred the past two days. These three people were entirely flabbergasted by these events, and they were trying to stop their heads from spinning. Whiffer was filling Jackson and Brooke in on all of the details regarding the find they made. He also had to fill them in on the details of his quick trip to Andrews Air Force Base. Before they could get through a complete and thorough briefing, Jackson's cell phone vibrated. Jackson pulled the phone from his pants pocket and looked shocked. Jackson looked down at his iPhone 5 screen and saw the caller ID listed as UNKNOWN.

He answered the call with a tone of guarded hesitation. "Jackson Reynolds…"

The voice on the other end of the line identified himself: "Hello, Mr. Reynolds, I am Ronald Burnett. I spent some time with our computer gurus yesterday in a hangar at Andrews. I need to talk to you on a matter of national security."

Jackson was a bit concerned with having this conversation until he finished his briefing with Whiffer. So, Jackson continued, "Mr. Burnett, I am in a private meeting right this second. Could you please give me your number, and I'll call you back within the hour?"

Burnett agreed and promptly left his number. Jackson jotted the number down on his desk calendar along with the name RONALD BURNETT. With that, Jackson returned to the business at hand.

He looked at Whiffer and said, "Whiff, talk to me. I need the entire story about Burnett before I call him back." So, Whiffer spent the next hour telling Jackson and Brooke every single detail about the meeting between Burnett, Russell, Darian, and himself. Jackson and Brooke were now also aware that Darian Amir was coming into the Econ Lab 1. They were all too keenly aware that from this day forward, they would be entirely supervised and observed in everything they worked on and did. From this day forward, all work was being watched. Whiffer went back to work on the game floor, and Brooke had a class to teach. Jackson called Ronald Burnett again. Darian Amir was scheduled to report to the Econ Lab 1 at eight a.m. the next day.

It was not the fact, nor even the idea, that there was ever anything that happened that bothered Jackson; nor what was said in, or around, the MANOPOLY Project. Rather, it seemed that this sequence of events signaled the end of the innocence of the project. The relationships that grew from the project seemed very organic and pure to this point. Never again could he, nor anyone else on the management team, had any reasonable belief that there would be any privacy or confidentiality concerning the lives touched by the project. Now it would have to be assumed that everything that happened was not only seen and heard, but also recorded and/or written down.

Nothing would need to change except for some noticeable security enhancements. It was just a feeling that everything would be more formal, more dangerous. People would feel less free to express ideas as openly and freely. This was a moment of melancholy and a very bittersweet one at that to Jackson. Jackson knew he had to follow the course laid out before him, and he knew that the added security would be beneficial. However, he was just sad that his baby had ended up being treated in a manner that he felt was so unfair. Nonetheless, Jackson was bracing for an entirely new era, the turning of a new page in the history of the MANOPOLY Project. That night was indeed the last night in the passing of a chapter that had treated Jackson and his dream very well. Jackson looked at his watch and walked over to the coat tree in his office, pulled on his jacket, and headed out the door to meet Brooke for dinner.

That night, there was a formal dress affair at the home of the university president; Jackson and Brooke's attendance was expected, if not required. Northwestern University had a very loyal body of alumni that hosted an annual gala each year that hosted celebrity guest speakers who addressed many topics of interest to the university. This event was hosted by a group of professional basketball players from the Chicago Bulls. Tickets cost twenty-five hundred dollars per plate, and the Northwestern University Alumni Association had done a stellar job of advertising the event. A local owner of a radio station had donated airtime for advertising as well. It was a full house.

The formal dining room at the university-owned president's mansion was packed. There was a university chamber orchestra playing classical pieces from the Renaissance. Jackson and Brooke walked into the foyer dressed to kill. Jackson was dressed in a black satin tuxedo with tails and a fire-engine-red bow tie. Brooke was wearing a couture gown made by Chanel, the exact same shade of red as Jackson's bow tie. The dress flowed to the floor and had long sleeves and a plunging neckline that stopped just an inch or two above her belly button. Her hair was in an immaculate bun on the top of her head. The entire room halted and noticed Jackson and Brooke's entrance at the party. Most noticeable to their closest friends, on the ring finger of Brooke's left hand, was a stunning, 2.2-carat, brilliant, flawless, marquis cut diamond engagement ring. Tonight would be the night that Jackson and Brooke would formally announce their engagement. It was the moment that Brooke had waited her entire life to experience.

As they walked into the dining room, Brooke was glowing like a full moon on a clear winter's night. She was ecstatic when she saw Beau. Jackson had made sure that her big brother was there to share her night.

As the orchestra played, Jackson asked Brooke to dance. They were hearing a beautiful waltz. Brooke was now very thankful for the ballroom dance lessons that she took in Baton Rouge that the cotillion dances had required. Through her high school and college career, she had experienced only a handful of opportunities to use the dances that she had learned as a teenage girl. As she danced tonight, she felt like a princess.

She was amazed to learn that Jackson knew how to waltz as well. As the orchestra continued to play, they looked like a living Disney couple dancing at a ball. Life could be no better than it was at that very moment! The music faded down. Jackson took Brooke by the hand and led her to a twelve-quart, leaded crystal punch bowl. He picked up a cup of punch and reached out to give it to her. She had a different idea. Instead, he set it back down on the table. He put his arm around her waist while she turned her face toward his. Their eyes met, and Jackson kissed her with all of the love he had in his heart.

The moment was abruptly ended by someone tapping them on their shoulders. Whiffer smiled like he had brand new teeth and wished them his most sincere congratulations. Brooke's heart was full; she was surrounded by everyone she loved in her life. Whiffer took her hand and took a long look at the engagement ring. He looked at Jackson and said, "You sure did a good job on this one, Jack!"

He continued, "Where did you find a rock like this in Evanston?"

Jack smiled and replied, "Whiff, remember when you called us both about fifteen times apiece the day before yesterday? We snuck off to Chicago and picked out the ring." Jackson smiled as though he had never been so proud of himself in his life.

Whiffer, on the other hand, was worn slick from the day he had as a result of the missed calls. Nonetheless, this was a beautiful night, and the thought about work and phone calls was quickly drowned out by the dynamic sound of a rumba. Life was good tonight, but tomorrow, Darian Amir would begin at Econ Lab 1.

It had been a fantastic night for Jackson and Brooke. They had a great time with friends and family, but they were at the university, and at any university event, there always seemed to be some expectation of work lurking in the dark. The university president's wife came over to wish Brooke her best and wanted to see her ring. The president wandered to Jackson's other side and engaged him in small conversation. The university's newspaper, *The Daily Northwestern*, always had a photographer on hand for events such as this one. The president and his wife with two department chairs was a great shot, so they posed together and smiled. As the girls walked away chatting, Jackson thought that he should use this moment to let the president know that things might be changing in the Econ Lab 1. He approached the topic with some trepidation. He was very conscious that about fifteen different federal laws bound this disclosure, so Jackson chose his words very carefully.

Jackson excused himself and stepped into the closest nondescript corner in the room. He began by telling the president that things were moving very well with the MANOPOLY Project. The report that had been done for the federal government regarding the Haitian economic recovery had been very positive. However, he continued, they anticipated that coming projects would be highly sensitive. Since they had a very mutually beneficial arrangement here, and the government had a lot of taxpayer dollars invested, the government would be mandating some additional security protocols. The president seemed to act as though this news just rolled off of his back like water from a duck's back. Jackson was very relieved. He felt as though the weight of the world had been lifted off of his back.

The boys found the girls and exchanged a few parting lines. Jackson and Brooke snuck out to spend a special night alone together. Eight in the morning would be there too quickly.

At 6:30 a.m., Whiffer was at the control panel in the crow's nest at Econ Lab 1. He was a bit uneasy about the arrival of Darian Amir today. He, too, felt as though the dynamics of the project were about to shift or change. When he was nervous, he worked. Jackson and Brooke came into the lab together but parted ways in the lobby. Jackson was heading to his office. Brooke was rushing to hers, to give a test. Brooke was carrying a semester exam in her arms for her Economics 405 class. Jackson was anxious to get to his office and get through the Human Resource maze that was coming this morning. Figuring out how to hide a government spy in your payroll seemed a duty that should have been completed before Darian arrived. He called the Human Resource manager and his legal counsel into his office for a meeting to make the necessary arrangements and accommodations to add a new executive-level employee.

At exactly eight a.m., Darian Amir walked through the door to the outside office of the Director of the Department of Economics. Jackson's secretary escorted Darian through the door into Jackson's office. Jackson had never seen Darian Amir, but he had been described to him by Whiffer. He was taller than Whiffer had recalled, like six-foot-two, but Whiffer had only seen him sitting in a car. Jackson guessed his weight at two hundred ten pounds, olive complexion, jet-black hair, dark brown eyes, and a big smile. He looked like a kindly man. He thought to himself that this might not be so bad. The secretary closed the door behind her, and the gentlemen sat down. Jackson picked up the neat pile of employment paperwork in the middle of his desk and arranged it for his meeting. Darian reached into his jacket and grabbed a pen from his shirt pocket. He picked up the top sheet of paper from the pile in front of him, preparing to fill them out.

Jackson was observing his every move and watched as he took the pen into his left hand and started filling out the application. He stopped him from filling out the paperwork just this moment and cleared his throat. He started slowly and proceeded with measured intensity.

"Darian, I want you to understand that I am an economist that has enjoyed playing board games my entire life. My ability to play games, to anticipate the moves of others, and to observe many moving parts at one time has always been my gift."

He continued, "The one thing that stupefies me more than anything regarding the matters that have brought you here is that I missed the entire thing! I fancied myself as a man who saw things before me and anticipated what was going to happen around me... I missed this all! And that fact bothers me more than you can know!"

Darian looked at him contently and listened as Jackson continued, "I find myself at a new crossroad that I also never anticipated. I now have to have a government intelligence asset here in my project, and I failed to prevent that from happening. I just don't understand how this all will work."

Darian looked into his eyes, paused, and saw that this was

all very unfamiliar to a very educated man, and he moved slowly to speak. He said, "Mr. Reynolds, please understand that I take no pleasure in the failures of security that your project has experienced. It is my understanding that you have never met Ronald Burnett. I would strongly recommend that you meet with him and have him tell you his personal story regarding how he ended up in the employ of the NSA. I think your mind would be very soothed." Jackson smiled and nodded in acknowledgment that he had heard and understood what Darian had just told him.

Darian was referring to the circumstances by which Ronald Burnett happened to become employed by the NSA. Burnett had owned a very successful computer networking firm in Seattle. The company was selected through a very secure bidding process to set up a secured government network for the Seattle FBI office. Everything had gone smoothly until the FBI decided that they would require a full biometric security protocol for specific secure computer networks. Burnett was pretty unfamiliar with the newest biometric hardware and was searching for an engineer who could program new equipment that he had never seen.

This was very early in the development of biometric security, and there were only a handful of experts on the topic in the world. Burnett received a resume from an English engineer who professed to have ties to MI6. He hired the engineer, and the install was completed in a timely fashion. The project seemed to be working well. However, the NSA had picked up a faint, intermittent beeping from the biometric control panel. They sent an engineer into the project and left with a rudimentary recording device. This was how Burnett met his boss with the NSA. Burnett had experienced a very similar experience and had used the experience to move up the ranks inside the NSA. Darian would call Burnett after Jackson left the building and ask him to contact him and tell him his story.

Darian really liked Jackson. He even believed they might one day become terrific friends.

Jackson had work in the crow's nest that he had to get done. He instructed Darian to complete the paperwork. He was instructed to give it to his secretary and then have her call him into the crow's nest. Darian shook his hand and sat down to complete his assignment. Jackson headed out the front door of his office, thinking to himself, *Perhaps, this will be fine.*

Chapter 21

Salomon Agassi had poised himself in a waiting room in the lobby of the Economics building. He had selected this exact seat so he could see the door of Jackson's office down the hallway. It would give him the strategic advantage of knowing when Jackson was alone. It would also allow him to see who came and went from the office. Agassi saw Jackson walk into the hall, headed for the elevator. Jackson was alone; Agassi made a rapid approach. Using his position on the finance committee, he began a conversation.

"Jackson, what the heck is going on around here? Have I missed something?" he inquired.

"What do you need, Salomon? I am swamped right now," Jackson glibly responded.

Agassi pressed, "I am the man with budgetary oversight of your little fiefdom. I demand some answers!"

Jackson stopped in his tracks, slowly turned his head toward Agassi, and calculated his exact response. "We had a bug in our hardware. We are still trying to determine what has happened. Whiffer is evaluating the situation as we speak. You are aware that my project is under military oversight?" Jackson continued with a touch of snark, "I will inform you of any financial expenditures as they arise." He then began walking away. "We are finished." Jackson stepped onto the elevator, and the door closed.

Whiffer seemed to be the key man. Salomon had to get a tail on him immediately. They also had the Iranian device. He had to get this intel back to the general.

Chapter 22

2015

About six months had passed since Whiffer had located the Iranian spyware in the junction box on the game floor at Econ Lab 1. Russell Emming and Whiffer, while doing the diagnostic computer work that tracked the origin of the Iranian device, had become a dynamic working team in locking down the network security for the MANOPOLY Project. They were implementing a far more automated process. In the beginning, fifty tables of four graduate students sat at game tables and manually operated the game pieces. After the Iranian espionage event, a number of improvements had been made. Increasing advancements in adding systems along with deeper levels of data collection were put in place. Finally, circuit boards and CPU's were added to minimalize human interaction. Artificial Intelligence (A.I.) was becoming the preferred method of collecting data, factoring rational decision making and actions. With fewer required humans around, the MANOPOLY Project was more secure than ever. It also was effectively minimizing the potential for leaks.

Additionally, Darian Amir was also now keeping watch

over the actions and modifications. In addition to Jackson, Brooke, Whiffer, Northwestern University, and the United States Department of Defense, the NSA now had a crucial position in the oversight of the evolution of the project. So, this was the new set of dynamics that was currently in effect. As a result, Russell and Whiffer had been working like crazy to keep the evolution moving toward these goals, while still being able to run scenarios as the need required.

On a parallel track, Darian, with oversight by Ronald Burnett and persons in offices much higher and unknown to Jackson, Brooke, Whiffer, and Beau, an exhaustive operation was progressing in Iran. The information regarding the source of the Iranian circuitry that had been traced to a retail store in suburban Tehran was forwarded to Ali Assad at the CIA's Middle Eastern desk. Assad had initiated highly classified contact with Colonel Muhammad Arman (a CIA asset under deep cover) in Brigadier General Aziz Nasizadeh's office, Commander of the IRIAF. Nasirzdeh answered directly to General Qassem Soleimani, Commander of the Quds Force. Soleimani was only answerable to the Supreme Commander of Iran himself. Quite surprisingly, this operation had reached to the very top of the government of Iran. The view from thirty-thousand feet of all of the players in the Iranian battlefield required a quick review of all players involved. This would give a structured reference so one could follow the actions as they happened on the ground in the Middle East.

The places the Iranian spy purchased the electronic computer components for the device were forwarded to Ali Assad. Assad was tasked with mobilizing local CIA assets to track down the retailer who sold the parts. Once the retailer was found, a top-secret operation was authorized to access the books, electronic records, and Internet access of the computer supply shop in Tehran. Once access to the economic and customer data was laid bare, it was possible to hack into and search the database of the retailer's customers. This information yielded four likely individuals who had made purchases that could have built such a device. At that juncture, the names were provided to Ronald Burnett and Darian Amir at the NSA. They had cross-referenced the possible builders with a list of known computer engineers/programmers in Iran that had access to the hardware, bandwidth, and freedom of movement to build and pass such a device through to the United States of America. This search found that two of the four purchasers could have passed this first means test.

It was now time to pass this information onto someone on the ground in Iran much closer to the two possible suspects. This information was given in a highly confidential meeting in the Embassy of the United Arab Emirates between Darian and Colonel Muhammad Arman. The report was now in the office of General Nasirzdeh. Currently, all the power and resources that Iran's own military possessed were coming to bear in search of the perpetrator. With an inside searcher, the team was very close to having the man who built the Iranian spy device in sight.

Arman entered the shared data in the Iranian National Security database, and the computer took all of about twenty-two seconds to spit out the name of Freyredoon Adipour, a computer engineer associated with the Iranian Revolutionary Guard Corps (IRGC). However, knowing who built the device and being able just to go pick him up and arrest him for extradition to the United States were two destinations that were very hard to drive between. The IRGC and the IRIAF were very closely associated inside Iran. The IRGC was the army that was formed by students in 1979, when the United States Embassy was overrun and the occupants were held hostage for 444 days—an action that cost Jimmy Carter the United States presidency.

Conversely, this was the same event that brought Ronald Reagan into the White House. The Shah was expelled from Iran immediately thereafter leading these students to set up a theocracy that took the Iranian country back to the Stone Age relative to civil and human rights. This group also set up the Supreme Leader as the head of their government. The point here was that reaching a computer engineer that was *this* close to the head of the IRGC was a level of complexity that had to be considered very carefully and handled with the most delicate of kid gloves.

2016

The information that Freyredoon Adipour had built the Iranian spy device found on the floor in Evanston was devastating. The fact that he was placed very high in the IRGC was a spy craft nugget that was passed like a hot potato from Arman back to Burnett. Here, the ball was stuck in time.

Chapter 23

The entire spy novel intrigue that had been running for almost a year at Econ Lab 1 in Evanston was daunting. The drama had brought the opportunities to run more scenarios through the MANOPOLY Project to a standstill. There was very little demand for sending confidential data to an entity that had just discovered an Iranian spy leak. These events had put Beau back into his position at the Federal Reserve full time. He had gotten very used to the autonomy and the freedom that being the Federal Reserve's primary had given him. Coming in and sitting at the desk every day was wearing very heavy on him, giving Beau a great deal of time to sit and stew in the mystery of knowing and meeting his father.

Patsy Benoit had been diagnosed with stage four metastatic breast cancer in 2010 and had passed away after a double mastectomy in 2012. Brightwell Benoit had not taken her death well at all and had struggled with depression and loneliness. Bright had let his health go, and his hypertension, left untreated, had led to a stroke that could have probably been avoidable. Although he had survived his stroke, his left side had little feeling. Moreover, the left side of his face had fallen, and his speech was tough to understand. He was staying in his Baton Rouge home because Beau and Brooke had hired an in-home nursing company to care for him around the clock.

They had farm and ranch staff that maintained the crop and livestock businesses. The family farm, along with all equipment and buildings, had been paid for long ago. The farm was a very profitable and self-sustaining business. So, keeping Bright comfortable in his home was not a hardship for the Benoit children. The Colonial-style plantation was very imposing and had many rooms on two stories. Most of the upstairs bedrooms had been closed and the furnishings covered with dust covers. The heating and cooling ducts had been sealed and the thermostats turned off to conserve on utility costs. Freezing water lines were just about unheard of in the Deep South. The heat generated for the main floor radiated up to the second story rooms to keep them temperate. The second story was closed; the children's bedrooms still contained family possessions from the past few generations. But the history and relics of the Benoit family were preserved.

Beau was suffering from cabin fever; he just could not sit at a desk day in and day out. The spare time he spent in his desk chair only put his mind more rooted in the mystery of his unknown father. It had been several months since Beau had been to Baton Rouge to see his dad. So, Beau leaned forward, pushed the intercom button on his desk, and instructed his secretary to book him a flight to Baton Rouge. He had her book it for the next morning and had her leave the return open. Beau walked out of the Federal Reserve Building in Midtown Manhattan and got into a car for his apartment in the Upper West Side. He packed his bag when he got home and made it an early night.

At seven a.m. the next morning, Beau was checking in at the American Airlines terminal to get his boarding pass. He took his carry-on to his assigned seat in business class, about five rows back. In his window seat, he peered out, leaned back, and mentally took flight. Beau's eyes were closed, but he was not sleeping. Rather, he was traveling back in time. Had he forgotten any clue that would help him find his missing natural father? His mind went to the high school football field, where he had been injured. It went to the hospital, where he had learned the news that had untethered his identity. He was trying to remember every word his mother had shared with him about Virgil William Bagley, his natural father.

Beau had fought an enormous struggle since he had learned that Bright was not his natural father. On the one side, he loved Bright Benoit. He was the only father he had ever known. Bright was a GREAT dad! But on the other hand, he felt empty and did not feel as though he knew who he was inside. When he discovered that his blood type had identified him as the son of another man, he wondered what else existed inside him. What was there, that he was unaware of, lurking in the unknown dark? He had tried with all of his might to shake this internal obsession, but when he woke up every morning, it was there, in his mind. He just did not have the strength to push it beneath the surface and keep it there. He had to know.

Beau's flight was very smooth. It was an excellent day to fly. The trip had taken just under two hours, and he deplaned carrying his only bag. He was able to avoid the baggage carousel. He walked through the Baton Rouge Metropolitan Airport (BTR), where the altitude was merely seventy feet. It was a tiny regional airport. His walk to the taxi stand, in front, was short. He caught a taxi, and within fifteen minutes he was riding down a long blacktop driveway. It looked as though the cab would drive straight into the front door of the vast white Colonial plantation house. Just as the doorknob was visible, the driveway swung to the right and came up alongside the wooden front porch. It was good to be home, and a smile slowly came across his face. The taxi stopped; Beau got out, grabbed his bag, and disappeared through the tall, twin front doors.

Beau immediately took a right and began to call out, "Dad? Dad, it's Beau!" Within a minute or less, Bright's nurse pushed him out of the sunroom in his wheelchair. Bright's eyes smiled, but the left side of his face moved very little. It appeared to be pulled by the right side. Beau said very warmly, "Hello, Dad! I love you!"

It was about 9:45 a.m. Beau walked into the large kitchen at home. He opened the refrigerator door and was looking for a bite of breakfast. He took out a pitcher of orange juice, sat it on the counter, opened the cabinet next to the fridge for a cup, and poured a glass of orange juice. He took a long draw from the tall glass of orange juice, quenching his immediate thirst, and then opened the refrigerator door again to replace the pitcher. He was looking for some protein. He found a carton of eggs, placed them on the counter, and opened the cabinet below the bar. He took a skillet out and sat it on the burner on the range opposite the refrigerator.

He turned the stove on medium and placed the skillet over the blue flame from the natural gas range. He turned back to the fridge, opened the dairy keeper lid, selected a stick of butter, and laid it on the counter beside the counter-top range. He opened the silverware drawer just above the cabinet from which the skillet came and selected a butter knife. He cut a pat of butter and dropped it into the hot skillet. There was a sizzling sound. He turned and replaced the butter and closed the fridge door. He opened the egg carton and took out two eggs, cracked them on the side of the skillet, and opened them into the bottom of the skillet. He closed the egg carton and replaced it in its original spot in the refrigerator.

The crackling sound of frying eggs sounded like home to Beau. The smell of the home-cooked sunny side up eggs smelled delicious to Beau's nostrils. He then realized that he would need a spatula to flip the eggs, and he found one. He then removed a plate from the upper cabinet next to the glass-fronted curio cabinet where the juice glass was kept. He removed a plate and sat it next to the skillet and scooped the eggs onto his plate. He turned off the burner, put the skillet into the sink, and carried the plate to the table in the breakfast nook. The routine felt so very healthy to Beau. It felt so good to be home!

Beau found it very comforting to be in the bosom of his childhood home. He walked out onto the front porch to enjoy the view that he remembered so well as a boy. The smell of the air was so familiar, but he remembered he was here on a fact-finding mission. He needed to find some answers to the nagging mystery that had haunted him since he was seventeen years old. He took a deep breath of fresh, Louisiana air and walked back in the door and headed up the stairs.

At the top of the steps, he turned right and opened the second door on the left. It was a storage closet that was the repository of all of the family photos, yearbooks, pieces of art, certificates, and awards. He flipped on the light switch. When the light came on, Beau's senses were flooded with sights that took him back into his memory years, if not decades. The boxes were yellowed with age. Beau felt that he had walked back in time. He began looking at his mother's handwriting on the box panels facing the center of the room. The boxes were organized with labels that had both names and years. The name indicated the family member to whom the items belonged, and the date stated the year the treasures were collected. He had never been in this closet without his mother standing in front of him, guiding his search; this time, he was on his own. He would have to do some guessing. He looked up and down, and he realized that he wasn't even sure what he was searching for. He was hoping for a clue, a voice from his mother, any thread that he could pull. Anything he could follow to some information that would lead him to a connection with Virgil.

Surely, a couple of hours had passed. Beau was still sitting in the middle of the hallway floor with several boxes on the floor surrounding him. Everywhere he looked, he saw his mother's handwriting and a collection of items that she alone had chosen to keep. She had organized the puzzle on the floor around him, and he wondered what she would say if he could ask her in what direction should he search. What clue would be the path to resolution?

He took a deep breath in through his nose, closed his eyes, and imagined his mother sitting there with him. His back was beginning to ache from his time on the floor. So, he started putting the family treasures back into the repository that his mother had selected. He finished packing each box, and then he replaced them one by one. He was shaking his head as he returned each box. "What am I missing?" he mumbled out loud.

He looked up at a hat box on the top shelf; the box that held her favorite Easter hat. He couldn't be here and not take just one peek at his momma's Easter hat. He reached up and pulled the box down, lifting it very gingerly. He knelt and sat the treasure on his lap. Gently, he lifted the lid. Then he saw the beautiful lace hat that he could imagine sitting on his momma's hair at Easter dinner. He gently reached in and cupped it into his hands. He suddenly felt tears running down his cheeks. He felt his momma beside him.

He sat there for a couple of minutes as memories flowed over him in a manner that he could never have expected. He wiped his eyes with his thumbs and gently picked the hat up to replace it. There in the box was a photo; an old picture. He laid the hat in the box lid, lying next to the hatbox, and he reached into the box to get a look at what he thought he saw. It was an old photo lying face down. It had two creases that were visible from the back. There was faded blue ink scribbled on the back. The scribbling looked like his mother's handwriting. He picked the photo up and drew it closer so he could inspect it.

The photo was faded black and white. There was a broad

white border with the outer edge cut with a scalloped design that resembled torn paper. There were three people in the photo. One was his mother when she was very young, perhaps high school. And two young men that looked a bit older. Behind them was a bass drum with what looked like faded letters painted on the front of it. The drum was standing upright on its edge.

Tears were running down his face again; he turned the picture over and moved it closer to the light. He saw his mother's name, the name Lyle Willis, and another name that he struggled to read. It was very faded: Randy Bell. Who were these people and was this a clue? Beau replaced his mother's hat just as it had been found, turned off the light, and closed the door. He walked down the stairs and went into the sunroom to have a pleasant visit with his dad.

Chapter 24

It was a year that was evenly divisible by four, which meant it was a presidential election year. In a program that was primarily controlled by the defense industry and the budgetary agencies of the federal government, the prevailing wisdom was that Hillary Clinton would be easily elected. Meaning, for the most part, Barack Obama's policies would remain in place.

Jackson, Brooke, Whiffer, and Beau felt confident in projecting that the scenarios most likely to come to the MANOPOLY Project would likely be military spending scenarios. It would be very similar to what had been coming from this administration and pose no great burden. Searching for and seeking funding sources most viable and efficient to fund military policies were easily found. The most likely scenario, it was rumored, was the probability of a war with North Korea.

It was widely believed that their leader, Kim Jung-Un, was a despot aching for war with the United States. North Korea had been saber-rattling regarding their nuclear weapon program since seizing power. The continued United States presence in neighboring South Korea was also a considerable bone of contention. The Korean War had never officially ended; just a signed armistice stopped the fighting and established the demilitarized zone. South Korea's close relationship with the United States, and the presence of American troops on their southern border, kept Kim in a constant state of agitation. North Korea had a closer alliance to China, making the two Koreas very much like proxies representing America and China. Developing a nuclear weapon to resist regime change had been the stated policy since the Kim family seized control of North Korea. Kim had even killed his uncle, so he could not have a claim to the dictatorship.

They were perpetually shooting missiles, testing delivery vehicles, and trying to perfect the miniaturization of a warhead that could successfully re-enter the atmosphere intact and functional. These missile tests that sent projectiles into the South China Sea and over Japan were constant international episodes. These episodes kept the United Nations Security Council in gridlock. The great quandary at the DOD, the Joint Chiefs of Staff, and the budgetary establishment in the federal government was on figuring out how to go to war without sending the economy into a tailspin. GDP growth had been steady at about 1 to 1.5 percent. It wasn't good growth, but it was growth. Everyone knew that growth was good.

The United States military had experienced six years of drastic funding cuts to make tax dollars available for regulatory and social justice spending. The realization that the military might now be required to fend off a nuclear threat was the "silent buzz" within the Washington establishment. Still, it was being kept very quiet during the 2016 election cycle.

Jackson and Whiffer had run a couple of economic scenarios through MANOPOLY that indicated that appropriations were going to have to be reorganized to strengthen the military before an advance against North Korea could be executed. It also appeared that tax increases across the board would be required to rebuild the aging and decrepit military.

The United States was already deficit spending to the tune of almost a *trillion* dollars a year. The Chinese were underwriting that deficit.

The earlier reference to the WOPR in the 1983 movie *War Games*, reminded Whiffer of the outputs coming from the MANOPOLY Project data. *"There can be no winner,"* continuously echoed through his mind. Perhaps he could load tic-tac-toe secretly onto the computers of Kim Jung-Un, the Joint Chiefs, and China for good measure. A tournament might make them understand that the only way to win is not to fight. But Jackson was an economist, so his main staples remained guns and butter. However, this was not an acceptable answer to the bureaucrats paying the bills at MANOPOLY. Thus, the scenarios were continually refined and re-run, to no avail.

November 8, 2016, arrived, and the American people went to the polls. *Newsweek* magazine had already printed a cover with a smiling Hillary Clinton; the caption read, *"MADAM PRESIDENT."* The cover was actually on newsstands in New York the morning that the polls opened. Before any votes were counted. There seemed to be a huge hunger for the first female president immediately following the first black president. There was a feeling across the nation that Hillary only had to wait until the polls closed to take her triumphant victory lap in the Javits Center in New York City.

All of the pollsters were reporting their data and assured the entire country that Hillary was the next President of the United States of America. Inside Trump Tower in Midtown Manhattan, the Trump family hunkered down and watched, fully expecting to lose as well. Jackson and Whiffer were in the crow's nest with the election returns playing in the background. They programmed new data extrapolations into the control panel to run another scenario, to produce a new report, for the brand-new Clinton administration when the DOD called in the morning. The background election returns were just ambient noise to comfort Jack and Whiff.

Evanston, Illinois, sat in Central Standard Time on November 8, 2016. The first poll closings occurred on the east coast at seven CST. The predominantly Democratic upper eastern seaboard states were the only states that reported early. There were no surprises in those reports. The quote of the day that the two men heard over and over was, *"There is no path by which Trump could reach 270 electoral votes."* For quite some time, that was all they heard. The noise seemed to move further into the background in the crow's nest.

While Jackson and Whiffer were racking their brains trying to devise new strategies to tweak the data for different results, the continuous droning of the newscasters in the background grew more and more interesting. The channel was CNN, and the *"No path to 270"* was alive and doing very well. However, these two men dealt in numbers and laws of statistical probabilities, and they were becoming intrigued. They had seen the data from the polls stating that Hillary Clinton would be the forty-fifth president. That was not what these mathematical geniuses were hearing as vote totals came in.

At six CST, Indiana and Kentucky went for Trump, Vermont for Clinton.

6:30: West Virginia went to Trump.

6:50: South Carolina went to Trump.

7:00: Alabama went to Trump.

Connecticut, Delaware, and the District of Columbia went to Clinton.

Illinois, Maryland, and Massachusetts went to Clinton.

Mississippi, Oklahoma, and Tennessee went to Trump.

New Jersey and Rhode Island went to Clinton.

The Electoral Map was: Clinton 75

Trump 66

7:30: Arkansas went to Trump.

8:00: Kansas, Louisiana, and Nebraska went to Trump.

New York went to Clinton.

The Electoral Map was: Trump 140

Clinton 104

9:03: New Mexico went to Clinton.

9:06: Missouri went to Trump.

9:21: Ohio, a bellwether state and considered a must-win, went to Trump.

9:30: Virginia went to Clinton.

9:35: Colorado went to Clinton.

10:00: California, Hawaii, Oregon, and Washington all went to Clinton.

Idaho went to Trump.

The Electoral Map was:Clinton 209

Trump 176

After Ohio, a bellwether state, had gone for Trump, it appeared that what had once been a horse race had shifted seismically. "The Blue Wall" had crumbled!

10:07: North Carolina went for Trump.

10:30: Florida, Utah, and Iowa all went for Trump.

10:44: Georgia went for Trump.

The Electoral Map was: Trump 244

Clinton 209

Suddenly the *"No possible path to 270 electoral votes"* narrative had collapsed. Jackson and Whiffer were no longer sitting at the control panel in the crow's nest. Instead, they were sitting on the sofa in front of the only television in the room. They were no longer just sitting; rather, they were leaning toward the screen in utter disbelief in what they were witnessing. They were watching the impossible happen right in front of their eyes! They were professionals in programming and in extrapolating data for the federal government. How could anyone have missed a trend like the one they had watched unfold? Whiffer looked at Jackson with a look of utter disbelief and just muttered, "I am so glad we didn't run this data! We would be toast!"

11:32: Nevada went to Clinton.

01:12: Alaska went to Trump.

At 01:40 a.m., Hillary Clinton called Donald Trump to concede!

The Electoral Map was:Trump 278

Clinton 218

Jackson and Whiffer looked at each other and shook their heads. They were wondering what this tragedy might mean to their government masters. What would it mean in the scenarios on which they were working? What would a brand-new administration even look like from their perspective? They were, indeed, in uncharted territory.

Chapter 25

Salomon Agassi had received word from General Soleimani that an Iranian operative of American birth was being sent to Northwestern. He was to follow Whiffer and evaluate his day-to-day routine. The fact that the silent circle of Quds Force operatives was growing on his campus made Agassi nervous. He thought it very lucky that the small Iranian circle of influence had maintained their anonymity. For some reason, he felt that this move was a bit too risky. But Agassi knew that it was never a wise move to question the strategy of the general.

Sitting in his office, waiting impatiently, Agassi was impressed when a tall, American basketball player walked into his office. "Are you Dr. Agassi?" he inquired.

"Yes? How can I assist you?" he replied.

The tall, all-American boy closed the door and replied, "I ride the carpet of Alibaba."

Those were the code words for which he had been waiting. The message was from the general, indicating that he was the messenger that was promised.

The two walked to Agassi's car, buckled up, and drove away.

Chapter 26

2017

Whiffer, Russell Emming, and Jeff Jones had been hard at work, refining the state-of-the-art of the MANOPOLY Project. They were performing the hardware and software upgrades that were so badly needed. Additionally, innovations became more complex as the process was growing deeper into A.I., and the migration toward absolute, airtight security was all-consuming. There had been three significant assignments that the United States government had submitted to Jackson, Brooke, Whiffer, and Beau; these scenarios had been very successful. As each of these scenarios unfolded, the paradigm shifted away from its original graduate-student-heavy testing program. It had evolved into a gymnasium floor with fifty pedestals having computer terminals, interconnected through an A.I. controller. This data stream was now hardwired through a sealed, stainless steel conduit to the mainframe.

The access was located in a locked room with armed guards posted at the entrance around the clock. There were no longer convenient accessibility junctions to make working on the fiber, coaxial, and copper wiring contained in the conduit easy. Any alterations would now require cutting saws and welding torches. The crow's nest had an entirely new look as well. It now had bulletproof glass overlooking the floor. A solid core steel door with biometric retina-scanning enabled entry was installed as well. The entire small family community vibe that had been the hallmark of the MANOPOLY Project was gone. Now it felt very cold, sterile, and like the sally port for a Brink's Truck Depot.

With each new layer of security and armor, it seemed like Jackson, Brooke, and Whiffer became less in charge of the progress and the steering of the future. Beau seemed very preoccupied with other things as well. If anything seemed inevitable at all, it was that change was in the air. Nobody was sure how things would fall. Everyone was uncomfortable and uncertain. What once felt like a family now was very cold and institutional. They had also just put their heads down after the unexpected presidential election and waited to see which way the winds would blow at the MANOPOLY Project. Their wait would not be very long!

Chapter 27

January 20, 2017, was the Inauguration of Donald John Trump, forty-fifth President of the United States. It had been a long wait for Jackson, Brooke, Whiffer, and Beau since Election Day. Things were about to change. One of the promises that the new president had made was a new tax cut to stimulate the economy. Beau was plugged in pretty tight at the Federal Reserve. He had told Jackson that the word was that the corporate tax rate was rumored to be the first target. He had heard it would be reduced to around 25 percent.

Trump believed that reducing the corporate tax rate would bring overseas industries back to the shores of the United States. Additionally, he believed it would cause repatriation of American investors' dollars parked in banks overseas due to lower tax rates. He was convinced that cutting tax and regulations on business and on small businesses would bring manufacturers who had moved overseas back to the U.S.

It sounded a bit simplistic, but crazier things had worked. Beauregard Benoit's information regarding financial data and fiscal policy had never been wrong. So, Jackson and Whiffer began researching the intricacies of the corporate tax law. However, they quickly found that reading tax bills and legislation was a task that would make watching paint dry an exciting proposition. Nonetheless, it had to be done, so domestic corporate tax law was the flavor of the month in the MANOPOLY Project.

Brooke was picking up as much slack as possible in the way of teaching duties and administrative responsibilities. This freed up Jackson and Whiffer to be positioned ahead of the curve. It would put them all ahead of the game when the appropriate policy people were in place within the new administration. They would be ready to liaise with them about the duties they would require, the formats of the data they would receive, and how that data outputs would need to be formatted and reported. Even though they had received no direct instructions or orders, guidance from Beau had never failed. The financial community, both on Wall Street and from the Federal Reserve, had always been reliable, and they were all looking for change. Taking advice from Beau had never left them in a tight spot.

Jeff Jones had filled a spot that had opened from the forward evolution of the MANOPOLY Project. The project had grown into many diverse directions—growth that required more and more intense programming and data formatting and reporting duties for Whiffer. Jeff was the only person that Whiffer trusted to pick up the reins that were left lying on the floor, unattended more and more frequently. It became evident that Whiffer had more duties than he had minutes in the day. He was simply unable to perform the voluminous workload. It had been almost five years now that Russell Emming had been coming to do the NSA mandated backups. The issue had popped to the surface in a manner that could not be ignored and had caused quite the uproar throughout the MANOPOLY Project.

Russell showed up, went down on the floor to begin the data backup, and after about an hour, still no Whiffer. Russell walked up to the crow's nest to see what Whiffer was doing.

Upon his arrival, he found Jackson there at the programming terminal by himself. Jackson was shocked to see Russell walk in. He asked why Russell was in the building. When Russell showed him the work order, Whiffer was immediately called on his cell phone. Whiffer answered and was utterly shocked by the fact that he had forgotten the routine backup task. He was in Chicago picking up some electronic components for an interface upgrade required to run the tax cut data.

The incident made it crystal clear that Whiffer needed help. Russell went ahead and completed the backup work. Jackson had called Jeff to be there as the secondary witness to the data transfer. The event was not a problem. Nonetheless, it did identify a weakness in the program.

Jackson sat down with Whiffer the next day, and the program was discussed. It was apparent to both that the position was not receiving the attention that it required. Both agreed that Jeff was the man for the job. Jeff was already a Northwestern University employee, so all of the paperwork necessary was internal transfer papers from one department to the other. So, Jeff was immediately transferred from the Department of Computer Sciences to the Department of Economics. Neither his tenure nor his benefits were interrupted. It also avoided bringing in someone new that everyone had to learn how to trust. Trust was a commodity that was very highly valued after the Iranian spy incident. Trust was possibly the most valuable attribute required at this juncture.

Chapter 28

March 2017

Beau was sitting at his desk in the Federal Reserve Building in the financial district of Wall Street. It was a pretty average day, nothing very much out of the ordinary. Janet Yellen was the Barack Obama-appointed Chair of the Federal Reserve. She was the first woman to serve in this position. She assumed this position from Ben Bernanke in 2014. During the entire Obama presidency, the Federal Reserve had kept interest rates flat. Now with a new president, Yellen was signaling possibly two interest rates in response to a tax cut being discussed by the new administration.

Holy cow! It was turning into a shit show! Why would a Federal Reserve chair do such a thing? The new president was a businessman. He was a self-made billionaire, and he had a working knowledge of financial policy that exceeded most politicians. This discussion had pretty much played out in the newspapers. That was, until today.

Steve Bannon, an extreme right-wing political activist, had been named to the Trump administration as chief of staff.

Today was the day that he would walk into Beau's office and declare open warfare against the Federal Reserve. Bannon had been a very influential member of the Trump team since the latter stages of the 2016 Trump for President campaign, and he was keenly aware who Beau was as well. Further, Bannon knew that Beau was the access point for securing the analysis of the MANOPOLY Project financial team.

Bannon stormed into the lobby and demanded to see Beau. At that moment, the generally recognized veil of independence between the Federal Reserve and the White House was shredded in a swift and flamboyant manner! The press was having fits over the White House demanding that the Federal Reserve surrender its independence to the president. It was reminiscent of an old WWF wrestling match!

The made-for-Hollywood scene in the lobby at Beau's Wall Street office needed careful mitigating. He decided on a strategy that would diffuse the bomb that was standing very loudly in his reception office. He walked out, cleared his throat, and extended his hand. He politely introduced himself.

"Hi! I am Beau Benoit. How can I help you?" Then he quickly ushered Bannon into his office and quickly closed the door behind them. He had at least stopped the current episode of *The Jerry Springer Show* that had been unfolding in his office lobby.

The next step of his plan was to get him seated and to calm his anger. He wanted to soothe him enough to engage him in intelligent conversation. He also aimed to deescalate the scene to a level that was not painful to his ears, and those of every other person on the entire floor.

Beau had heard Steve Bannon's name in many conversations around Manhattan. He was keenly aware that this man had the ear and the complete confidence of the President of the United States of America. Beau knew that being kind and gentle would serve him best in this situation. He spoke very softly, hoping that this strategy would make Bannon lean in to hear. He sought to eliminate the need to shout loud enough for the entire world to hear. It seemed to be working! After some more pleasant words were exchanged, Beau asked him what he could do to assist his boss.

"You might have heard that I am the president's chief of staff," Bannon started. "And you may know who I am, and if you do, you had better listen to me."

Beau nodded in anticipation. He also wondered what he wanted.

"Donald wants to get a tax cut through ASAP!" He had manipulatively used his first name to convey that he was tight with the president. But Beau already knew this, as did anyone else who had a news channel on their television. Beau just looked and waited for the next line.

"We are aware of your role in the Northwestern University think tank. Don wants you to run the numbers to locate the precise areas for a huge tax cut," Bannon continued. Beau heard what was said but was very amused that he had gone from Donald to Don to press the point. And he had thought the *Springer Show* had ended in the lobby.

Beau formulated a strategic response. "May I ask if the president has any specific ideas or goals?"

Bannon replied, "He wants the corporate rates dropped to stimulate growth. He also wants a decrease in taxpayer rates to give them money to spend." Beau raised his eyebrows and rubbed his chin.

"You gonna say something or just rub your chin?" Bannon smugly asked. "Oh, and by the way, he wants that Obamacare tax removed now, too!"

"I think I understand what you are requesting. What is your time frame?" Beau inquired.

"Soon! Damned soon!" Bannon replied and stepped out of the door.

Beau had now seen the Steve Bannon of whom he had heard. Beau could not believe that his demeanor could last very long in Washington. He went to work on the assignment.

━━

THE PRESIDENT WAS WORKING at a feverish pace to get a tax cut perfected and passed. He wanted to get it through Congress while the Republicans had control of both the House and the Senate. Bannon had been working on the team of advisors that were advising the president regarding the tax cuts. Word was coming out of the administration that Federal Reserve Chairwoman Yellen was toast. She thought that since the administration was considering tax cuts, the Federal Reserve would respond with a couple of rate increases throughout 2017.

The administration viewed this action as job-killing, deficit-increasing shots across the bow of a possible tax cut. The administration was looking for a combination of tax cuts that would stimulate the growth of American companies. They sought to reduce corporate tax rates to keep manufacturers from moving American factory jobs overseas into cheap labor markets. They also wanted to reduce regulation to the point that factories could re-tool, add manufacturing capacity, and build a blue-collar economy. Beau listened and sensed that he was about to hear the other shoe drop. He soon heard it.

Beau had never experienced an introduction and meeting quite like the one he had just experienced. He was not sure how he felt about it, what he thought, and most importantly, how to proceed. So, he picked up the phone and called Jackson. As the phone rang in Jackson's office, Beau was grinning about the made-for-television theater he had just seen play out in his office. *This might get pretty interesting*, he thought to himself.

Jackson had also heard the rumblings of a proposed tax

cut bill that was being discussed in the White House. A tax cut had been promised repeatedly on the campaign trail but given the odds in Las Vegas that Trump could actually win the presidency, fewer still had really considered what it might contain. Absolutely nobody had considered how it might really be structured.

The insiders in Washington, D.C., had really been busy concerning themselves with what they saw as the coming and unavoidable war with North Korea. But after his inauguration, Trump had reached out to the North Korean dictator, and the likelihood of war seemed to be remote. The mainstream media in Washington was far more concerned with the war of words over which president had a higher number in attendance at their inauguration: Trump or Obama. In this war, it seemed that all of the casualties would be Americans, both left and right. The media was pounding their chests, calling Trump weak for giving Kim Jung-Un an international platform. However, quietly, most people in the military circles were very relieved. Spending cuts and sequestration had decimated our military. The army was terrified at the thought of having to defend against a potential nuclear opponent and was secretly relieved.

Trump was also using his majorities in the House and Senate to restore the military. Funding cut by the previous administration was restored. However, it was done at the expense of fiscal responsibility. It was largely done on credit. The military employees that MANOPOLY Project employed in security often voiced their support for his policies. They believed that rebuilding the military would serve as a deterrent to other countries who might entertain military conflict with the United States. However, Jackson was an economics guy, and his eyes kept following the price tags. Could we actually do MORE deficit spending? So, while Beau had experienced a *Springer* episode, Jackson was beginning to find a sense of new direction.

Perhaps some of Beau's experience was the result of the perceived friction between the presidency and the Federal Reserve, as viewed through the lens of President Trump. Nonetheless, even though the Joint Chiefs of Staff had not given them an assignment, they now had a new project. Not even the Joint Chiefs could prevail in a jurisdictional dispute against the White House. So, Beau and Jackson proceeded to discuss how they could extrapolate the data necessary to put together a tax cut to stimulate the economy. Additionally, it would have to be designed to pass both houses of Congress.

Both of these factors had to be successful before the president would see it on his desk. So, they began plotting their strategy to attack this scenario.

Beau had taken copious notes of the details that Bannon had described as what the president was looking for in his new proposed tax cut: corporate tax rate reduction, governmental regulation reduction, increased personal tax exemptions, and the elimination of the individual mandate in the Affordable Care Act, which was perceived as an additional middle-class tax by most. It seemed very straightforward. But to the Democrats, it would be radioactive.

Jeff and Whiffer went to work on programming variables into the individual computers at each pedestal on the floor. As the MANOPOLY Process had evolved, rather than having people playing at each station, each station had a processor, a video monitor, and was networked through the steel conduit that ran under the floor. Where the junction box had been (where the Iranian spy device had been found by Whiffer), now stood a computer that received all of the incoming data from the fifty freestanding computers. This was the hub that collected all of the diverse data and fed it directly into the A.I. unit.

Each of these processors was running calculations on a specific aspect of the economy. Each machine was dealing with, or specialized in, one point of a macro economy. Inputs were streamed into an A.I. processor that applied "human-like" interpretations of the incoming data and compiled it into a single, massive stream of data. This stream of information was transmitted to the mainframe. The mainframe interpreted the data and ran the analysis of the data and funneled it into a database. The database could be accessed in any manner desired, by calling the correct tuple and attribute. To avoid any possible hacking, the system was isolated. It had no connectivity to the Internet. Hackers could only access this system by being on the gym floor.

So, over time, MANOPOLY had evolved into a very sophisticated LAN that worked on a unified goal. It did not "serve" files to each constituent computer. However, it received data from each station using its own independent operating system. Processing was done independently, with data only flowing from each terminal, to the A.I. processor, directly into the mainframe. The process had a hardwired one-way data flow. It was preventing corruption from one prompt to the next. This process simulated the fifty original games that were the unique concept of the MANOPOLY Process. The independent processing allowed for variances from processor to processor. Each computer desk had an assigned variable for the economic scenario running. This produced a global output that was unbelievably sophisticated, and the programming tasks were exhaustive.

The main variables for this tax cut scenario would be corporate tax, individual tax, sales tax, tax penalties, regulatory restrictions, employment tax, withholding tax, and income tax deductions, in addition to the entire battery of all of the significant economic variables moving from micro to macroeconomic repercussions. The goal of this run was to hit on as many different combinations of tax reduction scenarios possible and to isolate the best combination of tax policy modifications to have to generate the most substantial net effect on the economy. It took almost a week to get all of the data aligned for the test run of this scenario. A ping had now run through each terminal to the mainframe. The script was ready to compile its data and conclusions.

Jackson, Brooke, and Whiffer were all sitting at the control panel the following morning to execute the scenario. There was a great deal of emotion present in this particular project. It was the first time that the MANOPOLY Project had been assigned a situation specifically for the President of the United States, and one might argue, at his command. It was a genuinely weighty moment. While checking all of the parameters before executing the program, Whiffer wondered what the real-life consequences might be if they failed. Or, on the other hand, what might happen if they had a successful achievement for the most powerful man on earth. It was an exciting concept to contemplate. As he observed, Jackson pushed the start button.

Unlike in earlier days of the MANOPOLY Project, the scenarios did not require hours to process, but rather a minute or two. While looking through the glass in the crow's nest, each table was clearly visible. Each had a light on a pole that was elevated about eight feet into the air. When the computer was working on its delegated operation, the bulb was green. Once it had completed processing and sent its data to the A.I. process, it turned red. When all of the lights were red, the data was released simultaneously at the A.I. processor. Then the interpretation or "Human-Factor" operated very quickly on the data and sent it to the mainframe.

The mainframe only took seconds to sort and compile the data. It was a unique way to process data, but it was the most efficient way to get reliable predictive data that had proven to be very valuable over time. Jackson walked into the secured room, picked up the printout, and carried it back to the crow's nest.

All of the data was read, analyzed, interpreted, and checked for accuracy. After these quality control measures were completed, Brooke sat down to enter the conclusions. The policies that would be recommended to the president for his tax cut proposal were finished. It seemed very surreal composing a tax bill to deliver to the President of the United States. She was not sure if she loved it or if she feared it.

Chapter 29

Two weeks later, in the Oval Office at The White House, Steve Bannon walked in through the door opposite the resolute desk, carrying a briefcase. He walked up to the historic piece of furniture and smiled as the president turned around and met his gaze. "Mr. President," he stated, "I give you the Tax Cuts and Jobs Act of 2017."

Bannon smiled like a Cheshire cat and waited for a reply.

"Will it work?" the president asked.

"Everyone seems to think so, Mr. President," Bannon responded.

The president pushed a button on his desk, and an intercom phone was immediately ringing somewhere. Bannon had no clue where the phone had rung. "Legislative Affairs," a voice came in over the phone.

"Come to my office," said the president.

IN THE CAPITOL ROTUNDA, Mitch McConnell and Paul Ryan met in the center and were escorted to a limousine waiting to take them to the White House. The president had summoned them both together. They walked into the Oval Office. President Trump handed them each a copy of the bill, and he instructed them to get it passed. It was not a suggestion.

The Tax Cuts and Jobs Act of 2017 proposed that individual and business taxes be cut. The standard tax deduction was increased while reducing itemized deductions, reducing mortgage interest deductions, reducing the alternative minimum tax, and eliminating the ACA individual mandate. It passed the House Ways and Means Committee on November 9, 2017. It passed the House of Representatives on November 16, 2017, by a vote of 227 to 205. It also passed the Senate on December 2, 2017, by a vote of 51 to 49. It was signed into law by President Donald J. Trump on December 22, 2017. The MANOPOLY Project had just written its first piece of United States tax legislation. The overall morale in the crow's nest was jubilant immediately after President Donald J. Trump had called the team on the phone from the White House! It was the moment they had worked a very long time to feel! It was as sweet as life could possibly get!

On the gym floor in Econ Lab 1, the team of university employees and students that comprised the MANOPOLY Project was doing routine maintenance. For the very first time, a new computer sciences graduate was seen rolling up cables. This man was six-foot-eight, a former basketball player. He was a referral to the project through the university's administrative staff. Salomon Agassi had assigned him. Everyone assumed it was in exchange for budgetary lenience and fewer headaches from the Admin Office.

Chapter 30

It had been an exciting week for Beau, but even with all of the excitement in his professional life, he just couldn't shake the feeling that he had to make a connection with his natural father. He sat again, at his desk in his Manhattan loft. He was scrolling through the Halliburton data files trying to find the names Lyle Willis and Randy Bell. Not one of the personnel entries from the Halliburton file had either name. He had also done searches through accounts payable and receivable. They must not have worked with Virgil at Halliburton. But then where could they fit into this story? The entire set of circumstances was disheartening to him.

He opened the top left drawer and looked at his mother's handwriting again. It had undoubtedly faded over the years. He took his fingers and rubbed them across the surface where she once wrote on a fresh, clean photograph. For a brief moment, he could almost see her at seventeen years of age. He gently turned the photo over and looked at the faces. He stared at the faces, and he searched his memory with all of his might. But he simply did not recognize either of the boys. Then he allowed his eyes to wander over the surface of the picture.

"A drum, a lousy drum," he muttered to himself. Then, he saw something he had not seen before. It looked like faded peeling letters on the cover of the drum. What did it say? He reached into the drawer below where he retrieved the photo and took out his magnifying glass. He placed the picture under the magnifying glass. It was very dark, and the magnifying glass cast a shadow on the face of the photograph. He moved it under his desk lamp; it was faint. It looked like, T-h-e D-r-i-f-t-w-o-o-d. The Driftwood! It must have been a band name! He knew that he could not tell Brooke about his natural father, but he could certainly ask her if she had ever heard of The Driftwood!

Beau was pretty psyched about the new clue and could not wait to ask Brooke. But it was just too late to call tonight. She would be asleep, or worse, in the throes of passion with Jackson. In either case, he wasn't sure which would be more embarrassing to interrupt.

Beau knew Brooke and her schedule pretty well. He was very aware that her obsessive-compulsive tendencies made her early morning activities pretty easy to anticipate. She would be up at 6 a.m., out the door in her sweats by 6:10 on a 15-minute run around seven blocks of her neighborhood. Evanston was a small, safe town, and they lived in a lovely area. At 6:25, she was in the door, 6:27 her coffee pot was turned on, and in the shower by 6:28. At 6:35, she was at the counter in her robe. She was filling her coffee cup, after having put two tablespoons of cream and two teaspoons of sugar in the bottom of her beautiful china cup. She would stir three times. Then walk to the bedroom to the clothes she had laid out on the valet the night before. By 6:45, she was dressed and had the terrible habit of putting on her makeup while she was driving to work.

It was three miles to work. She pulled into her parking spot at precisely at 6:50 a.m. and spent the next three minutes putting on her bright red lipstick; it was her signature shade.

So, at precisely 6:53 a.m. Beau dialed Brooke's cell phone number. She answered the phone with a silly response that suddenly made him think about Imogene. She said, "*Hola.*"

Beau started immediately; he and Brooke were very close, and they had a verbal shorthand that nobody else really understood. Perhaps it almost sounded like a word association game, but Beau and Brooke spoke it with fluency. He shouted suddenly, "The Driftwood!" She quickly replied, "Hound Dog."

Beau scrunched up his face. This word association pair promptly went south for Beau. "*Hound Dog?*" he inquired. "Why Hound Dog?"

"It was mom's favorite song; we played it all of the time. It was a 45 R.P.M. record, vinyl, and the name of the band was The Driftwood. She taught me how to do the Twist to Hound Dog."

Being the big brother, Beau had to inform her that "Hound Dog" was a famous song done by Elvis Presley and that she was simply mistaken. She told him that she had the original 45 R.P.M. vinyl recording in her collection at home. She dared him to bet her a one-hundred-dollar bill. Brooke had *never* made a bet and lost. Beau knew that Brooke was as tight as the skin on a green grape; she never made a bet unless she was sure. He asked if she would be home over the coming weekend and told her he would fly in and visit her from New York on Saturday.

Brooke was always glad to see Beau, but she was now late, and she had to run into her office. Her brother would have to wait until Saturday.

Saturday came pretty quickly. Beau was on a red-eye from New York LaGuardia to Chicago O'Hare. O'Hare to Evanston was a very short flight. But he had a two-hour layover at O'Hare to catch a connector flight to Evanston. Beau landed in Evanston at almost 11:30 a.m. He hustled out to the front of the airport and found a taxi to Brooke and Jackson's home.

When he got into the cab, he turned on his phone and called Brooke. It was a short, sweet call. "Hey Brooke, see you in ten, max!"

He replaced his phone in his pants pocket. Adding the word "max" to the comment was part of their sibling short-hand; he was telling her that he was in a hurry, and she knew it. At 11:56 a.m., he rang Brooke's doorbell.

Saturday was the one and only day in Brooke's week that was not controlled by her obsessive-compulsive schedule. Saturdays, Brooke slept until she woke up, and that was usually way too early to suit Brooke. She would tell you that every Friday night, when she went to sleep, she planned to sleep in until at least noon. But it never seemed to happen. So, when she woke, she knew herself well enough to know that she might as well get up. She just never could go back to sleep. Her mind always started racing, and she had never mastered the skill of slowing it down enough to go back to sleep. She knew this because she had a lifetime of fighting the battle of covering her head with her blanket, struggling to keep her eyes closed, and falling back to sleep. The years had taught her to get up and become productive.

This particular morning, she was not having the *"woe is me"* monologue in her mind about why she just could not sleep late on Saturday. On this morning, she was excited to see her brother! After she got up, she ate a quick bite of breakfast (a strawberry Pop-Tart). Then she went into the living room, opened the base cabinet of the entertainment center, and knelt to access her vinyl record collection. She moved left past the LP albums to her collection of 45 R.P.M. records. She pulled out the stack and tenderly sorted through them. She read each label as she laid the previous disc on the carpet next to her. Almost half-way through the pile, her face lit up; it was "Hound Dog" by The Driftwood. *Ah-ha!* She thought; she'd known it wasn't Elvis Presley!

She placed the record on top of the entertainment center.

She picked up the stack on the floor beside her. She put the cover on top of the pile and replaced them in the storage cabinet. She looked at the clock on the living room wall and thought to herself that she had better get her butt into the shower. She would also have to get her hair dried and fixed, and her makeup put on so she didn't scare her brother. She took off bounding up the stairs on her mission to look presentable when Beau rang the doorbell.

Beau stepped out of the taxi wearing a nice pair of Levi 501 blue jeans, a red polo shirt with a pocket, and Nike jogging shoes. He looked very casual, and he was glad to see his sister. He pushed the doorbell and heard the chimes echo through the foyer. About fifteen seconds later, his sister cracked opened the door, peeked out, and screamed, "Beau, I am so excited you came down!"

The two moved into the living room and sat down and just started chatting as fast as anyone could comfortably listen to and understand. After covering some surface business topics, Beau's recent visit to see Brightwell seemed ripe on the agenda. They also discussed his most recent call with Imogene. Also discussed were the pitching prospects in the coming season for the St. Louis Cardinals, the Benoit family sports team. Then, quite suddenly, Brooke shot straight up, quickly walked over to the entertainment center, and picked up the record she had searched out earlier. She held it up, grinned from ear to ear, and said, "See, Beau! I told you Elvis Presley didn't sing Hound Dog!"

Beau rose from the sofa very slowly and walked toward his sister with very steady, measured steps. He never took his eyes off of the record. Beau had prepared for just this moment. He had Googled the cover of the Elvis hit release and printed a color copy. He had folded it and placed it in his back pocket. He smirked, reached into his back pocket, unfolded the photo, and rubbed it in his sister's face. She stuck her tongue out at him, shook The Driftwood's cover in his face, and said, "But

THIS is the one momma and I listened to! You lose. Nice try, sucker!" she playfully retorted. She held out her hand, grinned, and said, "One hundred dollars!" They both giggled.

Brooke handed Beau the record. She was a bit confused by the solemn look on his face. Beau looked down, and sure enough, the label said that the cut was Hound Dog. Sure enough, it was recorded by The Driftwood. He looked closer and listed below the title and typed in tiny letters was, PRODUCED BY RANDY BELL. Bingo! Beau had found a breadcrumb. It was about time that he had something to go on. He badly needed a small dose of hope.

Chapter 31

Almost a year had passed since Freyredoon Adipour was discovered to have been the computer engineer who had built the Iranian spyware planted in Evanston. Colonel Muhammad Arman, in Iran, and Ronald Burnett at the NSA, had been jointly working this piece of the jigsaw puzzle. Burnett might be a supervisor in the computer field, but he was also a very functional intelligence asset at the NSA. People often tended to think he simply worked on computers. However, they assumed that he didn't really know, nor do, any real spy craft.

The obvious nugget that everyone seemed to miss was the content of the data on the networks on which Burnett worked. He was responsible for operating top-secret programs containing eyes-only information and making sure that everyone had the correct access to the appropriate confidential files. Burnett maintained the repository of the most fabulous treasure trove of intelligence that existed in the entire world. To believe, quite naively, that Burnett was not a functional intelligence officer was a huge mistake. Burnett not only ran the most secure information systems in the world, but he also ran some of the most sensitive human assets. The computers contained lists of all existing intelligence assets and where they were positioned across the globe. His security clearance was as high as it went.

The fact that he was running Colonel Arman, a very deep plant in the IRIAF, would indicate the level of proficiency possessed by Burnett as an intel officer. In the interim, Arman had utilized his position and the trust that he had leveraged with General Nasirzdeh to run an entire dossier on Freyredoon Adipour. He now had a fairly good idea who else might be working with him to move spy equipment back and forth between international borders. Ali Assad, the CIA operator at Langley, had been taken a copy of the dossier. The Adipour Dossier was carried by Darian Amir the last time he had made a trip into Iran.

Darian had made a reconnaissance trip to Iran to follow Salomon Agassi on his annual trip for the summer. Darian had picked up the travel itineraries filed for reimbursement from Northwestern University in his cover position at the MANOPOLY Project in the Department of Economics. His access to all of the university employees was a prominent place to start in search of a spy. Who on staff might have taken a risk amounting to treason at the Northwestern University campus? The first computer search yielded the name of Agassi, due to the numerous trips to Iran, and the fact that he was related to members of the IRCG. One red flag was somewhat significant, two red flags in the same file were analogous to a fire alarm being pulled in a crowded theater.

Chapter 32

After Darian picked up the tip on Agassi's Northwestern University annual sabbaticals from the computer system, and the yearly trips to Iran, he contacted Ronald Burnett. He had successfully doubled the search potentials for useful information. Burnett, in turn, forwarded the search criteria to Ali Assad at the Middle East desk at the CIA in Langley. It formed a triangulation of data searching, and very quickly, Ghassim Kalani was identified as a known associate. A quick pull of CIA video that was collected at the Imam Khomeini International Airport turned up numerous video clips of the two together. Kalani was a known member of the Quds Force and was a suspected affiliate of Qassem Soleimani, second only to the Supreme Commander of Iran. Darian had learned as a cadet in the NSA, when a cursory data search yields such a direct and clear line of sight to a connection inside the government, one must act. Especially when it reached all of the way to the top of the Iranian State, it was worth investing some time in running the traps to see where it led and what it yielded.

In following Dr. Salomon Agassi through his activities and associates at Northwestern, Darian was able to utilize confidential human intelligence assets that were readily available from the NSA. Having three NSA undercover agents in Agassi's classes, in his social circles, and following him wherever he went paid one very rapid return on the investment. Very quickly, Darian discovered a young Iranian student named Muhammed Faruq. Faruq was located in a very systematic manner utilizing basic spy craft. First, Darian accessed a database of all of Agassi's students in all of his classes the past four years. He used a database search filtering all Persian, Arabic, or Middle Eastern surnames. This search yielded a much smaller list of possibilities. Of the handful of options, most were American-born of Middle Eastern heritage.

All of the American-born students were eliminated by doing a simple commercial credit report, clearing them after their credit in America was established. Those remaining were subjected to an NSA background investigation. Faruq was traced to Tehran. It was also discovered that he had close personal ties to the Quds Force, and had additionally been tied to the IRIAF air defense wing at Doshan Tappeh Air Base in Tehran. Further investigation also identified Ghassim Kalani as a close associate in Tehran, and when the familial connection between Agassi and Kalani were found, there were just way too many red flags to ignore.

After all of the reports had been compiled, Darian was convinced that there was something very much resembling a small terrorist cell on the Northwestern University campus. Having identified all of these nefarious connections and ties to the military regime in Iran, Darian decided that he should do a deep dive back to the beginning. The first known event that caused all of this national security hustle was the bug found on the gym floor.

Darian went back into the NSA computer files that Russell had kept through all of the MANOPOLY Project data file backups. He was building a basic outline of the actions that had been taken to secure data. He was also looking for any event associated with the need to change the data security protocol that Russell and Whiffer had maintained. This seemed the most traceable timeline of functions available to Darian. Nobody had ever expected this project to intersect with the world of espionage. Nobody had ever seen the need to keep notes on relevant measures taken to counter the actions of nefarious actors. The fact that there was no existing record, and the fact that Darian was responsible for creating a timeline and for evaluating the actions taken, made his job important for two reasons: He had to establish the schedule; then determine if the actions taken were practical and if they had circumvented further opportunity for encroachment. From the backup logs, and from the conversations that he had with Whiffer, the first event that was most obvious was the unknown man running from the gymnasium after the first test run scenario.

Based upon the information he had uncovered doing a deep dive into Dr. Agassi, he would bet that the man running from the gymnasium that night was Muhammad Faruq. It was pretty much in the middle of his intelligence skill set. But knowing that this event was the first *known* breach made Darian wonder when it had really begun. How did this small terror network end up in Evanston, Illinois, at a small university like Northwestern? How long had they been collecting data, and to whom was it being reported, and why? It seemed to Darian that undercover intelligence work was an infinite loop. Every time he turned over a stone to find a clue, it led to at least two more, and most frustrating, seldom, if *ever*, where all of the questions in his mind thoroughly answered.

So, Darian was now working on connections, personal history, family connections, political affiliations, and an entire array of questions that were necessary to determine any pre-existing relationship between Agassi and Faruq. These two became the known local face of the enemy. In Darian's experience, he could not learn, nor know, too much about them. He thought a few seconds and opened his secure government-issued laptop and composed an Interagency Memorandum of Inquiry. Darian's thought process was evolving as he processed the information that was coming into his stream of consciousness. *If these two guys have been active in Evanston, perhaps they are global players that have been assigned here by another intelligence agency! Perhaps I will find out,* Darian thought to himself.

The Memorandum of Inquiry (MOI) was addressed to MI6, Moussed, the 5-I's, NSA, the CIA, and the FBI. Included were their entire profile jackets with photos, prints, and every speck of information that he had discovered. The MOI was routed through secure servers at Langley and traveled at the speed of light. Darian was now hoping that someone else in his circle of associates had dealt with these players and might have keys, clues, and history of past operations that would shed light on their areas of expertise. He might get a better idea of what they were capable of pulling off in Evanston. He had done about all he could do for the day, so he headed back to the executive office in the Econ Lab 1 building. His curiosity had been piqued, and he was ready to move this ball down the field!

Chapter 33

Beau had tried to talk Brooke out of her Hound Dog record, but it had been her mom's, and she listened to it regularly. Because Beau did not wish to tip his hand and reveal that they had different fathers, he asked if she minded if he took a photo of the record label so he could attempt to find a copy for himself. Beau pulled his iPhone 8 Plus out of his pants pocket and quickly snapped a burst of several photos. He wanted to make sure that he had all of the information contained on the label of the record. He started to put his phone away and had another thought: *Perhaps I should also get the information on the flip side of the disc as well.* So, he pulled the record back and captured a rapid burst of photos of the reverse label as well.

He then sat back down and enjoyed the company of his sister, who had fixed him their childhood favorite for lunch: tomato soup and grilled cheese sandwiches. The sandwiches were on immaculate, beautiful china plates. The soup was in matching China bowls, sitting in matching saucers. Beau was very accustomed to Brooke's entertaining skills. However, it was the extra touch that melted Beau's heart. She had cut the crust off of the bread used to make the grilled cheese sandwiches. The sandwiches looked as though they had been surgically altered before they were cooked. It was a very loving gesture; it was not lost on Beau.

It was *exactly* how Beau had eaten his favorite lunch since before Brooke was born. It melted Beau's heart, but it made him feel a twinge of guilt for keeping a secret of this magnitude from her.

After a lovely lunch and visit, Beau excused himself and acted as though he needed to go by the Econ Lab 1 to conduct some unmentioned business while in town. He bent down, kissed his sister on the forehead, hugged her, and went out the door. Beau had texted for a car to pick him up. While Brooke was clearing the dishes from the dining room table, he walked down the street a block and stepped into the waiting car.

Beau had caught the next flight to Chicago O'Hare and booked a connecting flight back to New York LaGuardia. His car was parked in short term parking at LaGuardia airport, so he flew American to be close to his car. Beau always used the parking near the American terminal. He got into his car, pulled out his phone, and opened his camera roll. He used his fingers to pinch open the best photo of the A-side record label. He looked, and he looked, but he saw nothing else that resembled a clue. Then he swiped to the left and saw the B-side photo. Just for grins, he used his thumb and index finger to pinch that photo larger as well. Much to his surprise, the flip-side song was produced by Lyle Willis and Randy Bell! These were the same names on the back of the photo with his mother. These two men had been important enough to his mother for her to keep the picture in the box with her favorite Easter hat.

It had to be significant. It certainly was amazing, but how would he use this next clue? He was also amazed that in his haste at Brooke's, he had missed Lyle Willis's name written below Randy Bell's. But in looking closer, he saw the label had been played thousands of times. This spot on the label would have been directly in contact with the rubber pad on the turntable. There was some friction wear that had hidden the name.

Beau drove home. He was feeling pretty giddy about his day trip and the windfall discovery on the flip side. He pulled into the garage of his building, parked his red BMW in a parking spot closest to the elevator and rode it up to his floor. He walked from the elevator, thinking very deeply about how he could use his newly acquired information. How could he move his investigation further? Suddenly, as he put his key into the lock, it hit him: *The RECORD LABEL. Could the record label still exist and could they have any archived details of the talent in their company records?* He was pretty much beat from the quick trip but excited as well.

Beau walked to the office desk in his home and took a seat in front of the split-screen computer. He pulled his iPhone charging cable from the drawer to his right. Instead of plugging the male USB connector into a charging block, he plugged it into his computer CPU's USB port. He opened his iTunes account and uploaded the photos of the record labels he had taken today. He saved them to the hard drive of his home desktop computer. Once he had them uploaded, he unplugged his phone, and, this time, he did plug it into his charging block on a power strip between his split monitors. The phone had only about 22 percent of its full charge remaining. He then opened Photoshop and imported the photos. He was trying to see if any additional clues could be revealed under electronic magnification. He scoured the screen until his eyes seemed stuck in a permanent squint. There was nothing else to be found.

Beau opened the photos back up and dragged the side-A picture on the left monitor and the side-B photo on the right monitor. He carefully studied those photos side-by-side. The faded, somewhat discolored label was a washed-out purple color with a black band across the top. Across the top, printed in a white cursive font, 'NOLA' was written. At the bottom, 'Records' was written in italic font in white on the field of purple. Underneath that, in small black printing, was a 'C' with a circle around it and the number 1963 after it. It indicated that the recording was copyrighted in 1963 and gave it that approximate time of creation and printing. It wasn't an encyclopedia of knowledge, but it was a start. That was what he had been searching for. He now had two names, a photo, and a date … 1963! It wasn't a road map, but it was progressing.

Beau closed out of Photoshop and opened Google to see what he could find on the Internet. A cursory search told him that NOLA Records was a small, regional recording company from New Orleans, Louisiana. NOLA MIX Records was the property of Swallow Records and was owned by a gentleman named Floyd Soileau, who the Internet was telling him, still owned the company. It looked like it could, perhaps, be a thread that he could follow. Further research revealed that Swallow Records had at one time been a subsidiary of Ace Records. Ace Records began in 1955 in Jackson, Mississippi. Beau was praying that one of these companies still had an agent or an archives department that might produce some records. Hopefully, they might provide insight on artists and personnel who had made these records in the Big Easy in the 1960s. Surely if ten minutes with Google had yielded this many chances to find some information, then most certainly, a trip to New Orleans might do much better. Beau felt his spirit rise. For the first time in a very long time, Beau felt hopeful. Beau looked down at his watch, picked up his phone, and dialed Imogene.

Imogene was still in Mexico but was getting ready to move further south to Venezuela. There were many hungry Venezuelan citizens, and they were broke due to triple-digit inflation. The Venezuelan Maduro regime had nationalized the once-rich oil country. He then implemented socialism, skimmed the money out of the country, and left the Venezuelan population to starve.

Imogene's interdenominational missionary organization enjoyed the funding of some of the wealthiest people in the world. They truly were changing lives by keeping people from starving. Beau had not spoken to Imogene in a few weeks, and it was beautiful to hear her voice. Imogene was the sole person in the world that Beau had shared his secret regarding his search for his natural father. The events of his day of travel and research, for the first time, provided some information to share with her. She was thrilled with his news, and they shared great joy at that moment together. Imogene's voice always lifted Beau's spirit; she was his spiritual mentor, and he always sought her support and her continued support through prayer. They spoke for about ten minutes, then said goodbye, and Beau lumbered into his bedroom to end the day.

Chapter 34

In March and June of 2017, the Federal Reserve, under Janet Yellen, decided to reduce monetary policy accommodation gradually. In other words, the Federal Reserve reversed its policy and began raising interest rates, moving the rate from 1 percent to 1.25 percent. This measure was intended to cool off the economy when it looked likely that inflation might be rising very soon. Based on this move alone, the New York Stock exchange sold off. The markets interpreted this to mean that the Federal Reserve was shifting to an increased footing, which would tend to slow economic growth.

The president had made economic adjustments based upon the long-standing policy of the Federal Reserve that it would hold steady at the 1-percent rate. Yellen's willingness to do this ended the president's faith in her as the Federal Reserve Chair. Her term was to expire on February 5, 2018. On November 2, 2017, Donald Trump nominated Jerome Powell as Federal Reserve Chairman. The nomination was quickly approved by the United States Senate.

Meanwhile, on the gym floor at Northwestern, more and more of the day-to-day workload was being assumed by the tall grad student assigned to the program by Agassi. He was working closer and closer with Whiffer and was becoming a trusted worker in the program.

⊏▬⊐

2018

On February 5, 2018, Jerome Powell was sworn in as Federal Reserve Chairman. When Powell came into office, the Fed Monetary Rate was 1.5 percent. In the next eleven months, the rate was allowed to go up to 2.5 percent. The president cried foul due to the long period that the .25 percent rate had prevailed during the entire run of the previous administration. The Federal Reserve rate increase, and the Fed signaling a policy of increasing, had a considerable effect on Wall Street. If the rate went up, investors might choose bonds and Treasury Notes for decent yields without the risk associated with purchasing stocks. The president argued that providing a different harbor to invest funds harmed American businesses that were competing for investment capital.

Chapter 35

There was quite a raucous debate in the financial and investment sectors in the United States. The president was demanding empirical data to support his position regarding the correct posture signaled from the Federal Reserve. The Fed was trying to anticipate, and in turn, head off inflation. This was assumed to typically follow a long-running bull market. The administration was arguing that there were no signs of inflation. The signals being sent by raising the funds rate would become a self-fulfilling prophecy by killing stock market growth by Fed policy. Additionally, the ensuing reductions in the stock market cut GDP, employment, and many other associated factors. The administration believed this Fed policy had cost the United States economy a full point of annualized GDP growth. The administration decided to pay a visit to Beau Benoit.

Beau sat in an incredibly unique position regarding this matter. Beau was a topflight executive in the Federal Reserve but was also one-third of the brain trust that was the MANOPOLY Project. The president sent his chief of staff, Mick Mulvaney, to visit Beau.

Beau had all of the financial data required at his fingertips at his desk. Generally speaking, the fiscal policy at the Federal Reserve was usually based on arcane rules, policies, precedents, and human input from meetings. Never had all of the economic parameters used to determine where the Federal Reserve funds rate should be positioned been subjected to a computer-assisted process that accounted for hundreds of moving factors and calculated the correct rate. The software and computer processing prowess simply had not existed. The administration was hoping for a very weighty validation of their position regarding the Fed rate moving forward. Beau was keenly aware that this scenario would test his skills, and this result had to be right. Failure could cost him his position at the Federal Reserve.

Additionally, this scenario could substantially elevate the standing of the MANOPOLY Project with a valid and successful predictor. A result that made the correct Fed funds rate an amount quickly found, and movements easily identifiable, would make him the wizard of financial prognostication. Beau had a lot riding on this scenario! Whiffer and his new protégé had been double-teaming the effort around the clock. They were expanding the capabilities of the project. Even though they looked very comical working together, they were efficient together. His helper made him look like a small child.

The scenarios that had been completed by the MANOPOLY Project to date had been primarily in support of business or business practices, broadly stated. This scenario would require programming an entirely more specialized collection of data and analyzing exact financial data. This analysis would require going far deeper into the financial sector involving commercial, retail, and government interest rates; rates of return on bonds, stocks, futures; as well as the interest rates between countries that trade and carry balances with the United States government. The fluctuating amount of currency in circulation and the amounts minted, and a myriad of other financial factors, were now in play. They had never been isolated using this level of detail and these characteristics for any scenario before this assignment. Now the data would be considered as digital inputs.

Beau was sitting in the crow's nest in the Econ Lab 1 in the Department of Economics, Kellogg School of Business, Northwestern University, in Evanston, Illinois. The point of listing the entire description of where Beau sat is to give one the precise understanding of just how much economic and intellectual talent was at the disposal of the MANOPOLY Project. It took an all-star team to pull this massive amount of data together. After listing the pedigree of the financial side of the project at Northwestern, one would also have to marvel at the technical talent that the personnel brought to bear. Whiffer, Jeff Jones, and Russell Emming added incredible expertise from the Department of Computer Sciences, School of Engineering at Northwestern University.

Needless to say, Jackson, Brooke, and Beau pulled out all of the stops to bring the most available amount of talent to target this project. Never think that having the MANOPOLY Project on the Northwestern campus had not been responsible for the yearly migration of some of the best economic and computer talent in the world. This project had become the university recruiters' dream. Northwestern had become an intellectual powerhouse in the Midwest and had shown significant growth during its tenure.

Within a week, Beau had transferred all of the financial data required to run this scenario onto a hot-swappable hard drive. He personally carried it to the crow's nest with an escort by a U.S. Marshal, due to the sensitivity of the data. Whiffer, Jeff, and Russell had recruited the brightest students from all of the on-campus computer labs. They moved them to the gym floor in Econ Lab 1 and were ready to attack this project.

The entire Northwestern University team was hard at work updating and upgrading hard drives and memory modules on all of the computer terminals. These upgrades were allowing the hardware to process each piece of data as quickly and as efficiently as possible. Russell followed Whiffer and Jeff through the mountain of brute processing power. They were making sure that every computer's operating system was updated correctly and ready to roll. Additionally, the backup system for securing the data on each computer system was upgraded to match the larger hard drives. The firewalls were replaced with the very newest and most effective in the industry. Additionally, all copper, coaxial, and fiber optic cabling were replaced with new terminal ends.

In the secured mainframe room, upgrades were being done to achieve computing parity. The equipment in the MANOPOLY Project was now from three to seven years of age and needed a facelift. The beginning of a project as important as rewriting how the Federal Reserve determined the Fed rates were set was the perfect time to give the entire process a much-needed upgrade. Meanwhile, Russell had taken point on programming the necessary inputs for each independent computer. There was a vast array of independent processors on the gym floor. Russell was in the Computer Sciences labs vacated by the hardware students, using Northwestern graduate student programming power. Additionally, five of his best programmers from the NSA took the lead on the project.

If you were on the Northwestern University campus, it looked as though a new building might be starting. There was a huge presence of hardware suppliers, cabling contractors, and additional personnel from the Federal Reserve and NSA on campus. It was a massive project, and it was beyond any doubt that the United States government was very serious about this project.

Chapter 36

In the IRIAF headquarters just outside of Tehran, Colonel Muhammad Arman had been working quietly and invisibly whenever General Nasirzdeh was out of the office. He knew he would not be returning any time soon. Arman was using his contacts to seek out information on Freyredoon Adipour. Even though the IRCG and IRIAF were separate entities, the government of Iran was much smaller than that of the United States government. There was much closer intersectionality of the personnel data in the Iranian military servers. Arman had grown up in the IRIAF and had risen through the ranks. He was a smart manager with an American MBA. He was tech and business structure savvy, and he had been instructed by his CIA handler to get this information.

Finding Adipour was an easy task for Arman. He spent a whopping six minutes cross-referencing the IRIAF database with that of the IRGC. Adipour was an Oxford-educated computer engineer. His Oxford transcripts were scanned into the database, and he had maintained a 3.94 GPA and graduated with honors. Arman found two past addresses in Great Britain. Upon graduation he had moved back to his family home in Esfahan, to the south of Tehran. He had joined the

IRGC at age sixteen and the Iranian IRCG had paid for his education at Oxford. While scanning his personnel file, everything looked pretty uneventful.

Then he saw a very familiar signature on Adipour's appointment as a network administrator to the IRGC. He discovered that it had been a personal appointment by none other than Qassem Soleimani, the general in charge of the Iranian Special Forces Unit, the Quds Force. This nugget indicated to Arman that Adipour was going to be a risky target for him to approach, and even harder to eliminate.

Anything that pointed back to him would mean certain death for Arman, were anything to happen to Adipour suddenly. The proximity between Adipour and Soleimani indicated that there could be an extremely high likelihood that the fingerprints on the Iranian spyware planted in Evanston were more likely those of Soleimani and not those of Adipour. Further, if it were Qassem Soleimani that was working this operation, the fingerprints were most likely those of the Supreme Leader of Iran!

Arman had to do a sincere and honest self-evaluation about the level of risk to which he was now personally exposed. The level of risk had increased exponentially with the introduction of Soleimani into the threat matrix. At this juncture, Arman made a decision that he had to inform Assad at Langley. The extreme likelihood was that this was a Soleimani operation—meaning it had been sanctioned by the Supreme Leader himself. This revelation had national security implications all up and down the United States intelligence community. It was now more sensitive than one would have ever thought possible. Nobody could have suspected this when Whiffer found a bug on the gym floor in the middle of the Great Lakes region of Illinois. Sometimes life took crazy turns.

Arman purchased a non-traceable burner phone from eBay to make a call to Assad. He thought a moment and wondered: *If Soleimani had his thumb on the bug maker, does he have anyone else at Northwestern University?* He went back to his computer and began digging deeper into the other names that he knew in Evanston. He had two names with which he was familiar. He started typing names in the search field. Salomon Agassi and Muhammed Faruq were the names of which he was aware. Ali Assad had sent them their names electronically in the dossier. He entered the names and found a mixed bag. He pursued his hunch.

The searches executed by Arman were constructed to link the name of the person searched to subjects with whom parties could be electronically linked. He first searched for Salomon Agassi and assigned the affiliates Freyredoon Adipour and Qassem Soleimani. He hit enter. After about twelve seconds, Agassi was listed as a known associate and familial associate of Ghassim Kalani who was a "member of the IRGC and a known associate of Qassem Soleimani." Arman's eyes about popped out of his head when he saw the response that was returned. He typed in Muhammad Faruq with Freyredoon Adipour and Qassem Soleimani, and once again hit enter. In about ten seconds, he discovered that Faruq was also a member of the IRGC and the Quds Force. He was bewildered by what he had found within fifteen minutes, while sitting in his empty office.

He had flushed his last burner phone when Assad had called him unexpectedly. It would likely be two or three days before he could call Assad again. EBay was sometimes just too slow. Sometimes patience was the most challenging tool that a person in espionage got accustomed to using.

As Colonel Muhammad Arman was sitting at his desk, waiting on his burner phone to arrive, his mind was running miles ahead of where he was sitting. *How did these guys ever pass a background check to live in the United States? Do these guys know that the United States government funds the MANOPOLY Project? Was the one piece of spyware recovered, the only one planted? I have discovered people that are so close to the very top of the Iranian government. Has anyone noticed my searches?*

So many questions were flying through Arman's mind. Most had no right answer. He looked at the clock on his desk. Only thirty-five minutes had passed since he had read the search results. How would he ever make it until the arrival of his burner phone?

Since he had some time, he did some further digging on his computer regarding Agassi and Faruq. In running through Agassi's emails, he found an uncharacteristic email from General Qassem Soleimani. Seldom did the general use email. He found the fact that he was emailing Agassi on a secure email server fascinating. As he investigated, he found obscure references to 'Alibaba,' and to a plot to kidnap someone on the Northwestern University campus. It was *really* out of the ordinary! And there he was, stuck without a secure phone!

Chapter 37

Beau was inundated with getting the Federal Reserve scenario ready to run through the MANOPOLY Project. Beau had more at risk than anyone else in this entire scenario. If it was a huge success, he scored big at the Federal Reserve, and more significantly with his substantial interest in the MANOPOLY Project. Conversely, if it failed, his interest in MANOPOLY could take a huge hit. Additionally, his position at the Fed could make an awful turn, ending in him losing his job entirely. If he did not lose his job, it would undoubtedly flat line his career advancement curve within the Federal Reserve.

He could not empirically conclude that it might end his career in high finance altogether, but he strongly suspected that any firm he would want to work for would request a reference from the Federal Reserve. Beau had it all on the line. And there he was, right in the thick of it at Econ Lab 1 crow's nest. On the gym floor he oversaw the renovation of the MANOPOLY Project hardware and software projects. However, regardless of how busy he was and how much pressure he felt in the Fed scenario, he just could not shake the thought of his discovery on the record label.

Today, all of the hardware and software had been installed

and upgraded, in preparation for most significant challenge MANOPOLY had faced. MANOPOLY was an isolated system. Therefore, there was no Internet connectivity. The software upgrades had to be ordered from the software manufacturers on disc and manually installed. They received all of their software upgrades in this fashion. Before installation, they were scanned by a freestanding system to ensure there were no viruses or malware included.

It was the day that Whiffer and Jeff would be on the gym floor, and Jackson and Brooke would be in the crow's nest. This day they would do the diagnostic testing and running of trial data against data of known quantities and outcomes. Today was a day that Beau had been waiting for, a day that his presence would not be required at MANOPOLY. It was also a day that he was not expected in his Manhattan office. He grabbed the first flight he could get out of Evanston to New Orleans.

Beau was in a hurry and had not thought of bringing his laptop. Without his laptop, he caught a taxi and went directly to the New Orleans Public Library. He needed access to a computer and needed to see if they might have any old New Orleans telephone books. He told the taxi driver to go to 219 Loyola Avenue and settled back into his seat for the ride. Upon arrival at the library, he walked into the reference section and inquired about any old New Orleans telephone directories from the 1960s and 1970s. He was more specifically interested in the Yellow Pages. He wasn't precisely sure what he would find; therefore, he did not know exactly what to request. He was quite saddened to see that there were no physical directories in the archives. He was quite pleased to find that they were available on microfiche.

Beau sat down at the microfiche machine and began searching for addresses and telephone numbers belonging to Lyle Willis, Randy Bell, NOLA Records, Ace Records, Swallow Records, or James Floyd Soileau. He found nothing on Willis or Bell. He was not surprised. He had no reason to believe they had ever lived there; just that they had been present for the recording sessions in 1963. He did find a listing for NOLA Records, but the name had been picked up and revived as NOLA MIX RECORDS in 2011. The address they had was 1522 Magazine Street. Surely, his search couldn't be that easy, and it was not.

Their number listed was (504) 345-2138. Beau called, and his heart stopped when the girl on the other end of the line said, "Hello, NOLA Records, can I help you?"

She sounded to be in her late teens to early twenties. She spoke with a broad Southern accent, and he heard loud hip-hop music in the background. He asked her if the manager was in; she identified herself as the manager. He asked her if there was any connection between NOLA MIX RECORDS and NOLA Records in New Orleans in the 1960s.

He went on to explain that his father had recorded a record with NOLA. He was trying to locate the master tape and any information on the names of the musicians who made up a band called The Driftwood. She informed him that her dad had started the new business in 2011. They specialized in eclectic R&B and hip-hop music for a large group of disc jockeys in the Louisiana area. She went on to inform him that there was no connection to the NOLA Records from the 1960s. He was very appreciative and thanked her for her kindness and her time. It had been a dead end, so he soldiered on! He only had one day in New Orleans. His compadres were occupied testing their renovations in the computer hardware and software in Evanston. He had to keep moving. So many labels that had the common name NOLA! It made his head swim!

Next up on this list from his cursory research in his apartment office in Manhattan, was Swallow Records. Further research on Swallow Records indicated that its founder, Floyd Soileau, had merged, sold, or morphed into a record store known as Floyd's Records. Additionally, at some time in the past, Swallow had been acquired by a consolidated music interest known as Flat Town Music. They had a current address in Ville Platte, Louisiana, with a working telephone number. It seemed very unlikely that any records from the 1960s would have traveled that distance intact with the label.

He did find this Floyd Soileau to be a very likely human repository of the knowledge he sought. He moved on from the microfiche to a community desktop computer in a different section of the library. He thought that, given the time that had passed between 1963, the year of the recording, and today, and given that he must have been an adult to have owned a recording studio that Floyd might be in his eighties. So, the first search he made was a Google search for FLOYD SOILEAU OBITUARIES.

Beau discovered that Floyd was born in 1938, and, sadly, he had passed away on November 22, 2016. November 22, how fascinating! The anniversary of the day President John Fitzgerald Kennedy was assassinated. Then, he suddenly realized that his "conspiracy theory button" had been pushed. But he had no time, and he quickly shut it down. His heart sank, and he thought to himself, *if only I had begun my search just a few years earlier*.

Sitting there, ruminating on the nostalgic fact that the man in the obituary photo had known his father, Virgil, brought a tear to his eye. It occurred to him that while he was there, he should pause and read about Floyd's life. He was delighted to discover that Floyd was survived by his wife, Ann Marie, who was still in their home in Big Crane, Louisiana. But he broke out in a big smile when he learned that his son Keith was alive and lived in Baton Rouge! Beau now knew that his trip had born fruit and that he now had a clue to follow. He looked down at his watch, suddenly reminded that he had to catch a flight back to Evanston. His work had waited as long as it would on this day. He called a taxi and was off to the airport.

Chapter 38

The sun seemed to rise far too quickly for Beau the next morning. He seemed jetlagged, but that would be impossible from such a short flight. It seemed very crazy; he had never left the Central Time Zone. He rubbed his eyes and cleared his thoughts. He decided that the sluggishness must be from stress at both jobs and the excitement of being on the trail of his father. He stepped into the shower, and within an hour, he was walking into Econ Lab 1.

Beau's first stop was the crow's nest, where he found Jackson and Brooke. They both looked a bit frazzled and at the end of their wits. But this test had to proceed, and they were on task. Looking through the bulletproof glass pane of the control room, the lights on the gym floor were all on. He saw Whiffer, Russell, and Jeff working like the proverbial candle burning at both ends. They were making sure that every computer was ready. Jackson plugged the hot-swappable hard drive into the mainframe. It contained all of the financial data brought from the Federal Reserve's system. The hard drive started humming as the data transferred from the Fed hard drive to the memory of the mainframe. The program was ready to run.

The overhead speakers and microphones were hot. Jackson sat in the command chair of the control panel, and, over the intercom, he requested clearance of each member of the team.

"Brooke?" She was working the displays in the control room with Jackson.

"Check!" she stated.

"Whiffer?"

"Check!" he replied.

"Russell?"

"Check!" he responded.

"Jeff?"

"Check!" he replied.

Jackson looked Beau right in the eye. He paused before shouting, "*EXECUTE!*"

When he hit the start button, the entire system was running, but the sounds it made were all new.

Gone was the sound of the rattling bearings and bushings in the old hard drives and cooling fans. The sound was much less a WHIRRRRRING sound and much more a subdued hum. Brooke's screen started scrolling data on her display almost immediately. Simultaneously, the data was being copied onto a new hot-swappable hard drive for Beau to put in his briefcase and take back to the Federal Reserve. This drive would update their data files. The process had calculated data to feed directly and seamlessly into the Fed program. It would initiate the proposed changes for their evaluation. Suddenly, as quickly as the start button engaged, it was quiet. In less than two minutes, almost two trillion data combinations and scenarios had been tested, evaluated, and recorded. Then suddenly, after all of that work, it was finished.

All of the principal players had stood there, holding their collective breaths as the program had run. All heaved a sigh of relief. Whiffer's tall protégé seemed eerily on edge. After the run, he had excused himself and left the building. He quickly got into his car and drove to a vacant parking lot on campus. There, he removed a hidden cell phone from under the dashboard and dialed. On the second ring, there was a guttural answer in Persian. The tall man spoke quickly and only said, "Tonight, we go!"

Meanwhile, at Langley, Ali Assad had been tipped off by Colonel Arman about the potential kidnapping attempt. It was being planned by Soleimani at Northwestern. Assad had become aware of Agassi's new plant in the MANOPOLY Project and had been monitoring his actions. Assad had intercepted the call. He had traced it to a radical fringe Syrian Hezbollah terrorist pocket affiliated loosely with the Mosque Maryam in Chicago. It appeared to Assad that this group was planning to kidnap a MANOPOLY asset tonight. Assad had a rapid response team prepared for just such occasions. He immediately dispatched them to Chicago to address the incident. Nobody standing on the gym floor had any idea that Whiffer was the target of a kidnapping this very evening.

The program was designed to try as many different combinations and permutations as possible; economic factors and records combined to find the cumulative effect of the action on any financial outcome. The most successful combinations were printed and were now the potential economic recommendations of the new Federal Reserve Funds policy. The economy had been moving very well. The Federal Reserve Chairman, Jerome Powell, had been relying on an ancient set of criteria based more upon history and precedent than cold, hard statistical facts. The data provided by the MANOPOLY Project would attempt to place the U.S. economy on a course that would be the envy of the world.

The next week would be 2019. Powell had directed .25 percent rises throughout 2018, taking the Fed funds rate at 2.5 percent. These increases were viewed as counterproductive by the president. The rapid growth of real GDP was leveling off way too fast. This course was killing the recovery. The Dow

Jones Industrial Average, the NASDAQ, and the S&P were all slowing.

Unemployment was at historic lows; employed Americans were at an all-time high. New industries were starting, and housing starts were good. There was no inflation. But simply because of the length of the recovery, *historically*, inflation had to be coming soon. It did not!

This policy of rising Fed rates was killing economic growth. The president was livid and looking for ways to dump his new Fed chairman. The media was hollering about the independence of the Federal Reserve. It was a pretty crazy situation as 2018 came to an end.

The CIA rapid response team had quickly run down the source of the signal. At the opposite end of the call, they picked up four Americans. They had been radicalized at the local mosque and on the Internet. The time of the kidnapping came and passed. Whiffer was sleeping peacefully in his bed and was never aware he had been a target. Agassi's nefarious plant at Northwestern was picked up at Econ Lab 1. He was waiting for the four captured terrorists to arrive. He was apprehended without resistance.

2019

The data transmitted to the Federal Reserve from the MANOPOLY Project had been tested extensively by the Federal Reserve. The ensuing alterations made in their internal data calculations were producing spectacular results. Minor course corrections in the United States monetary policy were done very discreetly for a good reason. The Fed needed to know, in small increments, how the new program performed. Very few people within the United States government were even aware that MANOPOLY Project existed. Nor did they know that this highly sophisticated evolution of the

Monopoly board game was now taking over the fiscal policy of the most powerful country in the world.

The artificial intelligence component of the mainframe would, in and of itself, cause many conspiracy theorists to fear the program. The entire *Terminator* movie franchise had created a vast global following of people who feared A.I. because they feared it taking over the world. Additionally, there were religious groups that believed that artificial intelligence was the earthly incarnation of the Devil! This step forward in accurately implementing Federal Reserve rates would be viewed as blasphemous by some if it failed. There were so many moving parts to change. The changes were very substantial! The media continued to cover the friction between the president and the Fed chairman as an evil plan for the president to eliminate the Federal Reserve. This disinformation strategy served the secrecy that hid the changes being made in confidence very well. Fed Chairman Powell began 2019 lowering the Fed funds rate by .25 percent a couple of times, signaling a firm holding signal at 1.75 percent. Suddenly the GDP started bouncing back! Job numbers came back up in more significant quantities. Generally, the adjustment calculated by the MANOPOLY Project had remedied the age-old issue that economists had fought with the Federal Reserve.

Additionally, the stock markets came back up in higher weekly gains. The president maintained that losses in stock prices through this period had been in the neighborhood of $2 trillion. The program was incredibly successful.

Now that the administration and the Federal Reserve were on peaceful terms, the communications coming from the White House improved tremendously. After the first quarter-point cut and the signaling for continued cuts and a stable foundation at 1.75 percent, a new calm began. The president's chief of staff came in to visit Beau. To say that the president was pleased would be a gross understatement. Now that the monetary policy was stabilized and on firm footing, the president wanted Beau to know that he was very aware of what MANOPOLY had achieved. He was very grateful for their efforts. The investment the government had made in the MANOPOLY Project had paid for itself many times over.

Further, the upgrades that were initiated by the White House made MANOPOLY one of the United States government's greatest assets. Beau was very pleased. He could not wait to pass the word along to Jackson, Brooke, Whiffer, Russell, and Jeff.

Just as the White House emissary was getting up to leave Beau's office, his phone rang. He said a quick goodbye and answered, "Benoit, how can I assist you?" It was Federal Reserve Chairman Jerome Powell, who wanted to see him in one hour. Beau hung up and smirked a little bit. Life seemed very good.

Chapter 39

After the arrest and processing of the tall dark stranger that had been working deep inside the MANOPOLY Project, his history began to unfold. The Rapid Response Team took him to the Chicago field office of the FBI. Additionally, the four terrorists that had been recruited from the local Chicago mosque were taken to the same processing station. This made certain that there were no laws broken in apprehending the terror ring. Whiffer's protégé turned out to be Christopher Mizani, an American-born son of an Iranian immigrant and an American mother.

Mizani was born in Cincinnati. He had taken his mother's religion and was baptized Catholic shortly after birth. He attended public schools where he excelled in computers. He immediately went to undergraduate school at the University of Cincinnati. He graduated in only seven semesters. He had taken twenty-seven hours of dual credit Advanced Placement (A.P.) classes in high school. He graduated with a 4.0 grade point average. He applied and was accepted to graduate school at Ohio State University and graduated with honors with a Master's of Science in Computer Sciences. He was a wizard with computer hardware.

During his graduate school experience Mizani dated an Ohio State undergraduate who was an Iranian international student. This young lady had kindled a desire in him to search through his Muslim heritage. The two began attending services and prayers regularly at the Masjid Assunnah Mosque on Bates Avenue in Cincinnati. In their zeal to better serve Allah, they began studying with a radical Hezbollah group on the Internet. In the group, Mizani had become associated with Salomon Agassi. Agassi had shepherded his journey into jihad and established a friendship that would lead him to Northwestern.

In the cell at the FBI headquarters in Chicago, Mizani was coming unglued from his radicalized faith and spilling information about his associates. It began to appear that the hold Mizani's girlfriend had on him was not as strong as it needed to be for total radicalization. He revealed that he had arranged for the four men from the local mosque to participate in the kidnapping for money. What appeared to be a huge international Islamic terrorist kidnapping ring really boiled down to a kidnap-for-hire scheme. Mizani had gone outside of his jihadi principles and allowed greed to get the best of him. When he saw the money invested in all of the MANOPOLY equipment, he wanted it.

Mizani rolled over on the kidnappers in hopes that the United States government would show lenience in his prosecution and sentencing. The kidnap that never happened had certainly caused some very severe long-term consequences for the men held captive by the FBI in Chicago on this night. Only Salomon Agassi was aware that this plot had been initiated. He had managed to do this without tipping his hand one bit. He sat in his cushy home in suburban Evansville with total plausible deniability.

Chapter 40

Darian had received several communiques resulting from his Memorandum of Inquiry. Every major intelligence agency in the civilized Western world was gearing up. But since this was an ongoing situation and there was no imminent threat, the wheels of bureaucracy ground slowly toward resolution. Bits and pieces came in through secure channels; occasionally it was something that Darian found either interesting or helpful. When necessary, he passed intelligence along. What seemed very clear was that there was a powerful IRGC influence on the campus at Northwestern. However, what was lacking was definitive evidence of precisely who was involved.

When confidential human assets were concerned, there was always an information lag time. It took time to get assets placed behind "enemy" lines. These postings in places of trust were challenging to implement. It usually involved leveraging and turning a local person who was known to the target.

Last summer, Darian had followed Salomon Agassi on his annual trip to Tehran. As usual, he was met at the airport by Ghassim Kalani. Again, they got into his black Mercedes and drove through several checkpoints to the IRIAF Headquarters. This time Darian had made it into the hangar with some state-of-the-art spy craft. The equipment jammed all radio frequencies, allowing him to come in without being seen by their security scanners. He was able to disguise himself with the keffiyeh and agal (over headscarf tied with cord) in the pattern of a dominant local tribe. Darian hid on the wing of a fighter aircraft while Agassi and Kalani were in the building, and he caught a glimpse of Qassem Soleimani. He immediately knew that this plot was very sinister, indeed. However, after what appeared to be an annual check-in and debrief, Agassi seemed just to be visiting family and enjoying his time away from teaching.

While Darian was in Tehran, he visited Freyredoon Adipour's retail computer store. Adipour knew nothing of Darian's existence, nor that he was being interviewed. Darian sized up the store, the inventory, and all of the intangibles—things that a professional NSA agent sees in a picture that remains hidden to those without their training and instincts. Additionally, Darian was able to follow Adipour home one evening after closing his shop. He followed Adipour to a book café in Tehran. Adipour did some light reading, and he discovered that Adipour lived in a Quds Force barracks with approximately sixteen other soldiers. His life was tranquil and austere, and, to Darian, he appeared to be a nice person. He was never able to catch Adipour and Soleimani together, nor was he able to capture any of their communications. Darian had been very cautious in monitoring their electronic communications, being respectful of the technical aptitude that Adipour possessed. He just didn't want anyone to know he was there. Nor that he was observing both from afar in plain sight.

While Darian was in Tehran, he made contact with Colonel Muhammad Arman, and they exchanged a great deal of information. This trip had put Ali Assad in the CIA, Darian in the NSA, and Arman all on the same page. Now they all had the same knowledge. He also delivered a new, non-traceable burner phone to Arman and gave him a unique contact number to call that had to be committed to memory. The two weeks in Tehran went very quickly for Darian. He was ready to be back in the Economics Building on the Northwestern campus in the air conditioning.

Chapter 41

Beau was organizing the information in his "company" laptop and organizing the printed data from the scenario that MANOPOLY Project had run. Additionally, he was also evaluating the Federal Reserve program runs and subsequent monitoring of the United States economy. Circumstances were much improved since the hot-swappable hard drive had been plugged in and fed its data into the Fed's computer. The new data parameters applied to the data files in Manhattan. Many financial calculations were run daily, using all of the programmed adjustments that the MANOPOLY scenario had calculated.

The A.I. component of the processing was positioned on the back end of the script. The data reflected the simulated capacity for the computing processes to learn. They were tuning the interaction between changes in all aspects of the economy. The Fed System's printout was a printout from before the MANOPOLY upload and the one from today. The newly recorded data was much more in-depth and in detail and more accessible than previously. You could see the working interactions between functional areas of the economy. They had generally been "unseen" or "unknown" until the data changeover. He made sure that he had everything in his possession that Chairman Powell might request. Surely this presentation would be pleasing to the chairman. His phone rang again. Chairman Powell was ready for him.

Jerome Powell, the sixteenth Federal Reserve Chairman, was a Republican. He was appointed by President Donald Trump after Trump became disillusioned with Janet Yellen, the Barack Obama appointee. Powell had a Juris Doctor degree from Georgetown Law and was the first Federal Reserve Chairman not to have a doctorate in Economics. He was from the investment banking sector and had served on the Federal Reserve Board of Governors since 2012. Powell had traveled a rocky road as Fed chairman. His president had taken numerous public potshots at him due to his Federal Reserve funds rate policies.

The president expected Powell to hold the line on interest increases. Powell had raised the rate a few times. Each time he raised, Trump struck out at him. Each time this occurred, the partisan media threw up a big red sign and began screaming about the independence of the Federal Reserve. Powell was growing weary of the position and kept finding himself in the middle. Trump was about ready to try to remove him as Fed chair for failing to hold the line on interest rates. Trump saw the raises as personal assaults on his presidency, as deliberate attempts to sabotage the economic recovery that the United States economy was experiencing. Regardless of which side you believed, the constant friction and the subsequent reporting of the dispute in the national media was becoming a real drag for everyone involved. This was the exact reason why Trump had sent Mick Mulvaney to see Beau run the scenario on the Federal Reserve rates. It was an attempt to bring evidence supporting his position to Powell. Further, the president had been ready to fire the Federal Reserve chairman, who technically served at his pleasure. Congress was signaling that they would possibly impeach him if he fired him. Having calmed the seas between the two volatile branches of government was a real coup!

The fact that Beau, Jackson, Brooke, and company had come through, pleased both Trump and Jerome Powell. Powell, if he were candid, had been growing very weary of the constant pressure and humiliation that the situation caused. The president became very wary of the cyclical turmoil as well. Beau was walking into the office of the man who controlled his future with the Federal Reserve. However, he worked at the pleasure of the president. POTUS held the key to the success of the MANOPOLY Project. Congress kept the purse strings.

It would be challenging to find one individual on earth that had benefitted quite as much as Beauregard Benoit. Beau was walking into the chairman's office with the printed results in this briefcase. Additionally, he had the digital program on the "company" laptop. Beau had never quite been in such a position of strength.

After two funds rate decreases, followed by signaling that the Federal Reserve rate would remain steady, things leveled out. It indicated a propensity toward easing interest rates done after the MANOPOLY Project had run their scenario. Beau had brought the hot-swappable drive into the Federal Reserve and revised their economic data. They had run exhaustive testing around the clock before allowing the new data to flow into the pipeline, mixing with their data. The floodgates opened very carefully as testing began in the areas that were changed to ensure a positive and complete migration. At every juncture, the data proved accurate. Most were more precise than the data they had relied upon to make Fed policy in the past. As the information upgraded, and the new incoming data was processed using the latest processing capability, new, more delicate layers of data were discovered. This resulted in an unbelievably accurate ability to predict the outcomes of expectations across the entire United States economy. The data provided as a result of the MANOPOLY Project data was entirely responsible for the certainty used in executing the easing and cuts in the funds rate.

The net effect was the easing of tension between the White House and the Federal Reserve. Further, by eliminating this distracting friction, it also circumvented the Constitutional crisis Congress had threatened. Had the president fired Powell as threatened, Congress would have jumped straight to impeachment. It would undoubtedly have resulted in becoming the primary Article of Impeachment in a hostile, Democratic-controlled House of Representatives. The national news media and the Democratic House had beaten the drums of war every time President Trump and Chairman Powell had disagreed.

This peace was a welcome respite from the threats that had loomed very large for the first two years of Trump's presidency. Causing the calm before an impending storm of epic proportions had probably been the one most valuable short-term effect of the Federal Reserve Scenario. Beau was, indeed, looking very forward to this meeting.

Beau walked up to Chairman Powell's secretary's desk and announced his name and that he had been summoned. His secretary knew his name and knew he was coming. Beau grinned. He walked into the office, wondering if he would be promoted to Deputy Chair of the Fed. However, he mused, that would interfere with MANOPOLY. He was shocked when he came into the office to find that the meeting had an unexpected guest. John Bolton, the National Security Advisor to the president, was in attendance. Bolton was sitting in an armchair looking over wire-rimmed glasses that seemed to sit on top of a substantial grey mustache that covered his entire mouth. Beau had not expected this development.

Bolton had been instructed by the president to brief Beau on a top security assignment for the MANOPOLY Project. However, because of the security breach at Evanston, the

Federal Reserve Building had been deemed the safest place to do the briefing. Beau discovered that Ali Assad, the director of the CIA Middle Eastern Desk, had been supervising a deep cover investigation into a ring of IRGC operatives working within the Evanston/MANOPOLY vicinity. Bolton further informed Beau that an inside agent, Darian Amir, was working as an executive inside the Northwestern University campus. He was informed that Jackson Reynolds was aware of the operation. Jackson was aware that Darian had been placed there by the NSA. And Darian was working in conjunction with the CIA. Such interagency collaborations seldom occurred. Since Iran assets had deployed, the security of the MANOPOLY Project was under the jurisdiction of the NSA. Necessity had forged an unlikely alliance. Regardless of the rarity of the collaboration, the two agencies had found a way to work seamlessly together. They had managed to collect a fantastic amount of information.

Bolton proceeded to tell Beau that they highly suspected that the unholy marriage between the IRGC, Quds Force, and Hezbollah had led them to suspect that Iran, Iraq, and Syria were involved. Further, they believed the enterprise was run by Qassem Soleimani, who was believed to be the initiator of the plan. They suspected that Salomon Agassi had passed the information along as the MANOPOLY Project had progressed. Additionally, Muhammad Faruq had most probably placed the Iranian spy device in the circuitry on the gym floor.

Wow, Beau thought to himself. The Iranian spyware was something he had not thought about in quite a long time. Life had been so crazy with the quest to find his father that he'd completely forgotten the breach. It blew his mind that not one, but *two* agencies of the United States intelligence community were working in his company. Still, he'd been oblivious to their presence. Then he was suddenly angry. *Jackson? Why didn't he tell me?* Beau thought in a split-second. Immediately, his mind went back to the current meeting and the conversation in Powell's office.

"John," he asked, "why wasn't I informed of this investigation?"

John Bolton looked him square in the eye and said, very coolly and dispassionately, "It was need-to-know, and you didn't. Everyone that knows is under orders from the president not to speak a word. Now, so are you."

This conversation made him dizzy. His head started spinning with all of the wonders, fears, and apprehensions of how life would be keeping this secret. It already bothered him, keeping his secret about Virgil from Brooke. When he thought about Brooke, he began to worry about her safety. He wondered whether she knew any of this information. He couldn't imagine that Jackson had kept a secret of this magnitude from his sister. Geeze! Jackson and Brooke were about to be married. His mind flashed through hundreds of possible scenarios and outcomes. He could barely comprehend the events.

Beau walked out of Powell's office. He had not even opened his briefcase or his laptop. Nor did he discuss any data, nor any programming issues generated by the Fed Reserve Scenario. Instead, Beau had learned that what he believed to be true was not. How could he have been unaware of everything that was going on right under his nose?

This realization was, indeed, very humbling to Beauregard Benoit, who had planned his life very strategically. He had plotted his life to avoid such unplanned distractions. For the first time in his life, he found himself in a very unfamiliar spot. And he had no idea what would come next in his life.

Chapter 42

Darian was seated at his desk in the executive suite at the Department of Economics at Northwestern University. He was wearing a fashionable, tailored three-piece suit and a red power tie. In every way, he looked the part of a member of academia in the middle of a Midwestern university. Nobody would suspect him of being anything but an upper-level executive.

He appeared to be just shuffling the papers to run an economics department. Darian had a top-end Hewlett Packard desktop computer with a split display sitting on his desk. But he had pushed the keyboard under the twin displays and had set his non-descript black laptop in front of the monitors. The computer had a protective case that looked like a big Otter Box with absorbent rubber bumpers to protect it from shocks. It looked very out of place in an executive academic environment. But that was why it was sitting where it was, hidden by the twin displays. With its position where the keyboard had occupied, it gave the illusion that Darian was seated at his desk, just typing away on some meaningless report that nobody would ever read.

Russell Emming and Ronald Burnett came walking

around the corner in the hallway and walked into Darian's office and closed the door. About five minutes passed, and Jackson, Whiffer, and Beau came walking off of the elevator and walked down the hallway into Darian's office as well. Jackson entered last and made sure the door was closed securely behind him. He walked over to a cabinet on which a printer sat. The cabinet was against the wall, opposite the desk. Jackson opened a door and entered a code into a hidden security terminal. A jammer was now preventing any signal penetration, blocking signals in or out of the room. He walked back over and sat on the corner of Darian's desk, cleared his throat, and spoke.

"Gentlemen, allow me to introduce Beau Benoit to you all. You all know who he is. The National Security Advisor, at the direction of the president, read him into our operation. This will serve as his full briefing. He will be working on the same project; he will be in the Federal Reserve Building in Manhattan. Please welcome him!"

And just like that, in about twenty seconds, Beau was in the middle of an international spy ring! He was still not sure what was coming next in his life.

Chapter 43

Colonel Muhammad Arman was at his desk working. Brigadier General Nasirzdeh was readying himself for a business trip to neighboring Iraq for a week. Arman was hurriedly finalizing all of the documents and presentations that would be necessary for him to take with him. The general was standing behind his desk, shuffling through the telephone messages. His driver walked through the door, stopped, and saluted. The three exchanged salutes, and the general left with his driver. The door closed quickly behind them as they exited.

Arman continued his work uninterrupted for about an hour before the telephone on his desk rang. It was the IRIAF air traffic controller, verifying his portion of the security code to take the private military jet assigned to the IRGC. He confirmed the security challenge by reading the response numbers to those he had been given. The response matched the one required by the air traffic control. The man, on the other end, thanked him and hung up. Now Arman was safe to work on his plan. He was going to plant a bug to monitor the whereabouts of General Qassem Soleimani. He opened his desk and picked up the false top out of his pencil holder in his desk drawer and took a key out. He replaced the false top.

He called down to the carpool and requested an **IRIAF** car to take him to his destination. The car took him to a series of buildings that housed several embassies of the Gulf States, one of which was the embassy of Qatar. This series of buildings was a frequent destination for the officers of the Iranian military. His presence there was questioned by no one. He could have been going to any one of almost a dozen embassies. He sent the car back to the carpool and walked off.

He walked about two hundred yards, long enough for the driver to be long gone. He discreetly looked around, turned, and left. He walked into the Embassy of the Government of Qatar. Qatar was an Arab country in the Middle East that was much friendlier to the United States than some. They had some office space in their building that was rented out to international businesses and NGOs. Arman walked into the office of the Red Crescent and sat down to wait for the director to come to get him. The Red Crescent was the Muslim equivalent to the Red Cross in Judeo-Christian civilizations. It was a humanitarian organization that assisted the hungry, homeless, and those displaced by war and famine. These organizations are key NGOs throughout the world. A great many governments coordinated with them for humanitarian aid purposes.

Jacque Keller, a Swiss humanitarian aid specialist, was the director. Jacque had a long history with the Red Crescent, having served in both Gulf Wars. He had worked his way up through the ranks and appeared to have an excellent working relationship with all of the branches of the Iranian military. Arman and Keller had become friends during the second Gulf War and had maintained a close relationship as time passed. Nobody would ever suspect any nefarious motives within a friendship between these two fine men. Arman waited patiently to see his friend.

A Red Crescent nurse came out to the reception area wearing a white dress and a white burqa covering her head, hair, and face. She asked him to follow her back into the office. Once in Keller's office, Arman said nothing until approximately ten seconds after the nurse had left and walked off, down the hall. Both of the men were very savvy in the nuances of discretion; they both lived in Tehran, and they both worked around the IRGC. There was no need to speak so they could be heard. Arman unbuttoned his shirt pocket and pulled out the key that he had hidden in his desk. He raised it to about eye level so Keller could see it. Keller, without a word, walked across his office and took out a fire-proof box that was locked and sat it on the desk between them. Arman opened the box, looked inside. He pulled out a small envelope, placed it in his back pants pocket, relocked the safety box, and without a word, walked from the room and closed the door behind him. Arman walked out of the building and onto the street. He pulled his cell phone from his pants pocket and called the carpool for a driver. Ten minutes later, he was on his way back to his office.

Back at his desk, Arman pulled the sealed envelope out of his back pocket and carefully opened it to see what it contained. There was a communique in code, a capsule, and a high-tech Bluetooth device with which he was unfamiliar. He worked out the coded communique with a substitution cipher from a secure website that he accessed on the dark web. He accessed the cipher through a secret VPN installed on his computer. The code directed him to a one-time user link, also on the dark web. He watched the link, a video, and committed the information to his memory.

The capsule, he had just learned, was an odorless, tasteless, neurotoxin that was slow-acting and untraceable. The Bluetooth device was a tracking device that was so new and advanced that surely Freyredoon Adipour had not seen this technology. He would not know of its presence. The package's contents were for use at a later date in the near future. The capsule was designed to end Adipour's life without detection. The tracking device was intended to track the movements of Qassem Soleimani. There were also instructions on how to execute these directives. The information had come directly from Ali Assad, his handler at the CIA. And the instructions vanished from ever existing as soon as they were viewed.

Chapter 44

Beau had completed his briefing in the Economics Department at Northwestern University. He was still in a state of disbelief that all of this had been going on around him. He had been aware of the security breach when it occurred. But he was so naïve to have believed it had been resolved. He was speechless, and the briefing had driven that point home so far that he felt humiliated by his ignorance. How could he have missed all of the signs that were going on around him? He had become so engrossed in his direction of the Fed Reserve Scenario that he had watched an entire ballet of spy intrigue dance before his eyes and had no knowledge of its existence.

Beau had always fancied himself as an intelligent man who was ever vigilant and always keenly aware of what was going on around him. But the past twenty-four hours had devastated his perception of himself and his powers of observation. Beau needed some space and some time to clear his head. Beau walked out the door, across the parking lot, and got into his Porsche Boxster. He headed for the interstate.

Beau had few bad habits and even fewer sinful pleasures, but when he was up against a wall and needed to clear his mind, Beau loved SPEED! That was why he maintained a

Red BMW in New York and a Porsche Boxster in Evanston; he had to have speed as his stress reliever. He took Central Street, west to Old Orchard, and exited to I-94. Then he opened his glove box and removed an extravagant pair of leather driving gloves with open knuckles. He pulled them on tightly and downshifted. The whining sound of the Porsche engine winding up as the tires spun sounded like a banshee screaming into the dark! He hit 123 miles per hour in just a few seconds, shifted into high, and just settled back into his leather seat. Then, he reached down to turn on the music. About fifteen minutes later, Beau was about to enter Winnetka, Illinois.

He was thinking deeply about what he might discover from Keith Soileau and what he might be able to tell him. Would he have any of the remaining financial records, personnel records, or master recordings from NOLA Records? Would this be a lifeline or a dead end? Beau had experienced one hell of a day but taking his mind for a drive had been excellent therapy for him.

He reached for his cell phone, located Imogene's number, and hit dial. The Bluetooth captured the call, and it was now coming over the car stereo speakers. *Ring, ring…* "Hello, Beau! How are you doing?"

Beau needed to hear a friend's voice. Beau used this wind-shield time to fill Imogene in on all of the events that had occurred in New Orleans. All of the dead ends and the dead numbers were discussed. The vanishing of the past merging into the present, but he had a clue! Imogene listened very contently. She knew that she was the only other person in the world, except for Brightwell Benoit, who knew the deep, dark secret that Beau was carrying. She knew that this secret was a massive void in Beau's soul. She also knew that it felt as though he had a hole in his heart that could only be filled by discovery. Either in a meeting, or in the event of the very worst, Beau had to know his fate. If his natural father had passed, Beau would need to stand at his grave and pray. These two great friends enjoyed a conversation for about forty minutes, and then Imogene had to go.

Beau had slowed down almost to the speed limit and was just enjoying the solitude and his visit with Imogene. His blood pressure felt as though it was high when he left Evanston, but right this minute, he felt great. He looked down at his fuel gauge and saw that he needed to fill up. He signaled and turned at the next exit and pulled into a gasoline station. He pulled up to the pump, released the gas tank lid on the driver side, and stepped out of the car. He bent down and reached into the vehicle to twist the cap off the spout and reached for his wallet. He swiped his company gas card, selected the premium fuel, started the pump, and walked into the convenience store for a bottle of water. He came back in about three minutes. He placed the gas nozzle back in the slotted holder, closed the lid, opened the door, and started his engine.

He slowly pulled back onto the outer road. The tires did not spin, the motor did not whine, and the speedometer did not indicate that he was driving over the speed limit. The windshield therapy had been very effective in easing his nerves and lowering his stress. He was the man responsible for bringing the United States economy into balance and soothing the tension between the president and the Federal Reserve. Stress was not a stranger to Beau but missing something so obvious was. He headed back. He had a ton of work to get done.

Back in Evanston, Darian and Jackson were having a strict "Come to Jesus" conversation about the constituency from the IRGC that had taken up residency on campus at Northwestern University. After Whiffer had discovered the Iranian spy device, Jackson had assumed that getting Russell and Burnett involved had solved the problem. Additionally, he thought that the private placement of Darian in residence would plug the holes and their security. He assumed it was not an issue to consider. In Jackson's wildest dreams, he could have never imagined that there would be a local IRGC contingency monitoring his progress. He thought back to the day when Whiffer had brought the spy device into the crow's nest. That was a day that he would never forget. The subsequent upgrades and tightening of security, and the elimination of most of the graduate students that played the original Monopoly game, should have resolved the issue. But obviously it had not.

This event had also been the driving force to further evolve the game from a physical gameboard to a virtual game. It no longer existed as a game of human interaction, rather in a virtual computer reality. The more computerized, the fewer people, the tighter the computer facility, meant the MANOPOLY Project data would be safer. This event had indeed been a seminal moment in the MANOPOLY Project's development. The realization that the Supreme Leader of Iran, his Quds Force general, and the entire IRGC had their sights set on influencing or capturing their data stunned him. Further, it was beyond Jackson's ability to believe or understand.

He was due to meet with Brooke for dinner in about half an hour. He still had to tell her the details and the extent to which the assault on their MANOPOLY Project had experienced. Also, on the schedule for tomorrow was a meeting with a wedding planner. Brooke had booked the St. Nicholas Roman Catholic Church for a June wedding. He was concerned that his news might cause an upset in her plans and disappoint her. It had been fourteen years since Brooke began her residency at Northwestern. Jackson just didn't want to break her heart. Her mother had already passed away, and Bright was still living at home on 24/7 nursing care. Jackson knew that Beau would be her only family at the wedding. He just could not allow a bunch of revolutionaries from Iran to ruin her day. He just would not let that happen!

Chapter 45

Brooke Benoit started her day with an extra spring in her step. She found herself singing, *"I'm getting married in the mornin', ding dong the bells are gonna chime,"* the lyrics from Lerner and Lowe's Broadway classic, "Get Me to the Church on Time" from *My Fair Lady*. As a Gamma Phi Beta at Louisiana State University, she had participated in a sorority review performing the music of *My Fair Lady*. It was an opportunity seized to showcase her beautiful ballroom dance skills from her grade school cotillion days in Baton Rouge. As she stood in the shower, singing, she was also taking a mental trip back into her youth. She was basking in the sunshine of the wedding of her dreams becoming a reality.

Jackson had gotten up very early and rushed off to the office for a meeting. He had sworn to Brooke that he would meet her and Francine Hayes, her wedding planner at St. Nicholas Roman Catholic Church at 806 Ridge Avenue at 10:30 sharp.

She was having a perfect time, and she hoped that her day would just keep getting better and better!

Chapter 46

Back at the crow's nest in Econ Lab 1, behind the bulletproof glass with secured doors, and with a signal jammer operating, Jackson, Whiffer, Russell, Burnett, and Darian were having a meeting. They were discussing the actions under consideration in Tehran. They were briefed, without divulging any names or information that could compromise any operational details. They were discussing the plans to eliminate the man who engineered that Iranian spy device located on the gym floor. All they really knew was that the man who had developed this technology lived in Iran and was involved with the IRGC. Therefore, he had to be affiliated with the resident members on the Northwestern campus. Whether his involvement was direct or indirect was unknown to the men in Evanston and, really, irrelevant.

Additionally, they knew that a United States affiliated intelligence operative was now poised to make these bold moves. Further, they knew that a general very close to the Iranian Supreme Leader was going to be monitored and surveilled. His participation in this situation would be revealed. They were all quietly wondering what the repercussions would be in Evanston when these events unfolded in the

Middle East. As Burnett and Darian went methodically through the information that they deemed necessary to inform the MANOPOLY Project crew, they waited. They were cautious not to cause any undue concern or panic. But now recommendations that the Northwestern University campus be better secured were necessary.

The key issue driving the concern was the fact that with the IRGC and Quds Force, connections in the Middle East were present. How had two international academic employees passed a United States State Department background check? Why were no red flags raised in warning? American universities and colleges were very liberal in allowing foreign students to come into the United States. They contributed to the pool of knowledge that was a piece of the "university experience." The American university system generally, and the human resource departments individually, trusted that the State Department's background investigations were thorough and complete. It was imperative that the international students and teachers who came into the university community be safe and that they represented no harm to America's children. How did Iran manage to get these subversives past the American Secretary of State's global screening process? Did the failure to find any background information lie at the feet of the United States intelligence community?

How did the United States Embassy in Baghdad, Iraq, not know of these connections? This embassy was the Middle Eastern command center to monitor the pulse of the IRGC, the Quds Force, the IRIAF, Hezbollah, Al Qaeda, and the Shiite militias in Lebanon, Syria, and Iraq. This embassy generally referred to as "The Green Zone" from the two Iraqi wars was considered one of the most secure sites in the Middle East. It was broadly believed that this embassy housed contingencies from most all of the Western Intelligence Agencies. The CIA, MI6, and Moussed were all believed to have assets posted there to monitor subversive activities and any planned operations against Western civilization and Israel. Anyone would assume that all of these agencies would know the cogent players associated with the Supreme Leader of Iran, or at least those in trusted positions like those held by Salomon Agassi and Muhammad Faruq. These questions were the ones perplexing the men sitting in the crow's nest.

Jackson looked down at his watch. It was now 10:02 a.m. Jackson had to get to the church on time.

Chapter 47

The St. Nicholas Roman Catholic Church was an architectural masterpiece. The church was founded in 1887 by Luxembourgers, having masses held only in German. The church had twenty beautiful stained-glass windows constructed in Innsbruck, Austria, and were shipped to Evanston. The church, as it existed now, was built between 1904 and 1906 and was renovated in 2000. It was a beautiful example of classical Catholic architecture. As Brooke walked up to the entry from the curb, she felt her head leaning back to follow the spire toward Heaven. This was the original reason that churches were built with steeples.

When she walked through the door, the sun was projecting a mosaic of colored light throughout the auditorium. She heard the slight echo of her footsteps, indicating that the acoustics in the space were amazing. She looked toward the front of the church and was amazed at the hand-crafted artistry contained in the altar and the pulpit. On the back wall was an eight-foot-tall wooden carving of Jesus hanging on the cross. The crucifix was carved by hand and would have taken hundreds of hours of painstaking craftsmanship to sculpt. Her eyes transfixed upon the detailed work of each thorn contained in the crown of thorns. The crown that Jesus had worn on the cross was impeccable craftsmanship. She could not imagine the patience it must have taken to carve such a masterpiece.

Francine Hayes was very familiar with being in the church. She was, after all, a professional wedding planner. Additionally, she was also an intermittent member of the congregation at St. Nicholas Roman Catholic Church. Francine was more the kind of a congregant that attended on Easter, Christmas, and occasionally through the Lenten season. She was more familiar with the head pastor, Father Bishop, from working as a wedding coordinator. He was aware of the fact that she knew the facilities very well. It was a burden off of Father Bishop's shoulders. He would merely field the questions regarding the liturgy and Catholic Church doctrine issues. Additionally, logistics of dressing rooms, processional routes, etc. would be handled by Francine.

Brooke and Francine had met at the church a few minutes early by design so that she could get a feel for the space. Brooke looked down at her watch; it was 10:28 a.m. About twenty seconds after she looked up, she heard the front door open. Jackson was feeling a hefty weight on his countenance, but he was happy to see Brooke. He was even more pleased to see the beautiful smile on her face. One of Brooke's absolute best assets in Jackson's eyes had always been her smile. He would tell his friends that her smile would light up even the darkest room. He walked to the front of the church. Francine introduced him to Father Bishop, and the meeting began in earnest.

Chapter 48

Beau was aware that Jackson and Brooke had wedding details to complete for the rest of the day. From his office in Manhattan, Beau had been video conferenced into the meeting that Jackson had just come from at MANOPOLY. The program that had been engineered and installed by the MANOPOLY Project at the Federal Reserve was running very smoothly. Beau looked around and thought to himself that the rest of the day was his.

His mind quickly went to Baton Rouge and Keith Soileau. He sat down at his computer and Googled his telephone number and thought he would see if he was free today. Keith answered on the second ring, and Beau introduced himself. He told Keith that his father had been a friend of his dad's and that he had recorded a single with him on NOLA Records in 1963. Keith, as it turned out, was quite the talker and was a huge LSU Tiger football fan. Keith knew who Beau was from his college football career, and he wanted to talk Tiger football. Beau saw this as an opportunity and asked him what he had planned for dinner that evening.

He stretched the truth a tiny bit and told Keith he was going to be in Baton Rouge that evening, and his dinner plans had just canceled. Keith was beyond pleased for the chance to sit and talk football with Beau. They made a date to meet at a pizzeria near the LSU campus. Beau hung up, got on the phone, and booked the next flight to Baton Rouge.

Beau's flight was very uneventful, and he arrived in Baton Rouge about five minutes early. All he had brought was his briefcase and a backpack with some overnight clothes, if he decided to stay at his dad's overnight. His plans were pretty fluid. He had no idea where this meeting might take him. He was feeling very hopeful, but he also felt a tinge of trepidation. He knew that if this path were a dead end, then he had no further clues. No expectation or idea of when or where additional evidence might turn up. In any event, from the conversation that the two had shared on the telephone, Beau believed that he had made a new friend. Beau hailed a taxi from the airport and arrived at the pizzeria about ten minutes before the predetermined time.

Beau had a seat and ordered a Louisiana staple, a large sweet tea. He leaned back into the padded booth and relaxed. He was anxious to meet his new friend. Beau was so hopeful that he would shed some light on his path toward locating anything regarding Virgil.

About fifteen minutes later, a large man, maybe two hundred eighty pounds and probably five-feet, ten-inches, walked in. Beau guessed him to be ten to twelve years his senior. He walked in the door, looked carefully at all of the booths and tables, and smiled when he saw Beau. He walked over and said, "Beau? Beau Benoit?"

"Yes, you must be Keith!" he replied. He joined Beau at his booth. The very first thing they discussed was what pizza to order. They settled on a half-veggie deluxe for Beau and half-Hawaiian for Keith. Beau expected that they would have a great discussion. This was based solely upon the fact that they had carried on a twenty-minute debate over whether pineapple belonged on a pizza. The fact that half of the pizza for their table had pineapple was a reasonable indicator that the conversation had gone well. Keith had also ordered a sweet tea. The preparation time for the pizza was to be approximately twenty minutes. It was time for the talk to begin.

Beau took a deep breath and opened his mouth to speak. But suddenly Keith hit him with a barrage of about seven questions in a row about teams he had played his senior year at LSU. Additionally, he was interested in the general state of the SEC (South East Conference). Beau grinned and spent the next thirty minutes, answering the seven questions as fully as he could recall. The pizza had been delivered to the table. It sat idly in front of them about seven minutes before the explanation finished. Keith sat, nodding his head, hanging on Beau's every word until he finished.

Beau said, "Excuse me," and he bowed his head to pray. The two ate as passionately as they had begun their discussion. After about fifteen minutes of chewing and drinking sweet tea, Beau looked at Keith and asked him a single question: "I am a fan of your dad's recordings; did you share any of his passions?" Then Beau sat and waited for the answer he had been anticipating since the New Orleans Public Library. The formulation of this exact question was formulated throughout the entire flight from New York to Baton Rouge. Beau had probably considered maybe ten different items. He settled on this particular question because it was very strategic, and it allowed the response to guide the path of the subsequent conversation. Beau was a very proficient strategist.

As it turned out, Keith was a lifelong musician. He had played in the LSU Marching Tiger Band. Keith had sat in the stands playing a big bass drum and marched on the very same field on which Beau had played. He had often sat and watched the games and dreamed what it would be like to play on the hallowed ground. What it would be like to have all of the cheerleaders talking to him. He was more than a football fan;

he was an admirer. The conversation about Beau and football had Keith wondering what it was like to be a football star.

But Keith's real passion had been music, and yes, he had shared that passion with his dad. Beau was totally mesmerized as Keith told him many fascinating stories about the national parades the Marching LSU Tiger Band had marched in. Beau was not aware that they had even played in a Super Bowl in the Super Dome in New Orleans one year.

Beau had never made it to the field on a Super Bowl Sunday, and that statement meant an awful lot to Keith. The longer the two talked, the more he liked him. Beau intently listened to Keith's stories and was waiting for a strategic pause to ask some probing questions. Questions that might answer Beau's question he had carried since high school. The waitress came to the table to get the check settled. The pizzeria was about to close. The two men had talked for two-and-a-half hours. Beau asked him if he would like to get a piece of pie and coffee. Beau wasn't hungry, but he wanted to continue their conversation. Beau had taken a taxi, so he rode with Keith to a nearby Denny's to have desert.

In the car, Beau had found an opening to ask if he had ever taken the opportunity to record any music since his dad had owned a record label and studio. He told Beau that his dad had sold the studio to Ace Records while he was very young, but he had kept many of his master tapes. It was a response that sent Beau into a place of delight. But he tried to maintain his composure and asked if he still had the tapes. Just as this question landed, they pulled into a parking space at Denny's and got out of the car. The conversation paused while they walked into the restaurant and waited to be seated. The menus came, and there was another lengthy discussion about pie selection. They ordered, and when the waitress left, Beau asked, "Do you recall any of the musicians that your dad recorded?"

Then Keith's eyebrows raised, and you could see the light

going off inside his head. He replied, "Your dad recorded with my dad, isn't that what you told me?"

Finally, the door was wide open for Beau to walk through. Beau told him that his dad had played guitar and had recorded with a band called The Driftwood. The record released in 1963, and it was a cover of the Elvis Presley hit "Hound Dog." He told him that his dad's name was Virgil Bagley and that Lyle Willis and Randy Bell were listed on the NOLA Records label as producers. And he told Keith that he and his sister had grown up listening to the record, but he had always assumed it was Elvis. Beau explained briefly that his stepfather had raised him and that he was on a quest to discover who his natural father really was. And this was his only lead. Beau felt relieved to have unloaded this all. He no longer had to worry and wonder what he would say, or how it would be received. He wondered if it would be awkward, but he was comfortable with Keith and now sat waiting for some answers and some hope.

Keith was not at all familiar with the names The Drift-woods, Virgil Bagley, Lyle Willis, or Randy Bell. But that was not the end of the road either. Once Keith saw the agony behind Beau's eyes and heard the longing in his voice, the happiness of the conversation dissipated very quickly. Keith was now very forthcoming about the state of his father's affairs. Keith had not been interested in the early blues records that his father had done. He simply didn't like the blues. Keith was a brass and percussion kind of musician. He had heard a few of them, and it just wasn't what he liked. His dad loved the blues and liked a lot of the blues players. It had always seemed to his dad that blues players wrote sad stories from profound places, and those places shaped them as musicians. His dad had considered his master tapes to be his "Mona Lisa," his greatest musical achievement. Still, when the NOLA Record label was sold to Swallow Records and then again to Ace Records, he had lost the rights to the copyrights.

Therefore, he could not sell them or distribute them to radio stations for airtime play. This was how he generated royalties, thereby revenue.

As it turned out, it was an oversight in a contract between Swallow and Ace Records that sold the rights away. He had, however, maintained his master tapes. The tapes were kept in a box in the basement in his parent's home in Big Crane, Louisiana. They were located there at the time of his death. Since his death almost four years ago, Keith's mother's health had not been well. He and his siblings had moved her into a managed care facility. Rather than sell her home, the Soileau children had jointly agreed to rent her house. This arrangement offset the shortfall between the actual cost of her care and the long-term healthcare policy she owned. Selling her home would have created a spend-down scenario with Medicare. The income from the sale would disqualify her from receiving Medicare. The family transferred the home into the children's names, allowing their mother to receive the aid. So, they had a family rummage sale and moved several of their valuable family possessions into a climate-controlled storage unit. They had opted to pay twenty-five more dollars each month for a climate-controlled unit due to the master tapes. Keith had a key to the storage unit in Big Crane on his key ring.

So, at this second, it looked as though Beau had just obtained access to his father's master tape! However, it seemed unlikely that the tape would have any names or addresses. He needed to discuss the NOLA Record's business archives. As good as this felt, he had to stay grounded and authentic to his actual goal. Beau knew that Virgil had recorded in New Orleans in 1963. He also knew that possibly a connection existed to Halliburton, but that was it. Everything between them was just mysterious.

They had sat in Denny's for almost two hours, Beau was thinking about getting back to Evanston tomorrow. He had enjoyed the time he spent with Keith, and he, oddly, felt much closer to Virgil emotionally. It was amazing to sit and talk with Keith about a man that had been an excellent friend to Virgil. He felt a long-distance connection from bygone years.

They were saying their goodbyes, but Beau just had to breach the subject with Keith before they parted. Beau grabbed Keith's hand, squeezed it firmly, and said, "Keith, I cannot tell you what this visit has meant to me. But as good as this has made me feel, I am searching for clues I can follow. Do you have any clue where the business records for NOLA Records might be?"

Keith's smile dropped a bit. Beau knew this meant bad news, so he braced himself. "We do not have the business records. Dad never valued the papers, just the vinyl. I believe that they went with the sale to Ace Records."

Beau thanked him for his time. They exchanged phone numbers and email addresses and agreed to meet again soon. Beau took a taxi to a motel near the airport and booked the red-eye out at 7 a.m. the next morning. He would be in Evanston for his 9:30 appointment.

Chapter 49

It was 2014 when Whiffer discovered the Iranian spy device on the gym floor in Econ Lab 1. Almost five full years ago! Within a week of that event, Darian was assigned to the Northwestern University Department of Economics. The NSA and CIA had been involved in running this leak to ground. For almost five full years it had dragged. Granted, when hidden human assets are being utilized and are leveraging hostiles to participate, time has to pass to make things work. Still, this process was a marathon rather than a sprint.

This breach had caused the MANOPOLY Project to fortify its security and to internalize and move the process toward its inevitable state of being, much faster than had it not occurred. The utilization of the NSA's Information Technology personnel and resources had also improved and streamlined the growth process—growth toward where the technology had evolved. This opportunity recalibrated how the Federal Reserve monitored and adjusted its interest rates and altered how cash infusions and withdrawals from the economy occurred. They also created another tangible reason for the exponential growth that had occurred because of the process. Still, regardless of which contributing factor was selected, many factors had come together for many reasons to create this miraculous process.

It only seemed fitting that something so precious required such stringent security and protection. This process had the potential to evaluate the interaction between many divergent factors, to assess with unprecedented accuracy how they would all work together, and what the outcome would likely be. This process had been a very notable one, and had it not been classified, it would most certainly have been a Nobel Prize winner. Now in the waning days of 2019, the future looked very bright.

Chapter 50

In Iran, Jacque Keller, Iranian Director of the Red Crescent, was seen riding in a military vehicle with a Red Crescent moon painted on the roof and on both front doors. It pulled up to an armed military checkpoint somewhere in Tehran. The armed guard walked up to the driver's window, and the driver handed him a clipboard with government papers. The guard checked the documents and found them in order. Since he knew both men and dealt with them often, they were allowed to pass. They drove approximately another half mile, executed two very sharp turns, and pulled up to a red-and-white-striped pole. The pole swung down and blockaded the entrance to the Doshan Tappeh Air Base. Again, they showed the clipboard to the guard. Again, they were granted passage.

The large barricade swung up, and the truck pulled just past the blockade and stopped. The barrier dropped. Two officers came out of the guard shack and reached into the back of the transport and removed two wooden boxes about the size of a standard peach crate. Keller and the driver waited until they heard one of the men bang his fist against the tailgate. They proceeded forward. They had delivered medications for men on the base that Keller had acquired from the

Swiss for the Iranian military. They would need to be inspected and logged into inventory at the post.

The truck proceeded back to a very familiar, secure aircraft hangar. This time rather than getting out and swiping a security card, they simply honked. Within a few seconds, that hangar door began to pull open electronically, moved mechanically by a motorized chain, and the truck pulled into the hangar. Keller got out. The driver stayed in the transport. There were no planes or jets in the hangar. Instead, it stood empty. It was a large, clean pad of concrete. Keller walked into the air-conditioned office and the conference room; he had a seat at the table inside. Present at the meeting were Keller, a Major Muhammed, General Qassem Soleimani's Executive Officer, and an enlisted man who was responsible for the inventory of the base's medical supplies.

The Red Crescent had requested some medical supplies for a humanitarian aid project in a rural community north of Tehran. The request for supplies had to be approved by the representatives of the Supreme Leader. In Iran, the Iranian military was supplied first before any humanitarian needs were addressed. It was a process that Keller was very familiar with and had conducted many times. Keller had carried the clipboard in with him and had removed the papers. He was discussing them with Major Muhammed when General Qassem Soleimani walked into the room.

Everything stopped immediately, and everyone stood at attention. The major and the enlisted corpsman saluted, while Keller stood quietly at attention. Soleimani took the empty seat at the head of the table and nodded his head. When he nodded, everything in the room returned precisely to where it was when the door swung open. Soleimani listened as Keller continued to plead his case and seemed very attentive to the discussion. At the end of the presentation, the list of requested items was presented to the major for approval. The major looked at the number to make sure they reflected accurately the exact terms discussed, nodded his head, and placed the list on the tabletop. He slipped it across the surface of the table to the general. Soleimani glanced at the paper, nodded back at the major, and looked deeply into Keller's eyes. He paused, then looked down, took his pen out of his shirt pocket, and signed the requisition form. Soleimani nodded, stood, and exited the room.

The paper was taken out of the room by the corpsman. The major stood and instructed Keller to wait for a few minutes. He nodded; the major exited the room. In about twenty-five minutes, the corpsman returned and informed Keller that his truck and driver were waiting for him. Keller exited the air-conditioned office into the sweltering desert heat and got into the transport. Exiting the security was much more comfortable and quicker. The process was just driving slowly through the checkpoints in reverse order, while the driver was politely waved on through. The truck returned to the Embassy of the Government of Qatar. Keller went into the Red Crescent office and instructed his employees to bring the supplies in, out of the heat. The truck driver took off around the embassy and parked the truck in the garage. He returned to the Red Crescent's office.

The obvious takeaway from this event was the fact that Jacque Keller had relative ease of access to Soleimani. Also, Colonel Muhammad Arman, sitting in the IRIAF Brigadier General's office, was holding a state-of-the-art, high-tech miniaturized Bluetooth transmitter. It was designed specifically to monitor Soleimani. It would seem that the pieces halfway around the world, after five years of planning, were coming together. Every plan required an opportunity and an execution. It became clear that an opportunity now existed. The implementation would have to be carefully orchestrated and timed like a masterpiece to ensure the safety of all parties involved.

Chapter 51

Brooke and Jackson had enjoyed the meeting at the church. Brooke had grown up Catholic in Baton Rouge and had attended Catholic schools. It was easy for her and everything seemed to be flowing the way it was intended to be. Jackson was a bit more standoffish about the entire religious ceremonial rituals that were intermingled throughout the Catholic wedding Mass. Jackson held his cards very close to his vest regarding religion, his family, and his past. All anyone knew for sure was that he played baseball and was an outstanding hitter. That he had been caught using performance-enhancing drugs and lost his final year of NCAA eligibility. He had been forced to settle for a second-tier graduate school and that he had a fantastic IQ and a stellar work ethic.

Jackson had supported Beau in his transformation from an over-enthusiastic drinker to a born-again Christian. Yet, he had never discussed his faith with anyone. As Brooke sat in their living room, talking about the ceremony with Jackson, she sensed something that she did not recognize in Jackson. She sat down and looked across the room. She finally realized that in her zeal to plan and have her dream wedding, she had never asked Jackson what he wanted. Jackson was still just there to support her, and Beau. He never really talked about anything but his work and his ideas. Brooke sat there staring, and a tear started running down her cheek. She could not believe she had been so very selfish.

Brooke turned her face directly toward Jackson and looked all of the way into the bottom of his soul. She began, "Jackson, I have just had an epiphany. I realize that our entire life together has been about two things. It has been about my dreams and your work. For these almost fourteen years, I have never asked you what you thought, or believed. Jackson, I love you. I want to know how you feel about all of this."

Jackson looked down and had suddenly become very quiet. He had not seen this coming. Even though his life had been very hard, he had learned to survive by his wits. Jackson wasn't a whiner or a complainer and didn't need someone to check on his feelings every few minutes. Jackson was pleased with Brooke. And Beau was everything he could have ever wanted in a brother. His inclusion into their family had made him whole. It made him feel like part of a family that truly loved him. He had loved Patsy Benoit, and he loved talking to Bright Benoit still today.

Further, he accepted Bright as his very own father. He derived a great deal of pride from helping Brooke financially and logistically care for Bright after his stroke. Patsy's death had devastated them all. Jackson was very private, he was very guarded, and he was an exceptional young man.

Jackson was very uncertain about what to say to Brooke and how to say it. He began, and as he started, an unmistakable look of deep pain came across his face. Brooke was shocked and frightened. She struggled to understand what could be so painful. She knew it had not been murder or prison; he had top-secret clearance, and she had spent almost fourteen years with him without a single glitch. She knew about the steroid scandal. He had never been close to another performance drug. She was at a total loss. But Brooke had led a very charmed and protected life, one reminiscent of the belles in the Old South. Jackson was confident of one thing at that very moment. If he wanted to keep Brooke, it meant he had to bare all. He had to open up to her because he could not bear a loss that big.

"Brooke, I do not have the strength to tell you my entire story now. It may take the rest of our lives, but I will start, and I will try. I need you to work through this with me and love me through it all. I have never told anyone my entire story. Are you sure you want to know?" he asked her.

She had a very concerned look on her beautiful face, but she nodded affirmatively. So, he began to spill his heart to his future wife.

Jackson had been born to an unwed mother in Little Rock, Arkansas. She left him at a convent in North Little Rock. He was left in a basket of dirty laundry. There was nothing from which to derive a clue. There was not even a note. He never knew who either of his parents was. One of the nuns at the orphanage took a liking to him and kept him in her room. She called him Jackson. Her name was Sister Ann Reynolds. She had taken the baby to social services, who had investigated all of the area hospitals trying to find a record of the birth but found nothing. Social Services had assisted Sister Ann in procuring a birth certificate for the baby and applied for a social security number for him as well. He was not even sure of his date of birth. These revelations made Brooke better understand why he gaffed off his birthday each year.

Sister Ann Reynolds had attended Mount St. Mary High School in North Little Rock and had received a calling from God to be a nun. Upon graduation, she took her vows and went to college at the University of Arkansas in Little Rock. She got a bachelor's degree in sociology. She immediately took her vows and began life as a consecrated servant of God.

Her parents were very well off. Her dad was an executive vice president for Christian Finkbeiner Foods. Finkbeiner was a local meatpacking plant and a meat processor in Little Rock. They had a lovely home in Treasure Hills Subdivision off of Markham Road. Ann was an only child. Her parents fell in love with Jackson as well. When it was not feasible for Jackson to stay at the orphanage, he was welcomed into the Reynolds' home as if he were their grandson. In every way he was their only grandchild. They sent him to Little Rock Public Schools, and he went with them to services at the Cathedral of St. Andrew. Jackson did very well, and he had every opportunity that any typical kid could have wanted.

The summer after the sixth grade, he went to a Catholic camp for boys in the greater Memphis area. The camp was an all-boys camp. He had become friends with a Christian Brother at the camp who was studying to become a priest. They remained friends for almost two years. This man was Jackson's tireless friend. He went to his city league baseball games and caught for him when he took batting practice. Jackson was a gifted pitcher even in junior high school.

In seventh grade, he began playing Babe Ruth League baseball. It was a huge deal at that time. The Babe Ruth League had a world series and was a national youth baseball league. His Christian Brother friend, still in seminary, was home every summer to assist as a coach. On a trip to the Babe Ruth Regional Tournament, the Christian Brother molested Jackson. He never told a soul. From then on, he felt dirty and he felt abandoned by God. Jackson never told Sister Ann, never told Mr. and Mrs. Reynolds, and never went to church again.

As Jackson advanced through school at Parkview High School, he excelled at baseball. His senior year, he was throwing ninety-two miles per hour, and he had a decent curveball. The St. Louis Cardinals had a farm team in Little Rock at the time; the Arkansas Travelers, a double-A farm team. The coach was visible sitting there with a radar gun at any Parkview High School home game, clocking Jackson's pitches. He had talked to Jackson's coach, who had recommended that Jackson sign a professional baseball contract right out of high school.

Jackson learned from the Christian Brother, whose name he had never revealed, that you learn baseball from a coach. You never trust anything else they say. Jackson had his mind set on an NCAA Division I college baseball scholarship. He wanted an excellent education. He tried to make his way in life on his terms. He never wanted to feel helpless again. He was smart. And he tried to make his way in life. Since Jackson had been so busy playing baseball, he had only worked part-time jobs. Mr. and Mrs. Reynolds and Ann supplied all of his needs and were in the stands at every school baseball game. They were in awe at the dedication that the boy had toward his studies. His senior year, he was in the top ten of his high school class, a class of over six hundred students. He was on the Arkansas High School All-State Baseball Team. He was recruited very heavily by NCAA Division 1 schools. There were only two that were good enough at baseball and had a topflight school of economics. He narrowed his decision down to Arkansas and Arizona State. After having played on the diamond at the University of Arkansas several times in state playoff games, in the end, he felt like the field in Fayetteville was his baseball home. Jackson had pitched all of the way through high school. He was always able to see the movement on the ball better than most. He could hit the ball better than anyone around. So, when he went to college, he went as an outfielder so he could get more at-bats.

Jackson was a boy with a 135 IQ, a 4.0 GPA, and athletic ability running out his ears. Yet he still felt as though his mother, father, and God had abandoned him. Baseball was his tool to get the education that he coveted to become someone he respected. Then, during his junior year at the University of Arkansas, while struggling through a muscle tear in his triceps, a teammate injected him with an anabolic steroid. This happened just two days before the NCAA College World Series. A random blood test busted him.

It was all that he could bear to tell Brooke. When he looked up, through the tears in her eyes, he saw the one thing he feared: He thought he saw her pitying him.

Chapter 52

Colonel Arman was sitting at his desk at the IRIAF Head-quarters. He was working on a plan to create a need for Freyredoon Adipour's services. They needed to be required by the IRIAF. However, he had to devise this plan without Brigadier General Nasirzdeh knowing that it was a plot; a plot to draw him into proximity. In Arman's course of doing his duties as the executive officer for Brigadier General Nasirzdeh, he often composed communications, letters, and memoranda on behalf of the general. When doing so, and when it required a signature in his absence, he had a rubber stamp bearing a facsimile of the general's signature to use. Arman and the general had worked together for so long that he never questioned Arman about the usage of his name or his signature stamp. While the IRIAF and the IRGC was not the same military unit, they were closely related. The relation-ship was much like the United States Navy and the Seal Teams. It is not an identical analogy, but for the sake of understanding the trusted relationship between the IRIAF and the IRGC, the example will suffice.

The Quds Force was generally considered to be affiliated

with the IRGC. They were more like the Special Services of the IRGC. The Quds Force, through General Qassem Soleimani, was a direct extension of the Supreme Leader, Ali Khamenei. The IRGC linked directly back to the university students that stormed the United States Embassy in 1979. They were the same radical group that had held American citizens hostage for 444 days. Soleimani was the direct link to Hezbollah, Al Qaeda, and the Shiite groups in Lebanon, Syria, and Iraq. Arman was a crucial link in the communication chain that connected these entities. They shared a common need for the use of the Iranian Air Force's aircraft assets. In their hierarchy, Nasirzdeh held a crucial position in the supervision and maintenance of Iranian aircraft assets. He was also a required step in issuing launch release clearances to the air traffic controllers at the airbase. Arman had been secretly utilizing his trusted position and monitoring operations between the Quds Force and Hezbollah. He was searching for an activity that might require some specialized digital surveillance.

In Syria, Al Qaeda and ISIS (loosely affiliated) had been recently evicted by the United States military. They had staked a claim to a landmass by labeling it as a "caliphate," or an Islamic state under a caliph. A caliph was a religious prophet/leader with a link to the Islamic prophet Muhammad. The last recognized caliphate was the Ottoman Caliphate 1517 A.D., which ended in 1924. In 2010, Abu Bakr al-Baghdadi declared himself the caliph of an ISIS-supported caliphate. Al-Baghdadi was claiming to be a representative of God on earth. This caliphate would control entire cities in Iraq and Syria. They became notorious for their brutality and televised beheadings.

He was killed by the United States military on October 26, 2019, by direct order of President Donald Trump. The activities between ISIS, al-Qaeda, Hezbollah, and their financier, Soleimani, General of the Quds Force, put Arman right in the hub of communication between these entities. All of which required Iranian air support assets.

Hezbollah's base was in Lebanon under the leadership of Hassan Nasrallah, Secretary-General. It was believed that Iran was the chief financial and military backer of Hezbollah. In Beirut, Arman had discovered an operation to steal intellectual property kept on the computer networks of the American University in Beirut. The information was very high priority. It could be made to look as though it was needed by Soleimani for use in support of a Quds Force operation inside Damascus. The fall of the caliphate in Syria had created a need for additional security and intelligence processing in Damascus. The Quds Force was developing a digital link between Tehran and Damascus to fill the operational void left by the collapse of the al-Baghdadi caliphate. The software required to operate this digital link was on the servers at American University in Beirut. Arman saw this opening to construct a plan, and he seized it!

Freyredoon Adipour received a very official-appearing letter from Brigadier General Aziz Nasirzdeh. The message invoked the name and the authority of Qassem Soleimani for the use of his services. The services requested were for securing a piece of computer circuitry that would allow the Quds Force to intercept, and transmit remotely, great bursts of data. After capture onto magnetic digital media it could be smuggled. It was something he had done before for Soleimani for use in the United States against the MANOPOLY Project.

The request seemed very urgent and very authentic to Adipour. He was told to contact Nasizadeh's executive officer, Colonel Arman, to arrange a delivery at his earliest possible convenience. The request was urgent and seemed to be very time sensitive. The phrase that sold it as completely as authentic to Adipour was one he had heard Soleimani say many times himself: *"For the Glory of Allah and Ali* (a reference that Soleimani used personally to reference the Supreme

Leader)." He began making a list of required parts and sent an immediate response to Arman. Adipour went to work building his next masterpiece in his retail electronics shop just outside of Tehran. He had a job to get finished for his old friend.

Chapter 53

Imogene St. John was five-foot-ten, weighed about 125 pounds, and she was an avid runner. She had muscular legs, abdominals, and thighs that accounted for most of that weight. Everyone knew that muscle weighed more than fat. Imogene was the embodiment of this saying. Her hair was just about shoulder length and strawberry blonde. Her hair was layered and very neat. Previously she had sported a bright red mohawk. She was two years Beau Benoit's junior and grew up in Baton Rouge. She attended the high school where Beau had met her in the summer before Harvard.

Imogene's parents met in high school. They attended the same high school where she ran with Beau. They were married shortly after high school and had Imogene three years later. They were good Christian people and attended the First Baptist Church in Baton Rouge every Sunday morning and night. They went to Wednesday prayer meeting services as well. Additionally, Imogene had participated in the Baptist missionary youth group for girls, Acteens. She also partici-pated in the youth choir on Wednesdays. These activities all occurred immediately following a weekly sit-down family fellowship dinner, shared weekly by the entire congregation.

Even though a bit less than half of the congregation attended the mid-week services, this community served as a solid foundation for Imogene in building her Christian values and cementing her desire for a career in Christian service.

After high school, she stayed at home with her parents while attending Jimmy Swaggart College, a Baptist College in Baton Rouge. She received a bachelor's degree in Christianity and New Testament History and graduated Summa cum Laude. She immediately was assigned to a missionary post in Mexico. Then, she was assigned to South America by the Foreign Mission Board of the Southern Baptist Convention. Imogene had met Beau Benoit halfway through her college experience. Her heart belonged to Jesus, and she wore that honor very proudly. However, oddly enough, she had looked more like a punk rock swimmer than a Bible jock. Beau had seen something in her countenance that had attracted him. It made Beau desire that confidence she possessed in her eternal salvation.

Even though their relationship was based upon their shared faith in God and friendship, Imogene had always hoped that one day she would be Beau's wife. She was a virgin in her early thirties, and she was proud of her commitment. She had served in three different countries since graduating from college. Since she had minored in Spanish, her missionary assignments had all been in Mexico and South America. She had stayed in close contact with Beau through all of her appointments, finding solace in knowing when Beau needed to share a burden, he would always call her. In every way that mattered, Imogene was saving herself for Beau. She knew that he was struggling to find Virgil and that he was very busy with the Federal Reserve. And the MANOPOLY Project was another huge load. But she also knew that when he had a minute, her phone rang, and she *always* answered!

Chapter 54

Beau was in early tonight. It was a dark, rainy evening in Manhattan. Beau was sitting in his leather chair at his desk in his loft. He had a Moroccan leather journal in which he had tracked every aspect of his search for Virgil. He had been reviewing the steps in his quest and found himself sitting and staring at the name ACE RECORDS. He had circled it in red ink in his journal. He decided that now was the time to find something out. He was contemplating what business records that might or might not exist in the archives from the purchase of NOLA Records.

Ace Records began in 1955 in Jackson, Mississippi, by Johnny Vincent. Around the time The Driftwood recorded "Hound Dog," Ace Records went broke. It reformulated in 1971. It was sold in 1997 to the Demon Music Group in the United Kingdom. Ace Records had a marker on the Mississippi Blues Trail, which was commissioned in 2006. It was designed to memorialize the journey of the Blues in Mississippi. Jackson, Mississippi, was the location of the Ace Records marker. His evening had been filled with Google searches referencing Ace Records. He found countless references to their relationships with what seemed like countless small blues labels from the American South. After a couple of hours trying to map all of the names, he threw his hands up and began to look for an address or phone number.

Beau had discovered an old address at the library in New Orleans to Post Office Box 5982 in Pearl, Mississippi. But it led nowhere. Ace Records LTD., 46-50 Steele Road, London, NW10 7AS was listed as the headquarters. He figured that there was a six-hour time difference between Manhattan and London, so he shut down his computer, closed his leather journal, and dropped his face into his hands to rub the stare out of his eyes. He straightened up in his chair, folded his hands behind his head, and leaned backward in his swivel chair. He looked up at the ceiling, trying to clear his eyes. He closed his eyes and began to run all of the clues through his mind. His head was swimming, and he was frustrated.

He knew that patience was not his long suit. So, he reached into his pants pocket and pulled out his cell phone. He went to his favorites on his iPhone 11 Plus and selected Imogene's number and hit call. Imogene answered the phone on the second ring. Beau was delighted to hear the subtle southern drawl in her voice.

"Hello, Beau!" she replied. Beau filled her in on the events of his day and the status of his search for Virgil. He filled her in on the details of Brooke's wedding and then told her that Brooke had asked him to walk her down the aisle and give her away. It pleased him more than Brooke knew, just that she had asked. Imogene was really looking forward to attending the wedding. It was a great conversation; the wedding would be there before he knew it!

Chapter 55

Evanston, Illinois, was only fifteen miles north of Chicago. It was almost an hour drive if there was any traffic. It was right alongside Lake Michigan. While there were a few places in the Evanston area that catered to tuxedo rentals for weddings, Brooke wanted to find something very unique for her wedding. So, she and Jackson planned a day trip into Chicago to shop for tuxedos. Brooke had already been to Chicago, to Vwidon Bridal Boutique on North Franklin, and selected her wedding dress. Jackson was unaware of this detail; it would be a big surprise.

Brooke had done some looking while she was shopping for her dress and liked what she saw at The Black Tux on Armitage Avenue. She had selected Vwidon Boutique because they had close relationships with the Italian fabric mills. These were the mills that produced the fabrics she had adored her entire life. Brooke had fallen in love with Italian silk and chiffon as a girl going to cotillion dances. Patsy Benoit had loved the Italian fabrics and had inspired Brooke to fall in love with them as well. The most beautiful dresses she had ever seen were Italian silk. Those dresses were hanging in her mother's closet in Baton Rouge when she was a girl. Since her mother could not be there, Brooke was selecting the exact gown that she believed Patsy would have helped her select.

Brooke knew that Jackson was very busy. So out of necessity, more than surprise, she had gone and selected her dress. She was confident that Jackson was keenly aware that their wedding would be an emotional milestone. Her mother would not be there. Jackson had listened to her talk many times about picking out her dress with her momma, the colors they might choose together. Jackson was an excellent listener. He listened especially closely when Brooke spoke.

Now, more than ever, after Jackson's revelation about his childhood, Brooke was very keen regarding his feelings and protecting his heart. She never really knew how deeply Jackson had loved her. She now knew that she, indeed, was the center of his life. They had not spoken at any real length about Jackson's past since the huge revelation after the meeting at the church. It had been referenced a couple of times. But she was content to know, and she respected that Jackson had overcome much tribulation in his life and that he had conquered his demons. It made her very proud that he had just kept on pushing against every obstacle that he encountered. She was also so very touched by the depth of the love that he had developed and cultivated with Beau, her mom, and her dad. She had never imagined that such a man could ever love her to such a depth.

The revelation about Jackson's past had indicated to Brooke how delighted Jackson was to have chosen Brooke. A girl often wondered, *had it not been me, who might he have chosen?* After Jackson's revelation, she was convinced that there could have been no other for Jackson. That made her so happy and secure. She understood, for the first time, what Beau truly meant when he told her that she and Jack were blessed. It was such a wonderfully happy time in Brooke's life. If only she could have shared it with her momma!

Chapter 56

Beau was having different thoughts than Brooke regarding their mother. Beau loved his momma more than words could say, but the realization that hit him like a truck in the emergency room after that fateful high school football game had altered the course of his life forever. His life became a mystery. A puzzle that he had to solve in hopes that he might one day understand who he truly was. He had to reconcile this void to find peace in his life. The problem seemed so complicated that he compared it to a Rubik's Cube with all of the colored stickers removed. It always seemed unsolvable. Beau was up very early Monday morning. He was up at 3 a.m. to coincide with a 9 a.m. opening time at Ace Records, LTD, in London. A quick review of their website indicated that this company had roots deep in the past, and that they reveled in the delights of the sound of bygone years.

The deeper Beau had dug, the more hope grew in his heart. These people might just love the history, heritage, and background of the music enough to treasure archives. Perhaps even enough to have maintained all of the accounts that could come with the acquisition of a group of small American record labels. The three primary partners appeared to be

Leonard Chess, the Bihari brothers (number of brothers unknown, so counted as one), and Ted Carroll. From the professional biographies on the website and other subsequent searches, Beau suspected Ted Carroll to be the man to whom he needed to talk. Beau settled down into his leather chair and proceeded to dial the international number. The phone rang three times, and it was answered: "Thank you for calling ACE, the back catalog to die for!" This greeting almost made Beau giggle. But he suppressed his amusement and asked for Ted Carroll. The person on the other end cleared his throat and said, "You mean Teddy, right, you mean, Teddy?" Beau proceeded to tell the voice on the other end that, in reality, he didn't know who he wanted to speak to. So, the person rudely transferred him to Teddy Carroll.

Teddy Carroll was Ted Carroll's son. Teddy had taken his place in the business. Ted had been there since 1978, until about five years earlier when he retired. His son Teddy had taken over. Teddy was a chip off the old block and loved the old American rock and roll and blues. Teddy the younger had played in an Elvis Presley cover band in London. He not only loved the music, but he breathed it into his soul. He kept every piece of history about the music as a reference to history. He was a very different personality than the brilliant intellectual that was Beau Benoit, but they seemed to hit it off just fine.

Beau started by telling Teddy about how his search had led to this phone call. He told him that he and his natural father had been separated before birth. That he was searching for answers. Teddy was very receptive. He told him the history of The Driftwood, the history of the "Hound Dog" cover song, and the two names listed as producers on the NOLA Record label. Teddy was fascinated by the story and even more fascinated by the prospect of having a real music mystery. He was excited that he was going to have the opportunity to participate!

He was familiar with all of their master tapes. He indicated that they did not possess the master tape of a cover of "Hound Dog." Nor did they have a master by a band called The Driftwood. Still, he was familiar with the NOLA Record label and had recently seen some references to that label in their company archives. By this point, he was ready to join the search and help Beau. He was going to enjoy the trip!

Teddy told him that most of those business records had been scanned to microfiche years ago. They were in their warehouse in downtown London. The detective work would require Teddy driving down and spending a few hours breathing dusty air in an old warehouse. He didn't mind; it was a musical adventure, so Teddy was game. Beau left his name, number, and address so he could reach him at any time.

Beau hung up the phone and smiled. He felt a hope that he needed very badly. He called Imogene, woke her up, and told her about his progress. They were very pleased, indeed.

Chapter 57

In his small retail shop just outside Tehran, Freyredoon Adipour was sitting at his worktable looking through a circular magnifying lens with a circular fluorescent lamp. The light was strikingly like the one Whiffer used on his workstation in the crow's nest. Adipour was putting the final touches on the device that was requested by Arman. The device was designed to capture the software required by the Quds Force on the American University of Beirut servers. It was for use by Soleimani, to establish a data link between Tehran and Damascus. Adipour's work was meticulous, and he was confident that it would function as required, but he still needed to test the device.

Adipour's "retail shop" was filled with the latest and best cutting-edge computer hardware money could buy. He had the best tools, and his inventory of hard-to-obtain parts was abundant. However, as one looked around the "retail store," everything you could need or want was right there within arm's reach. Everything except the obvious and the most important for a retail store. There were no customers! In all of the surveillance reports of every intelligence officer across the CIA, NSA, MI6, and Moussed, not one report ever mentioned a customer having been in the store. An occasional Iranian military technician might wander in, or a visit from a friend, but never a customer.

The question that became strikingly obvious, when taking this observation into account, was how a retail store could afford the merchandise and equipment abundant in the shop, as well as paying the rent and utilities, all without any customers. One could only conclude that Adipour either had one very affluent customer that underwrote all of the expenses, or that the shop was a front for an Iranian military computer research laboratory. To the average resident of Tehran, it merely looked like a garden variety computer shop. Still, in reality, it was an enterprise funded by Soleimani for doing Quds Force technology work.

With the new device having been successfully tested in his shop, he was ready to reach out and contact Colonel Arman to set up a delivery. He needed to schedule an appointment to go to Brigadier General Nasizadeh's office at the IRIAF base.

Chapter 58

Jacque Keller was sitting in his office in the Red Crescent, in the Embassy of Qatar. He was on a burner cell phone talking to Colonel Arman, who was also on a burner phone. These men were both deep plant agents of the CIA. Both had been under deep cover for many years. Both were keenly aware that their moves would have to be executed perfectly, or their protection would be blown. Additionally, their murders would not be quick or painless.

They were planning to set up an aid request that would require Soleimani's presence in the air-conditioned office where Soleimani's executive officer, Major Muhammed, would summon him for approval. The office in the hangar was where Keller must place the Bluetooth transmitter on the leg of the chair where Soleimani sat. It had to be positioned right at boot level. As his boot brushed against the device and attached to the boot leather, it activated and sent Soleimani's location. CIA operators monitoring and logging his movements would immediately begin tracking. The timing had to be perfect. It had to coincide with the death of Adipour. It also had to coincide with the capture of Adipour's device intended for use at the American University in Beirut.

Arman had to coordinate a faux suicide bombing in a busy area outside Tehran to necessitate the humanitarian need that would trigger the meeting. It would also have to be organized at such a time to put Keller in the air-conditioned office on the right day to execute their plan correctly. Their conversation was very efficient, short, and concise. They finished, and both dropped their phones in a toilet.

Chapter 59

Jackson was standing in front of a mirror at The Black Tux in Chicago with his beautiful fiancée Brooke. She stood beside him and about a half-step back, looking at the front and the back of the tux simultaneously in the mirrors. *This was the tux,* she thought to herself. The tuxedo was the Black (Black Notch Lapel Tux) by Vera Wang. It included the jacket, slacks, vest, bowtie, pleated white cotton shirt, patent leather shoes, cuff-links, and the shirt studs. It was a classic black tuxedo. It was a stark contrast to the white Italian silk and chiffon wedding dress that was currently being hand-sewn for Brooke across town. The cost of the tuxedo on sale was $799. Jackson saw that Brooke was delighted and agreed to be measured for the tuxedo and to have it tailored. They checked out and left.

Jackson was a tiny bit uncertain if Brooke had loved the tux so very much, or if it had been the tremendous bargain that had hooked her. Either way, the job was behind them. There was a small sidewalk diner on the next block. They walked down and shared a chicken salad sandwich before heading back to Evanston.

Chapter 60

Back on Wall Street in Manhattan, Mick Mulvaney, acting chief of staff to the president, walked into the Federal Reserve Building. He rode the elevator to Beau's office. He greeted Beau's secretary and handed her his card. Beau was immediately summoned, and Beau walked out and greeted Mulvaney. Mulvaney followed Beau back to his office and closed the door. As usual, Beau walked over to the credenza and activated the signal jammer. Beau was seated in an armchair across the room from Mulvaney.

"What can I do for you today, sir?" asked Beau.

Mulvaney acknowledged that he was aware that the MANOPOLY Project input was vital for the design of the Tax Cuts and Jobs Act of 2017. He continued to inform Beau that the president was planning on seeking another tax cut to take effect in late 2020, or possibly as late as early 2021. The President was requesting that the MANOPOLY Project crunch all of the numbers. They were needed to isolate the exact combination of tax cuts to continue GDP growth at the optimum rate. Beau was very friendly and asked what the time frame was for the assignment. Mulvaney told him that the president would like to introduce the plan as early as March 2020. However, he would like an outline right away to begin discussions in the House and Senate finance committees. Beau agreed and saw Mulvaney out. He called Jackson and informed him of the new project.

Chapter 61

At Vwidon Bridal Boutique on North Franklin in Chicago, a bright yellow DHL delivery truck pulled up to the shop and double parked. The driver exited after watching for traffic to clear. He swung back the door and jumped out onto North Franklin and sprinted to the rear of the truck. He yanked the looped ribbon handle on the bottom of the door and jerked it mightily. It rattled noisily and rolled all of the way to the top of the truck. He jumped up into the truck and walked back between the shelves on either side. He pulled out two parcels addressed to Vwidon Bridal Boutique. He scanned the barcode and dropped them onto the floor of the truck. He jumped down, picked them up, and disappeared into the shop.

Inside at the counter, the driver sat the parcels on a shelf with a sign that said, "INCOMING PARCELS." He got the cashier to sign the delivery sheet and exited the shop. Both packages were from the same shipper, Taroni, in Milan, Italy. The fabric for Brooke's wedding dress was now in Chicago. Tomorrow, it would begin being hand-sewn and should be ready for the fitting within a week. The dress would be fashioned after a Bergdorf Goodman dress that she had seen. However, she wanted long formal sleeves, so Vwidon's in-house seamstress had agreed to custom sew it to size for her. The dress would have a mock neckline, an open back with gold chains between the shoulders, a column silhouette, and it would be floor-length with silk lining. The detail would be in white lace. The dress would be fashioned from Taroni white silk and chiffon. Brooke had seen a long version. She had tried on the short sleeve version and loved the profile in the mirror. The Italian silk was what she imagined her mother would have picked had she been alive to shop with her. Her mother's wedding ring would be hand-stitched onto the left sleeve. It would serve as her something borrowed. The wedding was scheduled for next month. Time would not be tight, but Brooke was very excited to see it and try it on.

Chapter 62

Beau was sitting in his office at the Federal Reserve in Manhattan, working through some tax cut scenarios that might be considered in a new tax cut bill. Being a CPA and a finance guy, sometimes Beau enjoyed toying with some of the scenarios that they were going to run through the MANOPOLY Project. It was a mental exercise to test his abilities. It was fun to see how close he could get to the same results the Project would produce. Beau had learned to be very respectful of the effects that the program rendered. While he always believed he had come up with a brilliant solution, the Project always picked up other aspects of the problem that Beau had failed to consider. This exercise certainly kept Beau humble. Still, he felt that it also honed his financial prowess and made him better at his job. Better than he might otherwise have become. Being able to compete against, and to be able to compare his results against, the best available minds in the world was exhilarating. It was an exercise that Beau had come to enjoy very much.

He had been digging into the deepest crooks and crevices of the United States tax code. He was searching for any vestigial tax policy that no longer served its purpose but might be relevant in this scenario. He loved the research, and he loved the numbers. He loved feeling the touch of his ten-key calculator. He loved the sound of each entry printing on the receipt coming from the paper roll. The sound reminded him of finance class at LSU. He loved the feeling of hunting through the numbers to find some magical sequence that made sense. Beau was immersed in his work when his cell phone vibrated in his pocket. He always put his cell phone on vibrate when he was in the Federal Reserve office. He thought little of the call until he pulled it from his pocket and saw that the number that was calling was from London. His heart jumped up into his throat! Beau hovered over the red answer button with his index finger for a second and answered.

"Beau Benoit? Teddy Carroll, Ace, London. You there?" the voice responded.

Beau replied with a speedy, "Yes."

Teddy began quickly telling him that he had found the microfiche archives. He had located the transaction when they brought the original NOLA Record label to Ace Records in London. There were several references found in the film that indicated that The Driftwood had been recorded in the original NOLA Studios in New Orleans in April of 1963. The song on the B-side of the record was a song named "Shakin' It Up," and the composers were listed as Virgil W. Bagley, Lyle Willis, and Randy Bell. Their address was listed on Main Street in New Orleans.

Teddy was very interested in why the master tape was not present at Ace since the old masters were his passion. Beau told him that he thought he knew who possessed the master tape. Beau informed him that he believed Keith Soileau had possession of the master tape in a climate-controlled storage unit in Big Crane, Louisiana. Teddy was very interested in getting a duplicate of the master tape to complete his collection. That would complete the entire set of NOLA Record masters. He had not known that The Driftwood tapes were in existence, and he was delighted to know that their possession was secure. Beau promised that he would get him a copy of the master.

Beau went to the browser on his computer while listening to Teddy talk and Googled the exact address on Main Street in New Orleans and discovered that it was now a city parking garage. It would mean that perhaps the City of New Orleans would have property records for previous owners of the property. Better yet, any real estate title company in New Orleans could pull an abstract of the property and reveal the history of the ownership of the property. It had been a great break, and Beau was elated!

Teddy was still droning on about some blues group from New Orleans that he was trying to hunt down from the 1960s in Memphis. Teddy's discussion had nothing to do with Beau's interests. Beau thanked Teddy and told him he had to get back to work. He promised to speak to Keith Soileau and check on the "Hound Dog" master tape. They hung up, and Beau replaced the cell phone into his trouser pocket and walked out of his office. Once inside the elevator, the door closed; he pushed 'G' and was gone. Once out the front door, he searched his favorites in his cell phone and touched the name 'Imogene.' The phone only rang once.

Chapter 63

Imogene seemed exceptionally happy to hear Beau's voice on this particular day. She was in Rio de Janeiro, Brazil. She had received a particularly beautiful bouquet of Peruvian lilies at the Catholic convent where the female missionaries were bunked. They were in Brazil while on a children's ministry trip. The two-dozen lilies were in a beautiful ceramic vase. The card was signed: *"I need a date to my sister's wedding, June 22. Love, Beau."* Imogene's voice was very light and almost a giggle when she blurted out, *"YES, BEAU, I WOULD LOVE TO!"*

Well, that was certainly out of the way! But Beau had momentarily forgotten that the flowers were to be delivered this morning. He had ordered them last week. He had just been engrossed in the beauty of tax codes and a phone call after that, and he now had an address in New Orleans for The Driftwood.

His instincts kicked in, and he suddenly gushed at the exuberance that Imogene radiated through the speaker on his phone. He engaged in the banter about the plans for the wedding, travel plans, and the excitement of seeing one another. There was a brief pause and Beau inserted what seemed an errant "*Imogene*" into the conversation. She suddenly touched back down to earth and said, "Yes, Beau?"

Beau told her that he had just gotten off of the phone with Teddy Carroll in London. He now had an address in New Orleans for The Driftwood. Imogene squealed and told Beau how very excited she was for him. He told her of his plan to have a real estate friend of Brooke's from LSU do a title search. The search would be for the New Orleans parking garage's address. This would lead to obtaining an abstract from that exact address before its condemnation and destruction. The parking garage was an entire city block. He only needed one specific lot in that block. Beau was very pleased with his fortunes, and Imogene was so happy Beau could see her smile in Manhattan from Rio on his cell phone!

Chapter 64

Jackson was starting to feel the crunch from all of the wedding plans converging on him. He suddenly seemed too busy running errands and *"doing Brooke a little favor(s)"* to even get the bare minimum demands of the workload at Econ Lab 1 completed. He was pretty sure that Whiffer was doing most of his work for him in the final push toward the wedding. The wedding was in just under two weeks.

Jackson had sent Whiffer, Beau, and Darian to The Black Tux to get measured for their rental tuxedos. He had also sent a local Baton Rouge tailor to measure Bright Benoit for his tux. Jackson had also arranged for a local limousine company to pick up Bright and deliver him to the Baton Rouge airport. He had hired a nurse to accompany Bright to the Evanston airport. Beau would pick their dad up for him and deliver him to their home in Evanston. Jackson had arranged for an around-the-clock nurse to be there while he was in for the wedding. They had bought a hospital bed for Bright in a ground-floor bedroom of their home. It would be a permanent change, a sign of their hope that Bright would spend more time with them after their marriage.

Brooke was using a couple of ladies that she had become

friends with inside the Department of Economics as brides-maids. Libby Ross from LSU and grad school at Mizzou and the School of Business would serve her best friend as maid of honor. Libby also happened to be the real estate whiz that Beau had in mind to pull strings required to obtain an abstract for the address he had discovered in New Orleans for The Driftwood. Brooke had made it a day, a couple of different times, to take the three ladies into Chicago to pick out brides-maid dresses. She selected a beautiful pink, Italian chiffon dress for Libby to wear as maid of honor. They had gone back on another trip for fittings, and the dresses would be ready to be picked up early next week.

Jackson had Ethan Lord Jewelers on Wabash in Chicago order in a 14k, yellow-gold wedding set. The set had a band to sidle up exactly with Brooke's engagement ring as well as a simple band for himself. The rings had also been sized and given to Beau for safekeeping as the best man. Beau would even walk Brooke down the aisle on her left arm while Bright rode on her right side in an electric wheelchair. Jackson had made sure that nothing was left to chance for Brooke's wedding!

Jackson had experienced an issue in dealing with his past. It happened when the pastor at St. Nicholas Roman Catholic Church had required a counseling session before their nuptials. The pastor had inquired about the faith of both the bride and groom; very standard questions for a Catholic wedding. The questions were not so very standard for Jackson. The Catholic Church was immaculate in the keeping of marital records. They always made sure that every I was dotted, and every T crossed. One of the questions was the denomination of the bride and the groom. The couple was seated at the pastor's desk in the rectory. He had handed them each a clipboard with a copy of the questionnaire. Then the pastor stood up to go into the chapel while they completed the task. Jackson had seen the question, dropped his head, and his countenance fell.

Brooke was very keenly aware that Jackson was struggling when she saw the question on her copy of the form. She looked at Jackson and assured him that she would handle the priest. Jackson stood up, rubbed his eyes with his index finger and thumb, and walked through the door on the opposite wall into the courtyard. The priest returned and was quite perplexed to find Jackson missing. He asked Brooke what had happened. She told the priest that Jackson had been orphaned, raised Catholic, and molested by a priest, and that his relationship with God was an ongoing struggle. The priest hung his head and picked up the clipboard on the desk. He wrote in the space provided, SAVED BY GRACE. The issue resolved, and Jackson never even asked what Brooke had told the priest. She had simply told Jackson that the problem was solved. Jackson trusted her without fail.

Everything was completed, purchased, addressed, reserved, hired, catered, and ready for the event of the year at Northwestern University. The wedding of Brooke Benoit to Dr. Jackson Reynolds was about to happen. Six hundred guests were invited, and tomorrow was the rehearsal.

Chapter 65

Beau had been delighted with the new information he had received from Teddy Carroll. All that Teddy had asked for in return was a copy of the master tape of The Driftwood cover of "Hound Dog." Beau was going to do everything within his power to return that favor and fulfill his promise. Beau sat down at his desk in his Manhattan loft and reached into his pocket to retrieve his cell phone. He scrolled through his contacts until he reached Keith Soileau and hit dial.

Keith was pleased to hear from Beau. Beau told him that he had called Teddy Carroll and that Teddy had done some research and had found an address in New Orleans. Beau told him that he was currently working on the address. He also told Keith that Teddy was a second-generation blues music fan and desperately coveted a copy of the master tape. Beau also said that Teddy would like a copy and offered to pay for both duplicates. He even offered to pay for Keith's time to have this done. Keith was pleased to do so and was also thrilled that Beau had found another clue. The call was not long, and Beau was getting ready for Bright Benoit to arrive in Evanston.

They hung up, and Beau was off to work on his list of duties assigned to the best man.

Chapter 66

Libby Ross was Brooke's maid of honor. They had gone to undergraduate school at LSU together. They also went to graduate school at the University of Missouri and worked together at Northwestern University. They were best friends. More than her friend, she was also a Benoit family friend, and Beau knew her very well. Beau knew that her specialty was real estate and that she was brilliant at every aspect of the real estate transaction.

Beau had called Libby the morning of the rehearsal. He had given her an address on Main Street in New Orleans. The address no longer existed. Years ago, the city had purchased the entire block and it was now covered by a city-owned parking garage. Beau was looking for an abstract for a single lot address that sat under this parking garage. He was looking for the history of the ownership of the parcel of land. Libby was very familiar with what Beau was asking for. Libby was a real estate professional and the Southern United States was right in the middle of Libby's specialty.

She left Beau and called an old Gamma Phi Beta sorority sister, who was in the recorder's office in New Orleans. Libby gave the address of the parcel to her sorority sister. Immediately, she was up to her neck in searching through microfiche, electronic scans, tax records, and GIS data, all querying the address. The parcel was on Main Street in New Orleans. The databases existed in several different offices, based upon the category of the search. Tax records were in the assessor's office, title transfers were in the recorder's office, etc. It would take a few hours to search for all of the data. The pages had to be printed, assembled from the data from in various offices, and compiled into a functional property abstract. When she had completed the task, she ran out to the local FedEx office and dropped it overnight to Libby. She shipped it in the care of Beau at Brooke and Jackson's house. The next piece of the puzzle was on the way to Evanston.

Chapter 67

Brooke was up very early on her wedding day. She was a brilliant woman with a top-flight education. Her professional accomplishments in building the MANOPOLY Project put her in an elite class of respected federal government contractors. There were few of her peers with top secret security clearances. But this morning, Brooke Benoit was a bride. Today was her day, and it began with pure superstition, in stark contrast with her qualifications. *Everyone* knew that it was bad luck to see your husband before the ceremony on your wedding day!

Brooke had spent the night with her college friend, work colleague, and maid of honor, Libby Ross. They had sat up the night before talking and sipping mimosas and reminiscing. It had been a fantastic journey they had traveled together. The tremendous progress made by the MANOPOLY Project had made them wildly successful. It was a fortuitous stroke of luck that had come with their move to Evanston. Their good fortune was beyond belief.

While discussing the rise of Jackson's dream child, the conversation shifted to a project that Libby had done for Beau. Earlier that day she had shipped the FedEx package and she related to Brooke that Beau had personally requested that she pull some strings in New Orleans to get a property abstract of an old address. It was a bit odd because the lot was now paved over in a New Orleans city parking garage. Brooke listened with great interest, furrowed her brow, and wondered why Beau was interested in a parking garage in the Big Easy. She found it quite perplexing. But Libby saw that she was not privy to the request and quickly went back to the wedding discussions. Libby was curious now. She hoped that Brooke was preoccupied enough today not to let the conversation register and trigger an awkward debate in the future with Beau.

The girls quickly noticed the clock and went to bed. That morning, they were immediately inundated with manicures, pedicures, and hairdresser appointments. They had to be at the St. Nicholas Roman Catholic Church by two p.m. for pictures. Brooke had secured the services of a Ph.D. and Dean of the School of Fine Art at Northwestern to do wedding photography. The dean was the winner of numerous national awards for photography. He was a fantastic get for their wedding portraits. They arrived about five minutes early with their garment bags and makeup bags in tow. The florist van was parked just outside the front door. The back door of the delivery van was standing wide open. The florist and two helpers, who were carrying candelabras, corsages, and boutonnieres, were busy. The beautiful bridal bouquet was done in tiny pink roses and baby's breath. The church was beginning to hum with activity. In the undercroft of the church, a magnificent feast was cooking. As one walked down the stairway, the pleasant aroma of roasted turkey and ham filled everyone's olfactory senses. Tables were being set up in the dining hall, covered with white paper tablecloths, and draped with a light pink ribbon. The wedding of Jackson and Brooke was in the offing.

Jackson had spent the night preceding the wedding in their home. Bright Benoit had arrived, and Beau had helped

Jackson get him settled in. Beau was in what they called the guest room. But for all intents and purposes, it was Beau's bedroom. As much time as Beau spent in Evanston, it just seemed silly for him to be in hotels that frequently, so Beau generally stayed with Jackson and Brooke when he was working in Evanston. Jackson was very appreciative of having Beau there to help him get Bright settled into his new room. Even though Jackson and Bright were very close and loved each other, there are personal care issues when bringing in an elderly stroke patient, best performed by his son. The three men had enjoyed their visit that night very much and had just really relaxed and talked.

They were all asleep early—all except Jackson. Jackson was lying in his bed, really missing having Brooke. He had grown so accustomed to having her there with him. She had been so very accepting of the revelation of his painful past. She had shielded him from questions and situations during the planning that would trigger a problematic situation for Jackson. He had never really allowed himself to dream about a whole, complete family life. Instead he had always invested 99 percent of his effort into being a success at his work. Now he found himself looking at the clock on the bed stand. He realized that within a matter of hours, he would take Brooke Benoit to be his wife.

Jackson had invited his "mother," Ann Reynolds and Mr. and Mrs. Reynolds to the wedding. He had made a trip to Little Rock with Brooke to introduce them after he had shared his story with her. He simply could not believe that his family would be on the right side of the church at the wedding as well. Jackson spent some very personal alone time with himself, time that he had avoided for many years. Jackson dared to feel an unrecognizable movement in his soul; could it be a revival of his *faith*? The evening had worn him out, and he fell immediately to sleep.

Jackson was awake about 4 a.m. and was then into his

shoes and out the door to Econ Lab 1. He had to make sure that everything was secure, and that the data gathered for the new tax cut scenario was on schedule. Jackson was a workaholic. So, before he could allow himself the indulgence of personal time, he had to check his baby. He found Whiffer there as well, having the same thoughts and insecurities. The two sat together in the crow's nest, and for the first time in their recent memory, they had a good laugh at themselves. They secured the office and were off to get Jackson hitched to Brooke.

Beau had assisted in getting Bright dressed and ready for the photos while Jackson was on campus. He had also gathered their garment bags containing their tuxedoes. He loaded them all into a handicapped-accessible van parked in the driveway, in front of the door. Jackson was on his way home from campus. Whiffer was on his way back to shower and get to the church for photos. Beau was checking the charge of the battery in the electric wheelchair when he heard the doorbell. He hollered, "*Just a minute,*" and ran toward the front door. He opened the door, and there stood a man in a FedEx uniform. "I am looking for Beau Benoit."

Beau's puzzle piece from New Orleans was now in his hand.

He stood there, looked at the package, and began to open it when he heard Bright cough in the front bedroom. He placed the box on the table in the foyer and went back to care for his dad. On his way to tend to him, Beau thought about how surreal it was to attend to one father while having a package containing a clue to the whereabouts of the other. And it was all happening in the same moment. He chuckled at the irony and settled back into the gallop to get everything to the church for pictures. Bright was making great progress but required assistance with his shoes. Beau went back into the kitchen and sat in the powered wheelchair and rode it back to Bright's bedroom. He helped his dad into the chair. He followed him out the open front door to the power lift on the side of the van. He loaded him into the van, and they were off to the church!

In the vestibule of the St. Nicholas Roman Catholic Church, Jackson, Beau, Bright, Whiffer, Libby, and the other two bridesmaids were gathered and ready to pose for their photos. The florist was standing at a folding table with all of the corsages and boutonnieres arranged in rows. She summoned each member of the bridal party as they gathered at the church. They each moved to the table to have their flower pinned to their dress or lapel. Brooke was sequestered in a parlor designed for just such occasions. The Dean of the School of Fine Arts walked out of the sanctuary. He began directing the participants for photos. Each couple walked through the door toward the tripod in the center of the aisle. About halfway to the altar, each paused and posed. The pre-ceremony photographs were completed in about twenty-five minutes, as they finished the pipe organ music began to play. The wedding started at 3 p.m. Everything was now in place.

It was 3 p.m. sharp, and the bells in the tower of the church began to chime. The ushers pushed open the sanctuary doors. The organ music volume came up and the first bridesmaid and Whiffer took off down the aisle. The time seemed to stand still while they took one step, paused; took another step and paused. When they were about halfway down the aisle, the second bridesmaid and Darian walked through the door. The music came up a bit while Beau, Bright, and Libby positioned themselves at the doorway. Whiffer and his bridesmaid had reached the altar, parted ways, and were standing on their rehearsed spots. They were on opposite sides of the platform. Darian and his bridesmaid were just approaching the front pew. Then, Beau and Libby began their step, pause, step. As they walked through the door, the door closed. Bright pulled his wheelchair up to the door.

Jackson entered the cathedral through a door behind the organ up front and walked to the altar.

Beau exited through a side door and rushed back to the door to assist Bright. From a portico to the left of the foyer, a door opened, and Brooke appeared. She was a vision of beauty; her Italian silk and chiffon white dress was form-fitting, and in the sunlight, she looked like an alabaster sculpture of a Greek goddess standing in the back of the church. Her veil covered the tears streaming down her face. She stepped forward and bent down to kiss her daddy's forehead. The organ music became deafening as it played "Bridal Chorus at Lohengrin" by Richard Wagner. Brooke took Beau's arm, the door swung open, and the Benoit family launched down the aisle. They were on their way to officially include Jackson into their family.

The rest of the day was a blur to Brooke and Jackson. Everything went as planned. The crowd of over six hundred attendees was a fantastic cross-section of people; a crowd far more diverse than one might see at an ordinary wedding. There were college students, graduate students, the president of the university and his wife, generals, admirals, and friends from all walks of life. The sit-down dinner was a feast enjoyed by all. Brooke and Jackson reveled in having the entire Benoit family on one side of the head table and the Reynolds family on the other. It was a first, and it was indeed a momentous occasion.

After the dinner, the cake was cut and served. The unwrapping of gifts was the last official event of the wedding. As the crowd thinned to change clothes for the dance, the Northwestern University Swing Band moved in to set up. The guests began shuffling back into the reception hall, and at 7 p.m. sharp, Beau Benoit picked up the microphone. He immediately introduced Brooke and Jackson for their first dance as husband and wife. The university ensemble had prepared the perfect song for their first dance. Dolly Parton's song "I Will

Always Love You," that Whitney Houston made a classic in the hit movie *The Bodyguard*, began to play. Brooke had planned this moment specifically for the opportunity to wrap her arms around Jackson and take off ballroom dancing with her new husband. Everyone stood and applauded and whistled.

At the back of the reception hall, wearing a caterer's uniform, standing in a dark corner, was Muhammad Faruq watching every move and taking mental photographs of all in attendance. It was a unique event in which every single person affiliated with the **MANOPOLY** Project had gathered in one place. He stood there through the entire dance, and as the lights came back up, he silently slipped back into the kitchen and out the delivery entrance door.

Chapter 68

Sitting outside the St. Nicholas Reception Hall was another white van parked next to the van that brought Bright and Beau. Sitting inside was none other than Ali Assad. The windows were very darkly tinted, and Faruq was oblivious to the fact that he was observed. Jackson would not allow the events surrounding the wedding to be altered by the espionage. However, the intrigue was radiating from the MANOPOLY Project in the parking lot. Ronald Burnett, Assad, and Darian had made additions to the guest list to make the wedding an event that the IRGC contingency on the Northwestern campus could not ignore. They had made the event such a precious intelligence collection opportunity that any spy would have to attend. Burnett and Assad had been busy setting up a network of operatives. They were strategically placed to observe the action in Evanston and put the assets into play to follow Faruq and Agassi. They had to follow so they could better understand how significant the local IRGC terrorist pocket was.

Darian was inside monitoring Agassi, who was a guest as a university faculty dean and advisor. Darian had managed to drop a listening device into his jacket pocket during the wedding reception. The command post in the van in the parking lot was recording every word he said all day for evaluation at Langley. It was a charming June night on Lake Michigan. Assad had parked a crotch rocket motorcycle behind the van to pursue Faruq if he ran. Assad started a video camera that monitored Faruq from the reception hall into his vehicle, and it would also capture the license plate number. Assad watched Faruq pull out and leave the church parking lot. Then he stepped out of the surveillance van while putting his smoked face motorcycle helmet on his head. He started the engine and followed behind him at a safe distance to remain unobserved.

Faruq was in a small Fiat 500, which was built to get in and out of small places. The low profile made it a perfect vehicle to disappear into traffic and become invisible. Before the dance, Darian had placed a miniaturized communication device into his ear, anticipating the operation that was planned. Darian had heard that Faruq had left. He knew that Assad had followed. Darian went out to the tinted van and entered through the back doors. He quickly changed into a black zippered jumpsuit. Immediately, he was off, chasing the tracking devices planted on both the motorcycle and the Fiat 500. While Brooke and Jackson were dancing as newlyweds, their friends were chasing the IRGC terror network down to find the source.

Faruq was using standard driving techniques of evasion while staying at a lower speed so as not to draw attention. Assad recognized them well. He had been trained the same way. His spy craft experience told him that Faruq was driving his route very easy and relaxed. This indicated that he probably did not suspect that he was being followed. He was, however, making frequent stops, left turns quickly without signaling, then back to the right. He was headed north, then turned east. The turn east was confusing to Assad and Darian. They assumed he would probably head west onto the interstate and then out to a remote country location. Perhaps he might head into the city of Chicago where it would be easy to get lost in the masses of people and traffic. They were both interested in where this chase would lead. After about five miles, it became pretty clear that Faruq was headed to a beachfront park with a picnic table on Lake Michigan. Assad followed and rode on past when Faruq pulled up to the picnic table on the beach. Darian was about a half-mile behind and pulled up to the shore before Faruq could see him. Assad sped around the next curve in the road and rode right behind a pile of brush that appeared to be there for a bonfire. He hid his bike and started walking, bent down, toward the picnic table. Darian was doing the same, coming from the opposite side.

It was tranquil on the beach. The moon was about a quarter waxing moon, so the light was usable but not too bright to worry about being easily seen. Faruq was sitting on the picnic table next to the shore at a public beach and appeared to be talking on his cell phone. Darian moved quickly to get in position to hear. Faruq was speaking in Persian; Darian was fluent in Persian. It took about another forty-five seconds to get into earshot. Assad was removing a 9-millimeter Glock pistol from his waistband and getting close enough to hit a target in the low light. Suddenly there was a small spotlight scanning the shoreline from the water. In the silence, they could hear a boat engine coming in over the surface of Lake Michigan. Seriously, a boat was where Faruq was headed? Neither Darian nor Assad would have guessed that their connection would come in via a speed boat.

Darian was still monitoring all communication channels in the area. He had picked up a radio channel on his walkie-talkie that was speaking in Persian. He assumed it was the men in the boat. Within about four or five minutes, the light on the water was very bright and shone on Faruq. Then, the light suddenly turned off after verifying his identity. The engine slowed, and they could hear conversational Persian. Then, the engine shut off. Faruq waded out into Lake Michigan to board the boat. Darian and Assad could not let them get away, so they both charged. By this time, both men had their guns trained on the boat. The occupants of the boat were unaware that they were charging. They had searched up and down the shoreline before turning the motor off.

Assad's feet hit the water first. The sound set off alarms with the IRGC members in the boat. A spit of machine-gun fire rang out, and a series of muzzle flashes were visible. The shots were aimed at Assad. Darian answered from the opposite side. The side where the boat's motor was exposed. He shot directly at the engine, and the metal against metal sound led him to believe that the vessel was disabled. Neither Darian nor Assad was shooting to kill. They needed these people alive. They both were running in the water as quickly as possible, alternating shots about two feet above their heads. The two men and Faruq, inside the boat, ducked behind the sides of the vessel. They both reached the vessel at the same time and jumped to catch the edge of the boat to catapult themselves up into the boat. Assad and Darian hit them in the face with bright light. The men were stunned.

Faruq was trembling in the bow. One man was bleeding and unconscious. The third was struggling with something in the stern. Darian was on that end. He quickly moved toward him. As he moved around into view, he immediately saw it. The other occupant was putting on a suicide vest. Darian screamed, "*VEST!*"

Assad shot the man through the head. Faruq was trying to crawl out of the boat; Assad grabbed him. Darian quickly assisted. They dragged him out of the boat and probably eighty-five feet to shore. Darian drove a sharp right jab into his jaw and knocked him out cold. Assad ran up the shoreline to the van and pulled it up to Faruq. They loaded him into the van, put a zip-tie around his hands and feet, and gagged him. Assad went and retrieved the motorcycle and brought it back to the van. They used the handicap lift to load the bike into the van. They left slowly. Not a sound could be heard except the waves of water lapping against the sides of the boat that contained two dead IRGC operatives.

As they pulled back onto the road, their first order of business was to contact that NSA and get a retrieval team dispatched. They required assistance to clean up the boat. The boat and the dead bodies were bound to wash up to shore very soon. The United States Coast Guard had a presence in Lake Michigan. They dispatched a boat and clean-up crew very expeditiously. Assad now had a bug in his ear buzzing with CIA chatter! They had to diffuse this situation quickly. They were working a plan to interrogate Faruq. They had to factor in that he would be expected at his post at Northwestern University on Monday morning. Further, they feared that Agassi might try to reach him before Monday.

The intelligence side of the MANOPOLY Project now found themselves in a very tricky spot! Neither the NSA nor the CIA could interrogate Faruq inside the United States. How should they handle this? They called Burnett. He was in the air within minutes. Once airborne, they were about forty-five minutes apart. They were all headed to Hansen Airport near Round Lake, Illinois. They were heading to an abandoned airfield that would accommodate their needs very well. Burnett was on the radio as soon as he was in the air. He was contacting the FAA to file a flight plan north into an airfield in southern Ontario, Canada. He was also on the horn to Langley. Langley was moving interrogators from Headquarters to the airfield in Ontario. Additionally, the Department of State had to be contacted regarding the encroachment into their sovereign territory. The United States Ambassador to Canada had to speak to the Canadian Ambassador. All of the bases were quickly being covered.

They were also sending transport to move the Fiat 500 to a safe place for the night.

The van was silent as Assad and Darian drove the last few miles to Hansen Airfield. The secure intelligence channels between Langley and Washington, D.C. were shooting message after message between the United States intelligence agencies. This was quickly becoming a huge operation.

Salomon Agassi was dancing. He appeared to be having a great time at Brooke and Jackson's wedding dance. Nothing had happened that would set off any alarm bells. The dance was a great time, and at 10 p.m., the dance was rounding up. Brooke and Jackson had left about 8:30 and had gone to the Hotel Lincoln in North Chicago to spend their wedding night. Bright was in town, so Beau and Bright went back to Brooke's house. They enjoyed a quiet evening.

Imogene's layover in Mexico City had a hang-up, so she had missed the wedding. Beau had spoken to her a couple of times during the day while she was waiting in airports. They were both very disappointed that she had missed the wedding. They were looking forward to sharing the day with family. Her flight was due to arrive at O'Hare International Airport at 11:48 p.m. Beau was going to pick her up. The constant care nurse would be there with Bright. Agassi left the dance alone and drove straight home to his upscale home in Evanston. Oddly, Darian and Assad were the first to know that he was home. When they took Faruq, they had confiscated his electronic devices. Now, Faruq's cell phone suddenly started dinging wildly.

The iPhone was locked, but as the incoming messages came in, they momentarily displayed on the screen. There was photo after photo of guests at Jackson and Brooke's wedding. All of the generals, admirals, Department of Defense employees, university employees, anyone who might play a vital role in the MANOPOLY Project had been photographed. The photos were followed by a list of names to match the photos.

Agassi had been very busy taking pictures to send to the IRGC in Iran. He had no idea that the images were being seen by an NSA agent and a CIA operative. Assad's connections in Langley would get the phone open. It was nice to know that Agassi had no idea that Faruq was a captive.

Chapter 69

Burnett landed first at Hansen Field and quickly killed the engines of the plane. He had landed without lights so nobody would see him land. Darian and Assad were only about eight minutes behind. Faruq was still unconscious and was still unaware that he had left the beach on Lake Michigan. The three men in the van transferred very quickly into the small aircraft. The engine started and they began to roll. Burnett had to turn the lights on to get positioned on the runway but quickly turned them off. He pushed the throttle, and the plane went rolling off into the dark. The liftoff was a bit rough. They climbed very quickly so they could get far enough away to turn on the lights. Within seven minutes, they were flying normally. It was about this time that Faruq roused and began to show signs of life. When he finally shook his head and opened his eyes, he tried to scream. The scream was muffled by the gag. His pupils were huge, and he looked like a wild, caged animal. Nobody said a word. They just flew straight to the airfield in Ontario.

Meanwhile, the plane that dispatched from Langley was flying over the northern point of Michigan, just heading out over Lake Michigan. The flight was about twenty minutes from the airfield. Onboard was an Iranian CIA operative that was a seasoned veteran in enhanced interrogation. His name was unknown to everyone, save the members of the Green Beret unit that he served within the second Gulf War in Syria. To everyone else, he was simply known as The Mongol. He lived up to his name. The pilot checked the instruments and banked left and prepared to make his descent into the private Canadian airfield. The plane touched down and taxied to a lean-to shelter that would hide the aircraft from the air. The Mongol got his bag from the plane and walked to the small hunting cabin. He immediately began to build a fire. Within minutes the rock chimney was belching thick white smoke. The pilot was sitting on the wing of his plane and heard the engine of another plane coming in.

Burnett's plane was on its glide path to land at the airfield. Darian had blindfolded Faruq to begin the sensory depriva-tion process. Sensory deprivation was pretty standard in inter-rogation of foreign nationals. The rocking and rolling of the small plane would also serve to disorient him. The aircraft touched down and taxied to the hunting lodge. Darian flung open the door of the aircraft. Burnett left the plane first and went in and had a brief, private conversation with The Mongol. Darian and Assad looked at each other as if they knew what song was playing on the jukebox next. Burnett walked to the door of the cabin and waved his hand. Darian and Assad pushed Faruq out of the plane. He stumbled and fell. They helped him up and pushed him toward the cabin. Once in the cabin, the door slammed closed. Faruq smelled the smoke from the fire, and he smelled another odor. It smelled like hot metal.

Darian and Assad were ordered to exit the cabin while Burnett turned and barked an unintelligible order in Persian to The Mongol. They moved quickly through the door and closed it behind them. As the door closed, they heard The Mongol scream at Faruq, *"You are a dog, I will make you bark!"*

The door closed. They joined the other pilot on the wing of the plane that was hidden from sight. They stared into the dark winter sky and watched bright orange embers suddenly fly up the flue from the cabin's chimney. Within a few seconds, they heard a blood-curdling cry from inside the cabin. It would be a very long night. But at least they were not inside the cabin.

Chapter 70

Since Salomon Agassi was a foreign national with a valid working visa, the CIA had no jurisdiction to arrest and detain him. They were on U.S. soil and did not have jurisdiction. Generally speaking, the NSA was more of a surveillance and intelligence collection agency. In a case that had international repercussions throughout the United States and the Middle East, Burnett had made inquiries at Langley. It had been decided that the FBI was required to pick up Agassi. They would detain him and make the appropriate contacts with the United Nations. The State Department would contact any interested embassies. The United States government did not want this case to be dismissed on a technicality. Nor did it wish to have the existence of the MANOPOLY Project become public knowledge.

Burnett walked out of the cabin and waved to Assad. He instructed him to call Langley. The appropriate people in the CIA chain of command needed to contact the FBI. They needed to have the Chicago field office pick up Agassi. They now had the smoking gun to charge him. The pictures of ranking intelligence and Department of Defense employees that he had texted to Faruq were sufficient for a warrant.

Inside the cabin, Faruq was singing like an entire chorus of birds. It would be a straightforward case to make in court. However, when arresting Iranian nationals, the amount of resistance from American allies in the Muslim world would be considerable. Every detail had to be tended to without fail.

Chapter 71

About forty-five minutes later, the FBI agent in command of the Chicago field office was standing on the driveway of Agassi's home in Evanston. There were three black Chevrolet Suburbans parked in the driveway. Each SUV contained two armed agents. The house was quickly surrounded, and the door was broken down with a battering ram. There, kneeling in front of the fireplace in the living room was Salomon Agassi, trying to light papers on fire with lighter fluid. He was wearing a robe and slippers and was cursing at the top of his lungs in Persian.

The six FBI agents moved with lightning speed and purpose to extinguish any evidence in the fireplace. Agassi was handcuffed and put into the back of the lead black Suburban. The arrest warrant had been read to him. He had a black bag over his head. They were on the way back to the field office in less than five minutes. The agents from the other two Suburbans were still in residence, doing a thorough search of the house for additional evidence. More than anything, they were looking for any clues that might indicate whether there could be additional members of the faculty or student body that were complicit in the conspiracy. The agents separated and tore the house apart from four different directions.

The field office was about a thirty-minute drive from the residence. Agassi cursed in Persian all of the way there. He had no clue that one of the men was from the Middle Eastern desk and spoke fluent Persian. So, every insult, every curse word, and every threat that Agassi spouted was understood by his captors. He was not aware of the American justice concept of having the right to remain silent. And he did not remain silent. They pulled up to a Federal Detainment Facility and honked. A sally port door opened. They drove into the void with the door closing quickly behind them.

Agassi was now trapped in the belly of the Great Satan. Now, for the very first time since his door had flown open, he wondered where Faruq was and if he had made his rendezvous with their handlers on Lake Michigan. He certainly hoped that the photos and list of names sent to Faruq were still secure. He also wondered how quickly Qassem Soleimani would learn of their capture and what the political blowback would be in Iran for the chain of events unfolding around him this very moment!

Chapter 72

In the IRIAF Headquarters in suburban Tehran, Colonel Arman had received the call on which he had been waiting. Freyredoon Adipour called him and informed him that the device requested for use at the American University in Beirut was ready to be delivered. Arman checked the Brigadier General's schedule and confirmed that he would be in Iraq the entire day. He directed Adipour to deliver the device to his office at 1:30 p.m. local time. The colonel had arranged for a weapons training seminar to be held in an old Quonset hut barracks on the base. This event would take the vast majority of the men out of the office and place them a safe distance from the office at an old barracks.

Arman was preparing for the meeting. He had taken the capsule of neurotoxin from the pencil box with a hollow bottom in his desk. He carefully removed the lid from a bottle of water without disturbing the factory seal and pulled the capsule apart. After having mixed the toxin into the bottle, he held it up to the sunlight in the window to make sure the mixture was precise. It was crystal clear. He replaced the lid and placed it in the small refrigerator on the table by the door. Adipour knocked on the door about two minutes early. Arman barked, "*Enter!*" Adipour walked in, carrying a small box that was wrapped in plain brown paper.

Adipour asked if General Nasirzdeh was in. Arman instructed him that he was in Iraq all day with General Soleimani. Adipour seemed quite pleased with his answer. Arman inquired, "Is that the general's package?"

Adipour responded simply, "Yes."

Arman instructed him to go in and place it on the general's desk so he would see it as soon as he returned. Adipour did as told.

"It's scorching out there. There is a bottle of cold water in the general's private refrigerator," Arman said coyly without looking up from his desk. Adipour opened the door, took the bottle, held it up to the window to check the seal, and opened the bottle of water. He drank it in about three long pulls. He told the colonel that he had work to do and walked out the door. Arman stopped him and had to remind him to come back and pick up the envelope that contained his payment for the package. The payment was an envelope stuffed with cash. He handed it to Adipour, and he left.

Arman smiled. Little did Adipour know that within the next twenty-four to forty-eight hours he would be dead! His death would appear to be meningitis, or some other insect-born disease. Further, the training event in the old barracks had prevented anyone from being present who might have seen him and recalled him being there. The colonel was very pleased with himself. He leaned back in his chair and smiled broadly. He then went into the general's office and retrieved the device. In reality, the general had no idea that the device had been ordered. It had been requested with his signature stamp and a smart request letter. Now, the device would be sent to Langley for analysis.

This evening, he would deliver the box to Jacque Keller at the Red Crescent Headquarters to be sent back to the United States. It would be compared to the Iranian spy device taken from the MANOPOLY Project floor. He spent the remaining hour until his workday was completed making sure that everything was perfectly back in place. The general would be arriving in the morning at 0700. He had no knowledge of the events that had just transpired in his office. Nor did he know that it had happened in his name.

Chapter 73

That evening, just after nightfall, Arman made his way under cover of dark back to the Embassy of the Government of Qatar. He went into the Red Crescent Headquarters. Once inside, Keller rushed him into a secure room in the embassy and took the box from him. Keller disappeared for a moment and placed the package in a safe in his main office. Arman informed him that the *"candy"* had been delivered, referring to the toxin ingested by Adipour. It indicated to Keller that the clock was now ticking until his piece of the plan was completed.

Keller took a burner phone from his pocket and made a quick call. The phone rang once, and he simply said, "Go to the well."

He hung the phone up, dropped it to the floor and crunched it into a million pieces with the heel of his shoe. Arman shook his hand and walked out of the Red Crescent office and out of the embassy. He had a walk of about a mile back to his barracks, and about three-quarters of the way back, he heard a loud explosion. He assumed it was the suicide bomb triggered at the "well." It would necessitate the humanitarian aid request for Soleimani the following day. He lowered his head and walked more quickly and with determined purpose back to his bunk.

Chapter 74

In the cabin at the airfield in Ontario, The Mongol had completed his work on Faruq. Darian had been asked into the room to determine if all of the questions to which he needed answers had been asked. As he entered, The Mongol was cleaning the "tools of his trade." A pot of water boiled on the fire in the fireplace. A roll of paper towels sat next to the water. These supplies had been brought in his plane. By now, his pilot had crawled into his cockpit and was sleeping. Burnett was sitting at the small table in the middle of the room, writing out a report by hand on a clipboard with a ball-point pen. Darian asked what he had already gotten out of him. Burnett nodded toward the report he was writing. Darian read as quickly as he could over his shoulder. He was up to speed pretty quickly. The Mongol had his tools packed up and headed back to his plane. The Mongol woke his pilot, and they were gone within ten minutes. Just the sound of his engine in the air remained.

In the corner of the room beside the fireplace sat a man. They were the remains of a man who had been completely broken. He was sobbing. His face was beaten and swollen, his mouth was bleeding. His hands were tightly tucked against his waist. Darian walked over to get a rag to clean him up enough to talk. He looked up and was missing two front teeth. Both index fingers had been severed. There was no fight left in this man. He was utterly broken. Darian handed Faruq the rag and asked him two more brief questions. "Was this directed by Soleimani, and is there anyone else besides you and Agassi at Northwestern?"

Faruq could only muster a small response, "Soleimani, yes. Nobody else."

Burnett looked at him and nodded. Darian shot Faruq between the eyes with his 9-millimeter Glock and ended his misery. The body was buried in the woods near the airfield. The three men headed back to the plane and readied for take-off. Once in the plane, Assad removed a secure CIA encrypted sky phone from his pocket. He texted a coded message to Langley. The message was, WE GOT A MOOSE IN CANADA, NO RACK. The aircraft engine screamed to full throttle, and they were gone. The encrypted message meant that they had killed Faruq and were not bringing the body back.

Chapter 75

In Chicago, Agassi had been moved from the sally port into a holding cell. Two guards were brought in for the express purpose of strip-searching him and putting him in an orange jumpsuit. Experience had taught the FBI that when dealing with Islamic terrorists who might have valuable information; it was prudent to treat them as high risk for suicide. If they would blow themselves up with suicide vests, the FBI didn't want to allow them an easy exit to meet their seventy virgins. So, Agassi was in a padded cell with nothing in the room but two huge guards. An armed guard also guarded the outside door. His orange jumpsuit was made of a soft paper so it could not be torn into strips and used for suicidal hanging.

The FBI agent in charge had been instructed to contact Darian Amir and Ronald Burnett and not to question the prisoner. They had also been instructed not to contact the United States Department of State and *not* to read the prisoner his Miranda Rights. That would start a clock that would trigger mandatory reporting to the myriad of inter-governmental and international agencies. They were also told not to allow him to speak to an attorney. They were merely holding Agassi for questioning in a matter of national interest. It was legal for twenty-four hours. The agent in charge had tried to call Darian and Burnett several times but only got to voicemail. Once in the air, Burnett's cell phone began dinging as the messages hit his cell phone repeatedly. He saw that the FBI had called, and he returned the call. Burnett told the agent that they were en route and would be there within the hour. He hung up. Darian and Burnett had to have a conversation about what they would tell Agassi about Faruq's whereabouts.

Assad listened and was very deeply in thought. He interjected, "His body will never be found, nor will the bodies of their handlers.... They all got away on the boat!" And that was the story they would all tell!

The three men looked back and forth at one another and nodded in agreement. However, before the aircraft landed, the stories of the three men had to be identical. Their statements that would be given within the next twenty-four hours could never change by a single word. It was as tight as an operation ever got. They all agreed, and the matter was settled for the remainder of all time. Even though the official story had just been written in the sky above the U.S./Canadian border, they all knew that Faruq was an IRGC Quds Force operative. The capture would undoubtedly be noticed and brought to the attention of Qassem Soleimani. Some ripples had been created that would travel a very long way and would return equally as significant.

Chapter 76

Assad had contacted the CIA using his sky phone and had an FAA flight plan cleared to put their small plane on schedule to land at Midway Airport in Chicago. They were due to land there in about fifteen minutes. Midway had fewer large planes. It was easier to get on and off the tarmac. Langley would have a car waiting there to pick them up and to transfer them to the FBI detention facility. The plane landed. Burnett, Darian, and Assad exited with the engine still idling. A CIA pilot taxied the plane back onto the runway and immediately took off for Langley Air Force Base. Any evidence that might remain with the plane would be disposed of properly. They would not be leaving any loose ends to come back and trip them up. It was about a thirty-minute drive to the FBI detention facility, and as they sat in the comfortable leather seats of the Cadillac Escalade, it finally struck the men … they were exhausted.

Chapter 77

The three men arrived at the FBI detention facility. Immediately, they were ushered into an office space that had been vacated for their privacy. All of the office tools they required were there. They immediately took the handwritten notes on Burnett's clipboard and began typing them in the standard government intelligence formatted report style.

Faruq had admitted that he was working for the IRGC and the Quds Force and that he knew and trained with Qassem Soleimani in Tehran. Soleimani had also sent Agassi to infiltrate the university as a professor of foreign studies. The Supreme Leader had used his connections with Saudi Arabia to keep Agassi's visa active as a guest professor. Faruq admitted to planting the Iranian spy device in Econ Lab 1. He also admitted that he was the one seen exiting the building by Whiffer. He also told them that Soleimani was looking for a way to hack into and access the MANOPOLY Project's results. He had been trying to obtain intelligence on what scenarios the United States government deemed essential; projects important enough to rate a MANOPOLY Project research evaluation.

Faruq was not high enough up the food chain to know the

reason why this project had been targeted. Even more importantly, how did they ever know that the project existed? When the Iranians began planting intelligence assets at Northwestern University, almost no agency in the federal government knew of its existence. It was a pilot program.

This time together to type and organize and share their interagency perspectives on what they had already discovered was necessary. They would only get one pass at Agassi before the State Department. Then a flurry of Arab embassies would flood the detention center. They had to be organized, and they had to be efficient.

Chapter 78

Assad, Darian, and Burnett walked into the interrogation room and were seated at the long table. The FBI agent in charge was with them. They were all seated, and the FBI agent read Agassi his Miranda Rights. This action started the clock on the stampede that was sure to follow. Darian began; Agassi knew him from the Northwestern campus. He started by telling Agassi what they already knew. Agassi continually interrupted by hollering for an attorney to call the State Department, etc. He was informed that they had twenty-four hours to detain him before allowing him a phone call, so they continued to pepper him with questions. They asked him about many of the issues to which they already knew the answers. It was done to check the integrity and truthfulness of his statements. Throughout the first four or five hours, he simply resisted and screamed obscenities at them in Persian.

The interrogators rotated in and out of the room, taking breaks, getting meals and drinks, and even resting. The strategy was to keep a full-court press on Agassi around the clock to wear him down. He had already been awake for almost forty-eight hours, so the four agents just kept repeating the same questions over and over and over. About nine hours into the interrogation, while Agassi was still protesting, Darian stopped. Darian got very quiet and whispered an unexpected question: "Ghassim Kalani is your cousin. You visit him every year and go to the IRGC Headquarters. Do you have other family members in Tehran whose lives you fear will be lost?"

Wow! They knew his family in Iran, and they followed him on his trips. The fear in Agassi's face was now visible. Agassi was prepared for hollering and verbal abuse, but he was not nearly as prepared for calm, dispassionate truth. They knew they had shaken him. It wouldn't be much longer now.

He began to say his Muslim prayers repeatedly as though he were preparing to die. He ran to the corner of the room and leaned forward on his knees, facing toward where he imagined Mecca might be. Then he came back and sat. This repetition went on for about another hour. Darian sat, staring him in the eyes the entire time. Agassi took a breath. Darian leaned in again and asked him if he would attend Freyredoon Adipour's funeral if he were able? Agassi knew that Adipour was Soleimani's computer engineer and that he was one of his most guarded secrets. *Now* Agassi knew that the jig was up. Agassi started sobbing. His head fell forward and hit the table. Darian pushed a button under the front lip of the table. The buzzer let the others know that he was talking.

Burnett and Assad came into the room, and the FBI agent left, as did the guards. At the door, they didn't want to see or hear anything that was about to transpire. They could not be accountable for what they did not know. Agassi was now spilling his secrets to the United States government. Agassi had believed that he was so very much smarter than all of the American faculty and students at Northwestern University. He really looked down his nose at them.

He looked forward to his trips to Iran each year. There, he could rejoice in his Muslim faith and enjoy the intellectual discussion about the Prophet Muhammed. He also liked discussing the interpretations of the Holy Quran. He had hated his time in America amid The Great Satan. He could not believe that he had just shamed himself, his faith, and his country by telling all of their secrets. What nobody had said was that Freyredoon Adipour was his mother's brother. Adipour was his uncle. That was why he had been trusted to execute the plan against the MANOPOLY Project. And Darian had just informed him that his uncle was dead. How could an infidel have been the messenger for such news? His faith had been tested. He had not yet discovered the extent to which his faith would be tested. Life had taken a terrible turn for Agassi. He was no longer walking between the raindrops in a foreign land. Now he was a prisoner of war.

Chapter 79

The explosion that Colonel Arman had heard on the way to his barracks was, indeed, the suicide bombers' vest. It had exploded at one of the checkpoints between the Tehran International Airport and the IRIAF Headquarters. Keller had indeed selected a target that would quickly get the required approval and attention of Qassem Soleimani. When he was approached with an application for humanitarian aid, this one would be near to him. Keller had waited until about 1300 to call the executive officer, Major Muhammed, to set an appointment. The appointment was finalized for 1500.

Keller opened his safe. He removed the ultra-high-tech Bluetooth transmitter and stuck it in the corner of an envelope, folded it in half twice, and put it in his shirt pocket. He called his secretary and told him he was ready to leave. His driver pulled up in front with the Red Crescent military transport to deliver Keller to the IRIAF Base. When they passed the checkpoint that had been blown up by the suicide bomber, they stopped. Keller was a humanitarian aid worker. He spoke with the guards and tried to soothe them. He asked about the families of those who were killed. The show of benevolence was very believable, and it appeared to be very sincere. After two more checkpoints they would reach the red-and-white-striped barricade. At each checkpoint they had to get out to be searched. Each time, the truck undercarriage was checked with mirrors all of the way around. They finally reached the gate. The barricade was slowly lifted. They were allowed entry. They pulled up to the aircraft hangar and honked. The suicide bomber had caused them to tighten security substantially.

The door pulled open electronically. They drove forward onto the concrete pad, and the door immediately closed behind them. The driver opened his door and walked around to open Keller's door. Keller reached into his shirt pocket and removed the envelope and quickly removed the Bluetooth device and placed it under the rim of his hat. They walked into the air-conditioned office building together. The driver was seated in the waiting room. Keller was ushered into the conference room. The oval table was their destination. Soleimani's executive officer would be in momentarily. Keller nodded and walked into the room. He pulled the door closed behind him. Keller hit the floor crawling as fast as he could go to the table leg next to Soleimani's armchair. He stuck it to the table leg and rolled out from under the table.

He quickly put his hands down to his side, onto the floor, snapped up, and was immediately on his feet. He acted as though he was tying his boot when the executive officer walked into the room. His clipboard was right in front of him. He reached out and picked it up from the table and handed it to the officer. He asked Keller to be seated, and they both took a seat. The clipboard was being discussed when Qassem Soleimani walked into the room. Soleimani nodded his head and took a seat. Keller tried to make his eyes follow the chair leg while not moving his head. He really needed to know that the transmitter was successfully deployed.

It was finished! The Bluetooth device was planted on Soleimani's boot. As soon as he got in his truck and messaged Arman, the device would be activated. Western intelligence was now tracking Soleimani in real-time!

Chapter 80

It had been about thirty-six hours since Freyredoon Adipour had been to Brigadier General Nasizadeh's office to deliver the device that he had designed. He was beginning to get a fever and was feeling very ill. He had a bad headache, his body ached all over, and he was incredibly thirsty. He decided to go to the back of his shop, where he kept a cot that he used when working very late on a project. He took a big drink of water, took a Tylenol, and fluffed his pillow and lay down. He placed his arm over his eyes, and he died. It would be the following day before one of General Soleimani's officers came in to get his computer upgraded and found him dead. Nothing looked suspicious, and his body was taken to his family. Foul play was never suspected.

Chapter 81

After the dance was over, Beau drove Bright back to Brooke and Jackson's home. He helped get Bright into the house, into his pajamas, and then bed. It had been a very long and exciting day. (He had no clue just *how exciting* the day had indeed been. The capture had gone on without Beau's knowledge.) He walked into the living room, undid his tie, and sat down in the recliner in the living room facing the door. He leaned back and stretched his back. As he was coming forward, his eyes caught on the envelope that he had laid on the table in the foyer. He had forgotten entirely about Virgil and his search.

He was thinking about getting ready to run and pick up Imogene at the airport in about twenty minutes. He rushed to the table, picked up the envelope, and tore it open. There in Beau's hands was a complete abstract of the piece of property that lay under the New Orleans parking garage. It was the last known address of anyone associated with The Driftwood.

He opened the abstract. It was a neatly bound compilation of copies, scans, and photographs of records that detailed the entire history of the ownership of the property. It listed ownership dating all of the way back to the Louisiana

Purchase. The abstract was arranged from most recent in front, to the earliest records in the back. The abstract started with the legal notice of the City of New Orleans exercising eminent domain over the property. It was followed by the condemnation notice, the last bill of sale, and each document was dated very neatly in the top margin. He quickly caught on to the dating scheme and thumbed his way back through time back to the 1960s.

There, in November of 1961, the home was purchased by Randall Joseph Bell. Included with the record was the application for the mortgage, the bill of sale, and the county recorder's appraisal. The mortgage application had his date of birth, his social security number, and his previous address. Beau had found the link for which he had been searching so very long. He had to get in the car and get Imogene. He could comb through the abstract more thoroughly later. Imogene would be thrilled. Beau finally felt like he might find a resolution to his quest.

Beau was on his way in his Porsche Boxster to Chicago O'Hare Airport to pick up Imogene St. John. Right at this moment, he thought that she just might be the woman of his dreams, and the love of his life. He downshifted, the engine whined as the tires spun, and Beau was off to get Imogene with a smile on his face. Today, he had given his baby sister away to his best friend. He had been there and watched their love grow. It had become something substantial and real. Being a part of their special day had made him forget about the void that he thought existed in his life. Perhaps love and marriage just might be for him and Imogene as well!

Chapter 82

Brooke and Jackson were just waking up in their honeymoon suite at the Hotel Lincoln in North Chicago. Jackson was vaguely aware that there would be some security-related issues that might trigger a chain of events after the wedding. However, he had not heard a word, so he assumed all was well. Brooke was floating on cloud nine, lying there naked in Beau's arms. Her nose nuzzled into the tuft of hair in the middle of his chest. The two had enjoyed an evening of passionate lovemaking and had fallen to sleep in each other's arms. They were both exhausted from the weeks of running to prepare for the wedding. Jackson had also been carrying the additional weight of the espionage episode in Econ Lab 1. Letting down and relaxing felt so good.

They were both very quiet, contemplating the events of the previous day. It had been very eventful. The Reynolds family had been folded seamlessly into the Benoit family. Jackson was feeling very pleased with his life. Brooke was very relieved that with all of the trials that he had endured throughout his life and childhood, it finally seemed that closure had found its way into Jackson's heart. And, she wondered, had that moment in the pastor's office been more substantive than she had initially thought? The moment when Jackson walked away, leaving Brooke to be his champion. Had the moment been an opening of the door to Jackson's faith? She certainly hoped so, but she would never push. She would pray for him to come to her. She believed that if not at *this* moment, that he one day would.

It was a new beginning for Brooke and Jackson, and she wanted to just soak in the experience. Check-out time was at noon. It was 10:30 a.m. by the clock by the bed. Brooke looked at the clock, looked at Jackson, grinned, and rolled on top of him and straddled him....

They would check out almost an hour later.

Chapter 83

Beau arrived at O'Hare International Airport about thirty minutes before the scheduled arrival time of Imogene's plane. He knew the airline and the flight number. He was very familiar with the airport since he flew in and out so regularly. It seemed he was always traveling back and forth between Evanston and New York. Sometimes, the schedules required that he take the flight he needed to O'Hare. Occasionally, they took him to Midway, and about half of the time to Evanston. Evanston was his preferred destination. It saved him time getting in and out, being a smaller regional airport. He never checked luggage, so the luggage carousel was a treat that he was usually able to avoid.

Beau was walking happily toward the American Terminal when he heard on the overhead speaker that flight 701 from Mexico City was running behind. Beau went to the terminal, checked the arrivals board, and went to the gate designated to unload the passengers. While he was at the terminal, a baggage handler had come out of the American office and told him the flight was running about twenty minutes behind. They had been delayed before takeoff in Mexico City. Beau was sitting down, glancing at the television screen. Beau was just filling some time while he watched out the window for Imogene's plane.

Beau remembered Randall Joseph Bell and his date of birth. He was about two years his mother's senior. He pulled out his iPhone 11 and searched the New Orleans phone directory for his name and found nothing. He tried the Baton Rouge phone book and found a Randall Bell listed at an address on the other side of Baton Rouge. This address looked very familiar; he had seen it before, and it was very memorable. He had seen it on several envelopes in the closet upstairs at the Benoit family home in Baton Rouge. The address was 101 Beauregard Street. That was an address Beauregard Benoit would not forget seeing! He thought for a second about touching the highlighted number on his phone screen and calling him, but he waited. Beau was nothing if not a polite southern gentleman. The practical side of him forced him to put the phone back into his pocket for now.

He looked up at the television again. Just at that moment, the spotlight on the front of Imogene's plane shone in through the window, into Beau's eyes. Beau was excited to see Imogene, and even more excited to tell her about his find! Imogene was the second person off the flight. She saw Beau and ran straight into his arms. To her sheer delight, Beau leaned her back and gave her a kiss that she would not soon forget. The two joined hands and took off walking like teenagers toward the luggage carrousel.

Imogene had not yet told Beau that she had taken a furlough from her mission assignment in South America. She wanted to come back to America and spend some time with Beau and some time with her parents. Imogene was to the age that her biological clock was ticking very loudly. Imogene had put God and her Christian vocation before everything else in her life. She realized that she was not getting any younger and was beginning to feel the need to put down roots. She was ready for a family, and she wanted a family with Beau.

Since the days running together around her high school track, she knew that when the time came, Beau Benoit would be her choice. She had prayed many times that God would save Beau for her. She had saved herself for him. She knew that he had been a partier in college and had struggled with alcohol. She knew that he had slept with other women in college, but she had saved herself. And she believed that God had saved Beau from marrying someone else. She had struggled her entire flight with whether or not she had done the right thing. She was bringing all of her clothes and coming back to stay. And she was doing so totally unannounced. She had hoped that it would not seem too forward to Beau.

They got to the luggage carousel. Imogene was wondering what Beau would say when her three big bags came through the gate onto the carousel for a ten-day stay. Before she could worry another second, Beau took her hand, spun her around, kissed her, and said, "Imogene, I have loved you for years. Would you do me the honor of marrying me?"

She cried, and through the tears, she whimpered, "Yes, Beau! I have always loved you!"

They stood there quietly together, waiting for the luggage. The luggage came, and Imogene told Beau that she had come home to stay. They both laughed at how funny it was that they had both come to the same decision at the same time on two separate continents.

At that moment, Beau decided that now was the time to reach out and discover what, if any, information was to be found about Virgil. Imogene was already up to speed. They were beginning their life together. Beau needed to find out something to put his mind at peace. They pulled the luggage from the carousel, placing it on a three-wheeled luggage cart. Beau stopped, touched Imogene's arm, and said, "Imogene, I have to call Randy Bell. Let's just call him right now."

Beau had saved the number he had located for Randall Bell at 101 Beauregard Street in Baton Rouge. He had waited as long as he could. There was nothing and nobody present now that he had to protect from discovering his mother's long-hidden secret. He looked into Imogene's eyes and said, "Cross your fingers, Baby! Here goes nothing?" Her face bloomed into a brilliant smile. She jumped up and said, "You bet I am!"

They turned their backs to the luggage carousel and faced a row of chairs. Beau stood nervously; Imogene sat on the very front edge of the chair facing Beau. She wanted to watch his expressions. Throughout this entire search for Beau's natural father, she had heard the whole story long distance. Now she was here, and she was his, and she wanted to watch his face when he learned any news.

Beau took out his cell phone and scrolled through his contacts. He had added Randy Bell to his favorites just a few minutes ago. He tapped the screen, and the phone began ringing. On the fourth ring, about the time Beau was becoming confident that nobody would answer, an older sounding man with a small, frail voice said, "Hello?"

Beau's heart skipped a beat, and he said, "May I speak to Randall Bell, please?"

"This is Randy," he replied.

Beau had played this scene through in his mind many times since he discovered the name in the abstract. But it certainly felt different to hear his voice. It felt like the voice of a ghost from his unknown past.

"My name is Beau Benoit," he continued. "Do you recall having known a Patsy Wilson or a Virgil Bagley?"

There was a pause, and then he suddenly said, "Those are two names I haven't heard in quite a while. But yes! They are both my dear old friends."

Beau was relieved, and Imogene was sitting on the edge of

her seat. She was beaming, sitting there in front of him. Beau asked him, "Have you kept in touch with Patsy?"

"Mostly by letter across the years," he replied and continued, "She asked me to keep an eye on the whereabouts of Virgil. She wanted to make sure she knew where he was in case of a medical emergency regarding their son. I am assuming that you are their son?"

Beau had gotten past his two big questions, and now, he was feeling much more comfortable and relaxed. He knew that Randy probably already had this knowledge, but he felt compelled to tell Randy a bit about his life. It was, after all, their first meeting of sorts. So, Beau filled in some details. Then he added, "I was raised as Bright Benoit's son until a high school football injury required blood typing. Mom was forced to tell me that Virgil was my natural father. I was devastated. I have spent my entire life since high school trying to discover who and where my natural father was."

Beau felt Randy already knew the story. He had seen a great number of letters in the upstairs closet at the Benoit family home in Baton Rouge. But there was great catharsis in saying the story out loud to his mother's confidant. He was reasonably sure that Randy was playing dumb to protect his old friend, Patsy. They spoke of fond memories of Patsy Benoit. They hit it off as long-lost friends. The conversation was coming very quickly. Then it hit him. What about Virgil?

Beau suddenly tensed up between his shoulders. Imogene saw this and wondered what he was thinking. As she opened her mouth to ask him what was wrong, he blurted, "Do you know where my father is?"

There was an awkward silence. Randy knew that Patsy had intended for Beau to believe that Bright was his dad his entire life. Would he be betraying his dear old friend? This question rolled through his mind in the stopped time of the paused conversation. He braced himself and decided to follow the Golden Rule.

Randy believed that he would want to know, so he continued, "Beau, Virgil went on to college on his G.I. Bill after Vietnam and became an engineer. He worked for Halliburton. He retired about ten years ago. He retired back in Baton Rouge so he could keep an eye on you from afar." He continued, "His wife, Lilly, is a beautiful woman who loves him dearly. But she was never able to have children of her own. So, they both watched you from afar."

Beau felt devastated for a moment, but then he remembered that all he needed was closure. Randy continued, "Beau, about five years ago, Virgil was diagnosed with Alzheimer's. They now live in a managed care home just outside of Baton Rouge. I think you should visit. Your mom is gone, which surely means this is not a betrayal. You went to a great deal of work to find him. Go see him!" He continued, "Go and find some closure, but don't expect him to know you. Last time I spoke to Lilly, she was the only person that he recognized."

Randy gave him the name and telephone number of the facility.

He had a dad that had loved him his entire life. He was good! He thanked Randy, and after a cordial conversation, they hung up. Beau had promised to visit Randy on a trip back to Baton Rouge soon. When the phone was disconnected, his shoulders slumped. He felt the weight from years of wonder and fear lifted from his back. He looked into Imogene's eyes, smiled, and said, "I love you!"

Finally, they loaded the bags into the Porsche, and the trunk was stuffed. They barely touched the ground all of the way to Evanston. They were so happy. Beau told her all about the wedding and that he had a telephone number to try in the search for Virgil. There was not a moment that they were not sharing every detail of their day and their lives. Beau thought to himself, *this is what living was all about.* He finally understood how Brooke and Jackson felt about each other. And while he was pulling onto the street where Brook and Jackson lived, the radio began playing, "I Will Always Love You!" They smiled and pulled up to the door. They hurriedly unloaded the luggage and stacked it in the entry hall closet. Beau took Imogene by the hand. And together, the two walked into Beau's room and closed the door. They did not speak a word.

Chapter 84

Colonel Muhammed Arman had set up a dark web Internet signal relay through the secret VPN on his computer. The signal being tracked from the Bluetooth tracking device on Soleimani's boot was relayed digitally to Ali Assad at the CIA's Middle Eastern desk at Langley. The entire Middle Eastern section and a computer support group had been tasked with monitoring the signal. They were transposing the signal onto a map so his actions could be tracked and logged.

He had the capability of knowing where he went and when. This allowed them to anticipate when and where he might be. Additionally, in the Middle East, borders between countries were non-existent for a man with the support and resources of the Supreme Leader of Iran. Iran was believed to be funding most of the terrorist groups in the Middle East. So, having a tracking device on his boot might be able to give Western intelligence some kind of a real idea into what extent the unrest in the region was tied to Iran, Soleimani, and the Quds Force. The information, believed to be accurate, indicated that this group was the primary source of funding. Iran funded a group of loosely connected terrorist organizations.

Groups like ISIS, al Qaeda, Hezbollah, and many of the jihadi groups throughout the region were growing rampant.

This group at the CIA in Langley was working around the clock. They were trying to put together a dossier of known actions, destinations, affiliates, and terror organizations linked to Soleimani. The intelligence activities in the Iranian theater looked better than they had in years. Real-time tracking on Soleimani and the assassination of his technology expert made the future look brighter. Additionally, it made the likelihood of the tracking device being discovered much more remote in the absence of Adipour.

Chapter 85

Brooke and Jackson were back in the crow's nest at Econ Lab 1. Darian and Burnett are there as well. Whiffer was there first, running some diagnostics. The room filled up pretty quickly. The topic got very serious, very fast. Darian and Burnett were debriefing the members of the MANOPOLY Project on the activities during the wedding dance. The developments had been very intense and were continuing to unfold.

Brooke seemed most shocked by the events that had been brewing around them for the past couple of years. She was pretty much absorbed in her work. Add in Jackson, her classes, and her area of expertise in the data consolidation for the scenarios that they ran, and she was swamped. She had never really taken the time to look up and pay attention to what had gone on around her. Jackson had been the critical contributor to all of the preventative actions that happened around Brooke when she was on campus. He was trying very hard to protect her and keep her as far from harm's way as possible.

Whiffer was the first to discover the intrusion on the game floor. He had been very much involved in protecting the program itself. Darian had worked with his aspects of security. Additionally, Russell Emming and Ronald Burnett had protected the lab and hardware. Whiffer was aware that there was a threat. He was on the lookout for that threat every day. But he was unaware that there were people on campus from the IRGC and the Quds Force. Honestly, he was quite freaked out. Each member of the team took their turn, reporting their contributions and findings to the group. It had been a full forty-eight hours.

Jackson pretty much just sat and listened to everyone in the crow's nest speak their minds. He took in everyone's perceptions and their reactions to the threat. He was taking it all in and trying to decide exactly how he felt as well. He had been there from the beginning. It was born in his mind. He had never imagined that an idea that was born in his mind would be an asset for which world governments would spy. As much as he tried to be angry, he was feeling kind of oddly proud. Brooke finally noticed that everyone but Jackson was talking. She directly addressed the issue to Jackson.

"Jack, you haven't said a word. What do you think?"

The entire room fell silent. Jackson looked up, smiled, and said, "You all about covered it!" and walked out of the crow's nest.

Chapter 86

The morning after Beau had picked up Imogene and stayed at Brooke and Jackson's house, Bright Benoit woke up bright and early. He had his nurse get him in his powered wheelchair. He decided to take breakfast in the kitchen. He was just taking his first bite of a country omelet, prepared by his nurse, when he heard Beau coming down the steps. He was excited to talk about the wedding and pushed the lever backward and to the left. The chair raced to the foot of the steps. Bright came to the bottom, just as Imogene stepped into sight with Beau's hand around her waist. He was walking beside her. "Well, Hello, Imogene!" Bright blurted out. And suddenly he spoke more clearly than he had spoken since his stroke.

The ice had been broken, and the family was all happy. Imogene and Beau went into the kitchen and fixed themselves some breakfast. They sat down with Bright to eat. Bright sat watching his son and Imogene. You could tell he was encouraged to see Beau happy. After breakfast, Beau and Imogene did dishes and walked out into the backyard for some fresh air. Bright laid down to take a nap. Beau snuck back in and picked up the abstract to the property in New Orleans. He took it out into the yard to share with Imogene. They both liked history;

the documents contained in the abstract kept them entertained for hours. They sat on the chaise lounges on the back patio and enjoyed the historical read.

After the meeting in the crow's nest, Brooke was beat and headed home. She walked in from the garage, into the kitchen. There, she found Beau and Imogene. They were locked in an embrace and kissing in front of the kitchen sink. Brooke squealed, "Imogene! You finally landed that slippery old fish?" They all laughed!

Brooke grabbed Imogene by the hand and dragged her into the living room. "Now sit right here and tell me how this all happened!" Brooke said.

Imogene was glowing. She began to talk. However, Beau walked up, placed his hands squarely on his little sister's shoulders, and said, "Brooke, I am not going to let someone else tell you this news! Imogene and I are getting married!"

Brooke and Imogene both busted into tears and hugged each other like the sisters they now were. Brooke could not wait to tell Jackson!

This romance between Beau and Imogene was not the surprise to the Benoit family that Beau and Imogene perceived it to be. Brooke had figured out long ago that if Beau ever found the time for a woman, it would be Imogene. Bright had spent some time with her as well in the early days, back in Baton Rouge. Jackson had probably spent the least amount of time with Imogene of any of the rest of the family. But Jack was quiet. When they were together, he saw a chemical reaction that he recognized from his feelings about Brooke. Jack was very pleased as well.

Chapter 87

In the next several weeks, the Soleimani Task Force at the CIA had received a staggering amount of data from the tracker in the general's boot. They had programmed a virtual map on a large computer screen and mapped all of his travels. Additionally, they had processed a satellite workaround to pull in the signal and take it off the dark web. Many patterns were beginning to develop regarding the places he traveled and the people he went to see.

There were far more trips to Iraq than anyone had ever previously thought. Additionally, Soleimani made several trips to Lebanon and a trip to Syria, which was less surprising. It was becoming evident that Qassem Soleimani was stirring trouble for the United States in the Middle East. More and more, it looked like Soleimani was carrying cash to Middle Eastern governments to fund terrorism against the United States. The United States President had implemented a policy of strict economic sanctions, and he had pulled out of the Iranian Nuclear Deal. He was also pushing America's European allies to isolate them as well. Iran had retaliated verbally by threatening to resume processing weapons-grade plutonium. The powder keg in the Middle East just kept getting hotter.

Chapter 88

Imogene stayed with Beau at Brooke and Jackson's home for about two weeks. Beau had to get back to Manhattan. Imogene needed to get her things back to her parents' house in Baton Rouge. Beau had made a plan to send Imogene's items via FedEx to her parents. She would spend a couple of days in Manhattan with him. They had discussed this thoroughly. Given the proximity to Brooke and Bright, it made calling and searching for further information on Virgil seem a fool's errand. It might hurt the family. There was simply no reason to hurt the family he had cherished his entire life. So, they waited and planned to go to Manhattan and do some investigating.

Imogene was tickled pink to get to be included in the visit with Virgil. She was even more excited to spend some time alone with Beau in his Manhattan loft as the lady of the house. In Evanston, that position was firmly taken by Brooke, and she was doing it admirably. Bright was still there. Brooke had made it her responsibility to make sure that her dad was pleased. Beau had also planned a trip after making contact with Randy Bell. The trip would be to the Benoit family home in Baton Rouge to inspect the letters in the upstairs closet. He was excited to further inspect the letters bearing a return address of 101 Beauregard Street. Things were looking perfect for Beau Benoit! And most importantly, he planned to meet Virgil.

Chapter 89

Imogene selected the necessities. She would surely need her toothbrush, hairbrush, deodorant, perfume, a dozen pairs of panties, and five bras. She could also use five shirts, three pairs of jeans, and one dress. The rest of her belongings were packed into two suitcases, then put in shipping boxes and sent via FedEx to her parents' home in Baton Rouge. Beau had assisted her in packing the boxes, during which she wrapped the items she was keeping with her. They were going into the one remaining suitcase for their trip. FedEx came to Brooke and Jackson's house to pick up the boxes. Imogene loaded the other bag into the trunk of Brooke's BMW SUV.

Beau pretty much lived between two residences: the Reynolds residence in Evanston part-time, and the remainder of the time in his loft on the Upper West Side of Manhattan. Brooke was running Beau and Imogene to the Evanston Airport to catch the American Airlines shuttle to LaGuardia in New York City. Beau only traveled with a small bag between Evanston and Manhattan. He pretty much had everything he needed, wanted, and used at both places. His furniture and works of art, his desk, and his books all resided in Manhattan.

Imogene had met Beau in New York once, but she had never been in his apartment, nor had she slept in his bed. She was very excited and very nervous all at the same time. After FedEx had picked up the boxes, they loaded up. Brooke took them to the airport. Their plane was on time. Forty-five minutes later, they were on the tarmac at LaGuardia. They both carried on their bag. Beau had texted an Uber driver he used often. They were in the car within thirty minutes of landing. The drive-in traffic was insane today. It took over an hour to get from LaGuardia to the Upper West Side. The driver pulled up in front of Beau's building, and the doorman came to help with the luggage. Beau introduced Imogene to the concierge and the doorman so she would not have any problems getting into the building. They went into the office and had Imogene's name added as an official occupant. Beau gave her his spare key. Because of fire codes in the building and Manhattan in general, emergency services like to have an accurate list of occupants living in the building and in what units they reside.

While Imogene had been spending time in some important cities in South America, none were as metropolitan as New York City. It was a bit intimidating and nerve-racking to her at first. After what seemed like hours spent jumping through endless hoops, they were walking into the elevator to their apartment. When they stepped off the elevator, Beau gestured for her to unlock the door. She did. She got her first look at their home in Manhattan. Beau followed her, carrying his bag and dragging Imogene's suitcase on the back wheels. He closed the door. She ran into his arms while pulling her shirt off over her head.

Chapter 90

The next morning, Beau was expected for a meeting at the Federal Reserve. It was Imogene's first day in New York. Beau felt terrible that he had a meeting. Imogene was very gracious. She said that she would find a place for her clothes in the apartment. She also mentioned that she had seen a couple of clothing stores and a grocery from the Uber coming to the loft from the airport the day before. She told Beau that she needed to find a cute dress and would stop and get a bag of groceries. She also wanted to fix them dinner for their first full day in Manhattan.

Beau headed off to catch his taxi. Imogene went back into the loft. She locked the door and dead-bolted it. She walked into the bathroom and turned on the faucet in the cast iron tub. She was going to soak in a hot bath.

Beau was a couple of minutes early to his meeting. While reviewing the itinerary for the meeting, he could not help but notice that the Federal Reserve was going to cut the funds rate another quarter percent. It would surely be good news to the president. He was very critical of expensive money policy. The Fed fund rate had been recalculated and sorted out by the MANOPOLY Project at the direction of the president. He wondered why he had not heard of the change before now. The meeting started. His questions were immediately answered by the news that the global economy had slowed. It meant that the easing would ease downward pressure on the United States economy from overseas markets. Next week was New Year's Day, and the New York Stock Exchange indices were on a tear heading into 2020.

Chapter 91

The meeting at the Federal Reserve was finished at about eleven. Beau had moved from the conference room into his office. On his frequent trips back into New York, he had always kept his messages and calls current. There were a couple of minor contacts that had to be made. He was finished up by about 12:30. He decided to stop and pick up Chinese to take home for Imogene and himself. There was a Chinese restaurant by his office that was locally owned by a Chinese family in the neighborhood. Beau loved their food and ate there often. He walked in. They greeted him very warmly. He selected Kung-pow chicken, brown rice, and crab rangoon. He also picked up a couple pairs of chopsticks and some sweet and sour sauce and caught a taxi.

It was only about ten minutes back to the loft at this time of day. He walked in. Imogene was sitting in the middle of the floor in his terrycloth bathrobe. She was looking out the picture window, taking in the sights of the city from her high vantage point. She was not expecting Beau home so soon and looked a bit startled. But as soon as she saw Beau, she jumped to her feet and ran over to greet him with a kiss. The two sat back down where she had been observing the city life and had a Chinese picnic in front of the loft window.

After lunch, Beau had something on his mind that he wanted to get done. There was a new number in his iPhone that was daunting him. He had waited as long as he could. Now, there was nothing and nobody present that he had to protect from discovering his mother's long-hidden secret. He looked into Imogene's eyes and said, "You want to call Virgil's nursing home?"

Her face bloomed into a brilliant smile. She jumped up and said, "You bet I do!" They walked into the home office. Beau took a seat in his leather chair. He was sure that Imogene would sit in the armchair in front of the desk. Instead, she shimmied in next to his chair and sat down cross-legged and looked up at Beau's face. She wanted to watch his expressions. She wanted to watch his face when he learned any news.

Beau took out his cell phone and scrolled through his contacts. He came to the name 'Sunrise of Baton Rouge.' He tapped the screen, and the phone began ringing. On the second ring, a bubbly young female voice said, "Hello! Thank you for calling Sunrise of Baton Rouge. How can I help you today?"

Beau's heart skipped a beat. He had played this scene through in his mind his entire adult life. He was finally calling where his natural father lived. "My name is Beau Benoit," he continued. "I am inquiring about my father, Virgil Bagley. Can you ring his room?"

The phone rang three times. A frail female voice answered, "Hello?"

Beau paused and took this second in before continuing, "I am Beauregard Benoit. May I inquire about Virgil Bagley?"

The voice on the other end quickly became noticeably broken, as though she were crying. "Beau, is that really you?" She continued, "I am Lilly, your dad's wife. Randy called and told me you two had spoken. We have waited so very many years to hear your beautiful voice! How can I help you?"

Beau was moved to tears. Imogene was sobbing as she was looking into his tear-filled eyes. Beau fought to hold his composure. He would have to be brief or cry out loud. "Can I please come to visit? No! Can *we* come to visit? I would like to bring my fiancée, Imogene with me."

Lilly sobbed and replied, "You come anytime, Beau! But you need to know that your dad only knows me, and not all of the time. We need to get a picture!"

Beau cried and mustered a short, simple, "Thank you, I will be in touch soon."

When the phone was disconnected, his shoulders slumped. Once again, he felt the weight from years of wonder and fear lifted from his back. He looked into Imogene's eyes. He fell into her arms and they cried. Imogene wiped the tears from her eyes and said in a broken cadence, "I love you!"

Chapter 92

Brooke and Jackson had invited the entire family to Evanston for the holidays. Beau and Imogene were flying in after visiting Imogene's parents the week of Christmas. They were flying to Evanston on Christmas Eve. Bright was still enjoying the company of his children. Being around them had helped his speech. Brooke had a ham glazed and sitting in the oven at 350 degrees. The house was starting to smell like Christmas. Brooke was cooking the pork tonight so that the turkey could go in first thing in the morning.

Whiffer and Libby would also be coming for Christmas dinner. They would each be bringing a plus-one. The year 2019 had been an incredible one for Brooke and Jackson. They were all very excited to spend the holidays together. Brooke had received a call from Beau earlier in the day asking if she would go with him to pick out an engagement ring for Imogene the day after Christmas. She was tickled to do so. The ham was finished, and she turned off the oven. She informed Bright's nurse that she was leaving. She headed to the Evanston Airport to pick up Beau and Imogene.

Since the Evanston Airport was a small regional airport, and Beau and Imogene had traveled back and forth between

New York and Chicago so frequently, they needed to pack very little when they traveled. Brooke pulled up in front of the airport about the time the flight was due to land. She put her car in park. She took her phone from her purse and texted her brother. He responded within about five minutes. They were out the door in seven minutes. They said their hellos and took off for the Reynolds' home. It had been a few weeks since Imogene had seen Brooke. They were talking about a mile a minute. It finally felt like Christmas.

Jackson was working on some new programs with Whiffer in the crow's nest. He looked down at the clock on the monitor and realized that it was about time to be heading home. Whiffer wanted to make sure that he had the time correct for Christmas dinner at Jackson and Brooke's. He knew he didn't need to bring anything, but he felt compelled to ask out of courtesy. Jackson told him one o'clock sharp and that he only needed to bring himself and his date. The two walked out of Econ Lab 1 together. They locked up the building, set the security system, and headed out to the parking lot together. They parted ways about halfway through the lot, got in their cars, and left. The weather was unseasonably warm this year for the Christmas season. The expected temperature for Christmas Day was supposed to be about fifty-five degrees, and there was no snow on the ground. It looked like a lovely Christmas.

Christmas Day came, and with it came a great day with family and friends. Great food and great friends made for an excellent first Christmas for Brooke and Jackson as husband and wife. Beau and Imogene's first Christmas together as a couple was perfect. And Bright got to spend the day with all of his children.

Chapter 93

2020

When the clock struck midnight, the entire family stood in Brooke and Jackson's dining room in Evanston to toast the New Year. They all stood to share a toast; all, that was, except Beau. The day after Christmas, Beau and Brooke had driven into Chicago. Beau had picked out a beautiful two-carat solitaire diamond engagement ring. So, rather than stand with the family, Beau had dropped beside Imogene to his knee. He had slipped his hand into his pocket to fetch the ring. Imogene turned to give him a New Year's kiss and saw the top of his head. She looked down and had a silly look on her face. She saw that Beau had a beautiful diamond engagement ring in his hand.

Tears of joy began to gush from Imogene's eyes. Brooke quickly followed suit. Jackson started clapping and immediately said, "Well played, Beau!"

The entire family rejoiced together. The commotion settled down, and Beau stayed on his knee. In front of the entire family, he asked Imogene to be his wife. She said yes, dropped to her knees, and kissed him passionately. It was how the new decade began for the Benoit family. It would be a trying year.

Chapter 94

The pace that the Soleimani Task Force was moving at the CIA Headquarters in Langley Virginia was phenomenal. The operation had quadrupled in size. The Task Force was now tracking a group of about six Iranian generals. All of the targets were throughout the Middle East. Jacque Keller had managed to get newer, smaller tracking devices into the leadership of the IRGC and Quds Force. The CIA had added an economic task force to track banking deposits in the cities that these men frequented. They began tracing deposits tied to government accounts and the banks from which the money was transferred and putting cases together. The trail that was being uncovered was almost frightening. It looked like a march to war.

By tracking withdrawals from the accounts of these men and matching them to deposits in the governments' accounts, a picture developed. This gave the CIA a pretty clear idea that the Iranians, General Qassem Soleimani, and the Supreme Leader of Iran were funding the enemies of the United States and Israel. It also seemed quite apparent that there was something big being planned. The threat assessment level in the

Middle East was raised substantially. United States Embassies were put on high alert.

Ali Assad had tasked Colonel Muhammad Arman to surveil the computer networks of the IRIAF. He was trying to glean any useful intelligence that might lead to a clue where the strike might be. The CIA sent confidential human assets into the field. Every known source that they had was sent to try and discover where and what would be the target. The CIA had also been tracking the radiation levels in the atmosphere above Iran. The United States was convinced that Iran was enriching uranium at unprecedented levels.

The Supreme Leader had made a speech. He announced that due to the economic sanctions imposed by the United States on Iran that they would surpass the agreed-upon quantity of enrichment, an amount prescribed in the Joint Comprehensive Plan of Action (JCPOA) between Iran and the Western world. On May 8, 2018, the United States President had announced that the U.S. was leaving the JCPOA agreement. However, the European allies continued purchasing Iranian oil and not enjoining the sanctions imposed by the United States. Their goal was to try to keep Iran in compliance with the agreement. They also continued to try and bring the United States back into the contract. The friction between the United States and its European allies was not making any changes in the American position. Things were agitated. Every intelligence agency in the Western world was bracing for an explosion in the Iranian theater.

Chapter 95

Darian, Burnett, and Assad were all in very close contact through this entire Iranian espionage incident at Northwestern University and through the continued tensions that ensued. Burnett had sent Darian over to connect with Colonel Arman to see if another Persian asset in the region could be of use. Ali Assad would be running Darian in the Iranian theater. Before Darian deployed as a CIA asset in Iran, the CIA's technology section requested a twenty-four-hour delay in his transfer. They were about to complete a device that would be handheld. It would also link to a United States military satellite and have an LED screen. The device would track Soleimani in real-time on the ground. They had one almost finished. They were feverishly putting another together. This allowed Arman and Darian to both track him in the theater. The CIA geeks would pull an all-nighter to make sure these handheld monitors could be deployed with Darian. Darian made his way to a bunk inside Langley, and he got some much-needed sleep. Tomorrow would be a hectic day.

The next morning at 0600, Darian was wide awake. He had been in the country of Iran probably twelve times since being assigned to the MANOPOLY Project. But somehow, today felt far more consequential. He was going in as an active player in the game. This trip, he would not just be an invisible observer. He would be looking for clues or running passive surveillance. At 0700, he was in the mess hall, having a very substantive breakfast. His experience taught him that this almost always meant that it was uncertain when he would have another substantial meal again. He savored every morsel. At 0730, he was in the Middle Eastern commissary. He was being outfitted with area-specific tribal clothing. Also, he was being equipped with a vast array of weaponry that would be required for this assignment. He was assigned a 9-millimeter Glock with no serial numbers, four magazines, and a case of shells. He was also issued a laser guidance pointer, and a coms set that fit tightly into his ear. The coms set was set to a frequency that was very difficult for the Iranian technicians to pick up. It was an ultra-low frequency that was usually mistaken for white noise. It was also very classified. At 1000 hours, he was in the CIA technology lab. He was being trained on the operation of the handheld monitors. They were now tuned directly to Soleimani's signal. By 1100 hours, he was on a C-130 Hercules en route to Andrews Air Force Base. At Andrews, he caught a C-17 Globemaster III and flew directly into Ramstein Air Force Base in Germany. From Ramstein, he was flown directly to Tel Aviv. He continued into Tehran in the back of a farm vehicle.

Once in Tehran, he was snuck into the Red Crescent office in the Embassy of the Government of Qatar. There, he met Arman and Keller, and there, he deployed the second handheld signal monitor. In a room behind a sliding file cabinet, inside the Red Crescent's office was a small room with a sink, toilet, and a bunk bed. It would be where Darian would stay to avoid detection. He lay down on the top bunk. He put his feet up and marveled at how much more efficiently his deployment into the Iranian theater was when his travel agent was the Unites States CIA. He grinned and went to sleep, exhausted.

Chapter 96

Tensions were quickly rising between the Iranian-backed rebels in Baghdad. The continued presence of the United States military in the Green Zone remained a thorn in the side of the Shiite rebels. However, since the two Gulf Wars beginning in the 1990s, the United States Embassy had been built as a robust fortified hold. The lessons learned by America when the United States Embassy in Tehran was overrun by the Iranian student group that would become the IRGC were taken to heart. Never again would an American post be overrun in any country. The United States spent big dollars to build this fortress in Baghdad. America also had support surrounding the region in allied countries.

Students took the embassy by force and held the embassy and fifty-two American diplomats and citizens for 444 days. The lesson learned by the United States Department of State was quite simple. If America is going to establish an embassy in a hostile Muslim country, it had to be a fortified stronghold that was impenetrable. The Iraqi people had primarily accepted the United States as a stabilization force in the country. There were, however, groups of Shiite extremists that were supported and funded by Iran. The groups were always on the edges trying to cause mayhem.

Chapter 97

The box that Colonel Arman had taken off of General Nasizadeh's desk had finally made it to Whiffer. Freyredoon Adipour had delivered the box to capture data residing on the servers at American University in Beirut. Whiffer had been the one that had disassembled the first device that he found in the junction box of the cabling on the game floor. He called his old friend Jeff Jones who assisted him in identifying the first device. Whiffer was carefully disassembling the new equipment. While doing so, Jeff was taking copious notes on architectural similarities. They were searching for any like components from known sources that would match the first device. They were trying to determine if the device had been designed and built by the same man. While Whiffer disassembled, Jeff was scratching out a rough schematic so he could compare the circuitry. The schematic would also make it easier to reassemble the device after their inspection and analysis.

In reality there had never been a program for this device to capture. The plan had been a red herring designed to ensnare Adipour. Whiffer was interested in how Adipour had achieved that expressed objective. He took layer after layer of the device apart as Jeff logged his findings. They wondered how he had intended for this device to capture and store the software. As he removed the second circuit board, he saw a device that he had never experienced before. He removed the device and picked it up. He lifted it closer to the magnifying lens of his work lamp. What he found amazed them both.

It appeared that Adipour had developed a memory storage device capable of storing up to five terabytes of data. What made it so incredible was that it was miniaturized beyond modern capabilities. The industrial and military uses were innumerable. Neither of the computer geniuses had ever seen such efficient use of nanotechnology. They now knew how Adipour had planned on capturing all of the data. Whiffer quickly moved to his computer to search the international Patent Cooperation Treaty (PCT) sites to see if this technology had been patented. To their amazement, they discovered that it was an original innovation that Adipour had created. It would easily become the next generation in computer storage and for use in any espionage data capture assignment.

This meant that Whiffer and Jeff were free to patent the device. Adipour was deceased and he had not applied for patent protection. The conclusion from the investigation concluded with great certainty that Adipour was the designer and maker of both devices. The deeper this entire Iranian connection went, the more fascinating it all became. Whiffer had always believed that he was far back behind the lines when it came to espionage and international intrigue. But the recent events that had transpired with the capture of Agassi and Faruq made Whiffer very keenly aware that the front lines were always moving. He had liked Agassi. He wondered what had become of him.

Whiffer made a schematic of the new device, and he and

Jeff patented it immediately. To the victor go the spoils. He then reassembled it and sent it back into the field, in Iran. He sent it to Darian through Ali Assad, his new CIA handler. He hoped it might find a home in a secure Iranian network. He knew of nobody to better achieve this than his friend.

Chapter 98

After several months of interrogation in CIA safe houses on the Baja Peninsula, the CIA was confident that they had extricated all of the information and intelligence value that Salomon Agassi possessed. Now, they had to consider where to store him.

Muhammad Faruq was buried in an unmarked grave in Ontario. He would not make his reports back to Tehran. Now Agassi had been captive for a few months and had missed his annual trip to Tehran to visit with Ghassim Kalani. Given Kalani's proximity to Qassem Soleimani, Ali Assad had to believe that the Iranians were aware that the two had been discovered. They probably believed them to be dead, if not in federal prison.

Assad had to determine what to do with Agassi now. He could not risk putting him in a federal prison with a Muslim population. The possibility of leaks was always to be expected from guests coming in to see Muslin prisoners. Fort Leavenworth seemed a lousy match. After many high-level discussions at the most senior levels at the CIA, it was determined that Guantanamo Bay was the only safe option, at least for as long as this Ayatollah remained the Supreme Leader. As long as Agassi had such a high value to General Soleimani, he had to be protected. Eventually, he might be required as a witness in the World Courts. Gitmo seemed the only safe place to put him. Leaking intelligence could not find its way back to Tehran from Gitmo.

So, without any knowledge of where he was going, Agassi was blindfolded, handcuffed, and his feet were shackled. He was loaded into a C-130 and took off from Mexico on a United States Air Force transport to a destination unknown. Four hours later he landed. His blindfold was removed. As it was pulled from his eyes, an American Marine said, "Welcome to Gitmo, soldier." Agassi's heart sank.

Chapter 99

Qassem Soleimani was sitting in Tehran and was livid with his failures in Evanston. He was even more angered by the loss of two critical intelligence assets. Faruq had been sent as the protector for the higher-ranking and higher-valued Agassi. It had seemed with the installation of the device built by Adipour he had scored a win. The high value of the data that had been transmitted to Soleimani had tapped into the main artery of American intelligence. Now Adipour was dead, and with him, the competitive advantage that his computer genius had provided.

He also believed that having Agassi in the administration at Northwestern University was a win. He had his organization positioned to pull American technology developments and information directly from its source. And he was doing this undetected. Piece by piece, his plan in the Midwestern United States had fallen into ruins. Agassi was missing in action and failed to make any of his scheduled contacts for months. The same was the case with Faruq. He could only fear the worst. His hope was that they were dead. It was far better for his purposes that they be martyred for his cause. Anything was better than them sitting in an American jail, singing about what they knew of his operation. Soleimani was getting more and more angry and indignant. Economic factors were also getting very tight in Iran. The United States had placed sanctions on Iranian oil. This situation was beginning to boil. It was just about to explode.

Chapter 100

On December 31, 2019, Iranian-led protesters in Iraq began a siege on the United States Embassy in Baghdad. Darian and Arman were monitoring Soleimani's movements and knew that he was in Baghdad. Darian hitched a ride in a goat truck across the border into Baghdad. Darian was in a building across the street from the U.S. Embassy. He was monitoring the actions and reporting back to the CIA. Since the Green Zone was highly hardened and fortified, this would not be a siege like in Tehran in 1979.

The "protestors" took up residence in front of the embassy and seemed to act as though they might try to outwait the Americans in the embassy. The protesters cited air strikes done by the United States against Iranian-backed militias (Kataib Hezbollah) in the area. The bodies of militia fighters were paraded through the crowd. A war of words and threats ensued. The Ayatollah threatened to escalate the siege. The United States threatened to increase troop levels in response to their warnings.

The United States had retaliated over an airstrike that killed a U.S. military contractor in Kirkuk on December 27. The United States sent in 750 additional troops in Osprey

Aircraft that were able to land inside the embassy compound. The arrival of the reinforcements pretty much ended the revolt. However, Darian had seen Qassem Soleimani among the protestors in front of the embassy, and he had followed him to keep an eye on his whereabouts. On January 2, Darian began following the general and followed him back to the local headquarters of the Kataib Hezbollah group. Darian had been able to get very close as a Persian man in full beard and tribal dress. He had been communicating with Ali Assad in Langley, apprising him of actions taking place on the ground in real-time.

Darian had been able to grab a local tribal guard just outside the tent where the leaders had set up their mobile command post. He grabbed his trachea and pulled it through his neck. It both silenced him and killed him instantly. He then dragged his body off and placed it in an abandoned car nearby. He had chosen this guard because he had a walkie-talkie with an earphone. He wanted to monitor the activities and movements of the general and the leadership of the Hezbollah group. As it turned out, this had been a very fortuitous decision. The walkie that Darian had captured was one of a set of four programmed to the same channel. The channel they were set on was the one that was carried by Soleimani's bodyguard.

Darian was getting live, real-time information about where they were going and what they were planning. It would prove to be a fantastic source of intelligence that would alter the course of the Iranian stranglehold that they maintained on the Shia militia groups in Iraq.

Chapter 101

Colonel Arman was utilizing his new hand-held tracking device to keep track of the movements of the IRGC and the Quds Force. Generally speaking, where Soleimani was, the Quds Force was not far away. Knowing this made his espionage activities less dangerous. While they were in Iraq, Syria, or Lebanon, Arman had free and easy movement between the IRIAF Base and the Red Crescent office. It made the transfer of collected intelligence much more comfortable to transmit in a timely fashion.

Darian was in a situation where the ability to communicate with Assad was limited. It was necessary due to the operational silence that was required to remain undercover. So, most of the operational reports of Soleimani and Quds Force movement were reported through Arman to Keller and relayed to Assad. The CIA also had their Bluetooth tracking device functional. Still, the data being picked up on the ground in real-time had added context that exponentially increased the value of the same information.

Additionally, knowing the movements of the IRIAF's aircraft and the orders that were being communicated through the IRIAF military network in Arman's office gave the battlefield map at Langley details that it never fully had in a battle such as this. It seemed that the confluence of this incoming information had given the CIA an operational advantage. They had been hoping for a break for many months. It seemed that the stage was being set for something massive to break wide open.

Chapter 102

In the United States, the president had shown great hesitance to engage in continuing, and becoming newly involved, in overseas wars. He was far more prone to a one-time massive response when pushed beyond ordinary provocation. He showed little interest in making any additional troop deployments for long periods. He had adopted a policy that any loss of American life would result in a response of deadly force. Iran seemed very determined to draw the United States into a protracted war by continuing to fund proxies that attacked U.S. assets in the area. The attack on the Iraqi Embassy created an embarrassment that seemed likely to demand an American response. The death of the American contractor at the hands of the Kataib Hezbollah militia groups would be the event around which an American answer might be based.

Chapter 103

In the Pentagon, the Joint Chiefs of Staff were discussing all of the options available. The standard options were all discussed. One was a cruise missile strike at the Hezbollah group headquarters. Another was a strike on the Iranian oil fields (especially after Iran struck the Saudi oil fields). A general military escalation that was typical of the industrial war complex, centered in Washington. On American op-ed television and in newspapers, conservatives were calling for the devastation of the Iranian oil fields. One even advocated that the U.S. take Iran out of the oil business entirely through extensive bombings of their oilfields. Calls from everywhere were demanding that America answer this provocation. A videotape was being run on the air of the 1979 siege of the United States Embassy in Iran with pictures of the hostages, and there was a thunderous drumbeat for retaliation in the United States.

Chapter 104

Beau Benoit had a very close relationship with many of the generals on the Joint Chiefs of Staff. He had worked with them extensively in running scenarios regarding military involvement. They trusted him as a top executive in the Federal Reserve. Not everyone in the military was aware of the MANOPOLY Project. It was pretty much a "need-to-know" security program. Beau had a great deal of insider information regarding the espionage activities by the Iranians. The Chairman of the Joint Chiefs was very close to the president. And he was aware of the Iranian issue that had occurred at Northwestern University. He also knew Beau. He was listening to all of the noise surrounding the response to the Iraqi Embassy attacks. He decided to visit Beau and have an "off-the-record" conversation. He needed to better understand the encroachment into the continental United States by the Iranians.

Most of what he had heard and seen was based on satellite imagery, typewritten intelligence reports, and age-old lines. He believed these tools had been worn out years ago. The chairman wanted to know just how hard the Iranians were coming at the United States. Few had the firsthand knowledge that an attack in your own company gives a person. Beau was surprised to see the four-star general walk into his office. He stood and saluted. The general sat and looked very solemnly into Beau's face. He asked, "Benoit, tell me about your Iranian breach."

Beau was shocked! Not a word of small talk, no jokes, no inquiries about family, just straight to the point.

Beau was reticent to say very much. The NSA and the CIA had told him that the events that had transpired in the MANOPOLY Project were top secret. The FBI had become involved in tying the facts up. They had also told him to keep a lid on it. The general saw that he was struggling to say anything. He took out his secure military cell phone and dialed a number. The general stated his name and read a security alpha-numeric sequence. There was a short pause, he said, "Go, Sir." It was the President of the United States! *The president!* Beau stuttered and said, "Yes, Sir!"

The president told him that the chairman was doing a threat assessment for him. He needed to know all of the details about the Iranian breach. Beau said, "Yes, Sir!" He hung up and answered all of the chairman's questions. The general left.

Beau sank into his leather chair. *WOW!* He thought. *WOW!* He was pretty sure that what had surprised the general the most was the brazen nerve that it took to live at an American university and while doing so, burrow into a top-secret, need-to-know security program. However, to do so with no regard for consequences indicated to the general a level of disrespect that he had not understood with the reporting through formal sources.

This had been why the president sent him to talk to Beau. He wanted honesty! He didn't want a bureaucrat to tell him what they thought he wanted to hear. He wanted to hear it in person while he watched the face of the man telling it. It had been what the general needed to hear. Beau had informed him that they had been assisted by a resident intelligence officer from the NSA, and that agent was in Iran on the trail of the person who was responsible for the attack. When the general got back to the Pentagon, he demanded to know who Darian Amir was and what he was doing in Iran. Everyone in the Joint Chiefs Office looked lost. They scattered off to their offices to find out who this man was and how he got into Iran.

The military-industrial complex was playing catch up to the intellectual assets that were radiating from the center of the **MANOPOLY** Project brain trust. This project had put very diverse people together from many different backgrounds and disciplines. They all coalesced around the growth of a program that made these people all a big family. These people were simply defending their work and their friends.

Chapter 105

When a communique went out to all United States military and intelligence agencies requesting information and whereabouts of any United States intelligence asset, the answer was very quickly on the way. The NSA had picked up the request. They contacted Ali Assad in the CIA, and his boss was on the phone to the Joint Chiefs. Within the hour, a secure teleconference was starting in the Situation Room in the White House.

Darian was in an operational status that was critical. Ali Assad was the briefer on the teleconference. He informed the chairman and the president that Darian was in Baghdad. He had visual contact with Qassem Soleimani. It appeared that Iran and/or its proxies were planning some sort of escalation in the Iraqi Embassy siege. They were briefed that Brigadier General Aziz Nasizadeh's executive officer, Colonel Muhammad Arman was an undercover CIA informant inside the IRIAF. They were also informed that Jacque Keller was also participating. He also informed them that he was from the Red Crescent office in the Qatari Embassy. The men at the conference table in the Situation Room had no idea that United States assets were sitting in the middle of this hornet's nest. This information voided all of the options that had been discussed before this revelation. It also brought into focus an entire new array of possibilities that they rarely had at their disposal.

They asked operational questions. They wondered how Darian was armed and how he was equipped. They hung up and had a brand-new discussion. They discussed the plausible options in response to the Iraqi Embassy issue. The conversation quickly moved from a military response to an opportunity for an army assassination. It could radically change the Middle East for years to come. The question had, in a short time, gone from a military response question to one of American morality.

Chapter 106

The dilemma that the two men, sitting at the conference table in the White House Situation Room, was considering were being judged by two very different thought processes. The Chairman of the Joint Chiefs of Staff was a thirty-four-year military veteran. The foremost thoughts in his mind were the lives of American soldiers and the most efficient use of American power in the theater. To this man, the question was a very clear-cut academic one. It was simply one man's life versus an unknown number that would play out over an unknown period of time.

The president faced a much larger and less clearly presented fact pattern. The president had to consider what the American people would think was best. He had to consider the constituency that had elected him. Would they support his philosophy on the topic? Then, he also had to consider the Americans who did not vote for him. Would these people understand why the decision was made? Would they understand what the benefits were versus the costs?

He also had to consider what the people who write history would think. Would the academics in high schools, universities, and think tanks truly understand the nuances that were weighed before making such a weighty decision? So, the two men processing the facts were looking at the problem from the opposite ends of the problem. Ultimately, the choice fell on the head of the president. The chairman had a fiduciary responsibility to present the facts from a perspective not seen by the president. The decision, whatever it would be, was imminent. The target was very time-sensitive.

Chapter 107

Darian was in a small outbuilding next to a small machine shop in Baghdad. He was nestled behind a cart full of junk parts. They looked as though they were being collected to be taken and sold for scrap metal. The cart was covered with an old canvas tarp. The tarp appeared to be a former military tarp. It was the three colored analog camouflage. All of the new army camo was the digital pattern. However, the cart, junk metal, and the canvas provided Darian a good, safe hiding place. It was next to the mobile command post where Soleimani and the Hezbollah militia leaders were plotting their strategy. He had the earphone from the walkie stuck in his ear. The volume was turned down low enough that he could hear the discussion. He could still hear any ambient noise in the shed. He was on a hair-trigger. He was focused precisely on the opening of the shed.

Across his lap was the automatic rifle that he had taken from the guard with the walkie. The automatic had a round chambered. It was ready to fire. The Glock had one chambered and was cocked as well. He was controlling his every bodily function with his mind. He was counting his heartbeats and his respirations—all exercises he had learned to keep himself calm. He was passing the time while performing his duties. His actions were like those of a long-shot sniper. That was the mindset he was in … sit motionless and wait for any information that would indicate what the enemy would choose to do. The night was getting very late. Darian was getting very sleepy when he heard Soleimani on the phone in his earpiece. He was arranging an airline ticket for the next day from Baghdad to Tehran.

He was going to come out into the open. Darian waited until he heard the time, and the flight number. Then, he silently snuck out of the shed and off into the darkness. He was completely undetected. He made it to a safe house outside the city. He contacted Colonel Arman and Ali Assad. Now, the CIA was aware of the window that would open and the corridor in which it would open.

Chapter 108

Ali Assad quickly contacted his supervisor. They began running logistical calculations on how the mechanics of a hit on Soleimani could work. The suspected route could present a lot of unknown variables. Would the vehicle be armored? What path would he take? Could he also send decoy vehicles? The matrix of possibilities seemed endless.

Where would be the one place for a sniper to take that ONE perfect shot? It had to be a kill shot! How do you get a sniper rifle into the theater on short notice? How do you get a scope dialed in in such a short time? All of these questions seemed impossible.

From the back of the briefing room, in the most secure briefing room inside the CIA Headquarters in Langley, a dry, stoic voice said a straightforward word: "Reaper."

The room fell deadly quiet.

Chapter 109

The use of a Reaper drone in the Iraqi theater was an obvious option. A Reaper drone is not a small aircraft. The General Atomics MQ-9 has a 66-foot wingspan. It travels at a speed of about 300 miles per hour and has a range of up to 1,200 miles. It can hover at the height of 25,000 feet using a propeller engine that is almost entirely silent. The deployment of a Reaper would require the use of the United States Air Force. It was usually tasked out of Kuwait. A smart missile could be tasked. But a person on the ground would need to be present to "paint" the target with a laser pointer for the avionics to follow. Darian was equipped with such a device. However, Darian would need to be on foot to remain invisible. The exact route he would take could be changed in a second's notice. The point of execution would have to be where the different paths converged into the road going into the airport.

This option would create its own unique set of obstacles to overcome. First and foremost, it was an *airport*! All airports are equipped with the best radar in the area. Using an aircraft to hit Soleimani next to an airport would eliminate the element of surprise, if the radar picked up the drone. If the element of surprise was eliminated and the target was tipped off, there would no longer be a kill zone. The best way to work around this problem would be to hover below the radar. There was an area that was uninhabited. However, it would require a more extended missile shot. These Reaper drones had a per-unit cost of approximately sixty-five million dollars. Losing the drone was not an option. It would appear that with the options available, the Reaper was the most feasible, and it would have the highest percentage probability of success. But they would have to use a smart missile and a long, low shot.

Chapter 110

Darian had reported all of the information that he had gathered to Arman and Assad. Now he had to wait for the CIA to evaluate the options and decide the best possible way forward. Darian had established a check-in schedule. He had kept it up-to-date in case any variables changed. Darian figured that he needed to put some space between himself and the Iranian general. He also knew that Soleimani was flying out at a predetermined time. Whatever decision was reached in Langley and then in Washington, the travel time could be done during non-mission time. He let Arman know that he was moving close to the airport.

Chapter 111

In the White House Situation Room, the options that had been discussed at Langley were boiled down to the best probability of success. The intelligence community was prepared to render their best scenario for success. The Reaper strike using the human asset on the ground appeared to be the very best possible scenario. It was fourteen hours until the target was available. Ten hours until the Reaper needed to depart Kuwait. The president was running out of time to decide.

The president called a United States senator from his party to the White House for a top secret meeting in the Oval Office. When he arrived, they walked into the Oval Office and closed the door. The president sat behind the Resolute Desk. The senator sat on the end of the sofa, closest to the president.

"I need to have a discussion with you that is private. I need your personal and political opinion," the president said. "We can hit Soleimani in nine hours. What are your thoughts on political assassination?"

The room hushed. Suddenly it felt as though the temperature dropped a couple of degrees.

"Generally speaking, I am against assassination, Mr. President. But for Qassem Soleimani, I can make an exception."

The senator continued, "He has the blood of hundreds of American soldiers on his hands. It goes all of the way back to the first Gulf War." He looked at him, set his jaw, and said, "Kill him, Mr. President! The American people would expect you to do this."

The president was very stoic and somber with this message. He had been advised to do this by the Chairman of the Joint Chiefs. He had been told to do this by the senator that he trusted the most. But could he sleep at night? And would his God understand the concept of "the greater good"?

He called his Secret Service detail. He told them that he wanted to go to the Pentagon. They left immediately. In the Beast, the presidential limousine, he used his secure cell phone and called the Chairman of the Joint Chiefs. He told him he was on his way to discuss the operational details of the Reaper strike on Soleimani. He hung up and looked solemnly ahead. It was three hours until the Reaper launch and five hours until the hit.

Chapter 112

Darian had made it to a safe house and had eaten. He had been able to get a couple of hours of sleep. One of Assad's men had snuck into Baghdad to assist him. He monitored the walkie while Darian slept. There was no real chatter. There were a few bursts that had nothing to do with their operation. Assad had been advised at Langley that the Reaper would launch in three hours. The truck carrying Soleimani should be pulling into the kill zone in five hours. Darian could sleep for another hour. Then he needed to get to his nest on a building. It was on the only road into the airport. Assad had also informed Colonel Arman of the timeline. The operation had been given the code name "SCORPION." It was a go!

Chapter 113

At the United States Air Force Base in Kuwait, a Reaper drone was pulled out onto the runway. A weapons airman rolled out a guided smart missile and mounted it on the bottom of the fuselage. The drone was fueled up and inspected for flight. The pilot was sitting in an air-conditioned room on the base. There was a video camera on the hangar. There was another that viewed down the runway. The pilot hit the start button on his remote control. The propeller spun quietly up to speed. The camera eye on the nose turned 180 degrees, then back. The operator was checking the clarity of the view coming back through the lens. The picture in the monitor on his desk showed a great, full-color, high definition picture.

The operator looked up at the clock. He checked his coordinates for his target. He reviewed his weather and radar reports. Then, he slowly moved the joystick forward. The Reaper began to roll across the tarmac. It taxied onto the runway. The propeller buzzed to full speed, and the Reaper sped down the track. The drone took off and flew silently on a northwestern course. It was about an eighty-five-minute flight to the hovering destination.

Chapter 114

Darian was now up, briefed, dressed, and out the door. He was on the way to his destination. He no longer had the automatic weapon he took from the guard outside the Iranian command post. He did have his 9-millimeter Glock. Before he left, he filled the magazine, pulled the slide back, and chambered a round. This time he put the safety on. He was not expecting anyone to see him. He would be in native dress, walking on out-of-the way streets to the Baghdad airport. He planned to walk to his chosen spot, undetected and unnoticed. He would do nothing to stand out. He would walk in crowds, and he would always walk right behind cars as they pulled away from an intersection. He had timed his route the night before in case this was the operation. It would take him seventeen minutes to walk to the spot. He was on the way.

Chapter 115

Qassem Soleimani was doing his final duties before walking out of the mobile command center. He walked right over the streak of blood that was left by Darian. It was done inadvertently while pulling out the guard's throat and dragging his body away to an abandoned car. He paid no attention to the streak of dried blood.

His driver opened his door. Soleimani stepped into the truck and settled into his seat. The driver jumped up into the driver's seat, started the engine, and adjusted the rear-view mirror. He put the truck in drive and pulled out. The general was talking on his cell phone.

Chapter 116

The Reaper drone was circling the target zone at about one thousand feet. It was over an industrial area that had been abandoned after the second Gulf War. Darian was in his chosen spot. Soleimani was driving right into the target.

The two had a mutual appointment with destiny.

Chapter 117

Qassem Soleimani's driver turned left onto the paved drive to the airport. The road was just short of a mile long. As he made his turn, Darian saw the truck that had brought the general to the mobile command center. He turned on his laser pointer and held the light steady on the top of the truck. It seemed like hours had passed and the clock had stopped.

But suddenly, after about ten seconds, there was a *SWISH* sound. It was followed by a massive explosion. The truck carrying Qassem Soleimani had been completely destroyed. There were no survivors. Darian turned the laser pointer off and dropped it onto the roof where he sat. He stomped it with his heel, and he took off as quickly as he could move, away from the blast. The scene of the explosion was soon swarming with a motorcade that was moving toward him. Chaos ensued! Darian escaped in the mayhem. Project SCORPION had been executed.

Chapter 118

Immediately upon the impact of the guided missile and the explosion, Shia Muslim citizens of Baghdad were on their cell phones taking pictures. They were texting and calling the news around the Muslim world, complete with photos. The news of the demise of the great General Qassem Soleimani seemed to cover the Middle East like a massive tsunami. It set the Muslim world ablaze. The Quds Force was suddenly rudderless. Nobody had ever imagined the Iranian Shiite government without Soleimani. Who was now running the military arm for the Ayatollah?

The Supreme Leader had lost his right arm. He was immediately angry at the United States, and more specifically, the president. Within minutes, the United States news media was breaking into regularly scheduled programming to announce the assassination. On the left, the media decried the action as an immoral political assassination. On the right, they were waving the flag while invoking the memories of the hundreds of United States military personnel killed in both Gulf Wars.

Embassies around the Middle East were bracing based on how tightly they were affiliated with the United States. Israel was pleased. The Quds Force was known for lobbing missiles into the West Bank and for supplying Palestinian forces with rockets and small arms. Meanwhile, in the White House, the president was monitoring the reaction. He wondered if he had been a visionary or a butcher.

The Supreme Leader put out a scathing press release. The Iranians and the Iraqis began airing the funeral activities to inflame the Muslim world. Only time would tell how this all played out. Soleimani was succeeded by his second-in-command, Esmail Ghanni. Soleimani was executed on January 3, 2020; Ghanni replaced him the very same day. The United States pledged that if he killed American citizens that he would be dealt with in the same fashion.

The Iranians were a very pragmatic people. Having seen a brazen midday murder in the streets of Baghdad made them believe the rhetoric that was coming out of Washington. The funeral was televised. The required mourning period was observed. Tensions remained very high.

Chapter 119

Immediately after the explosion, Brigadier General Aziz Nasizadeh's cell phone rang. The Supreme Leader's office was calling to inform him of the assassination. He was instructed to begin an investigation to see how someone got so close, and who had the intelligence required to hit the motorcade so easily.

Nasirzdeh was angry, and he was driven to right this terrible wrong. He drove straight to his office and stormed inside to demand answers. Nasirzdeh walked in on Colonel Arman deleting files and shredding documents.

The general immediately pulled out his sidearm and shot Arman in the temple. He called the Quds Force intelligence officer. They immediately began an exhaustive investigation of Arman's computer. They also began searching his residence and possessions. He had undoubtedly been a mole. They needed to run it to ground. The Supreme Leader's office was notified and was anxious to receive any news.

Chapter 120

Jacque Keller was sitting at his desk in the Red Crescent on the telephone. He was speaking to reservations with Ukrainian Airlines. He was booking a flight from Tehran to Kyiv for January 8, 2020. Darian was carrying a fake Iranian passport under the name Babak Farhat. A ticket was booked for Flight 752 departing from Imam Khomeini International Airport to Boryspil International Airport in Kyiv, Ukraine. Babak Farhat was the scheduled passenger.

Darian was in a safe house. He had made his way to an old family member in Baghdad to lay low. Jacque sent the ticket to the safe house through a messenger. To make sure Darian got the ticket, he sent a secure message to Colonel Arman's personal cell phone. When the message came in, a computer forensic expert was sitting in his old chair. He was scanning the hard drive for any information that could uncover the plot.

As the forensic expert sat there, Arman's cell phone began to vibrate. It was an incoming message. The message read, "FARHATBUKRAINE1-8752." It was somewhat cryptic. It looked more like shorthand between friends in a hurry. Nonetheless, it was enough information to let the Quds Force know that something was happening. The message was sent up the chain of command, and the computer forensics expert was back to work.

Chapter 121

In the Supreme Leader's office, his intelligence officers were doing database searches. They were looking for every combination of names, letters, numbers, and country names that might solve the puzzle. Ukraine was undoubtedly in the code. Farhat was a common Iranian name. What could the numbers mean? The number of permutations that the computers produced was dizzying.

The funeral of Soleimani was a huge, made-for-television event in the Muslim world. His martyrdom for his beloved Quds Force was being turned into a major recruiting event. The funeral was unfolding on international television. The Quds Force intelligence service was working around the clock to break the mystery. What was this cryptic message that was sent to the traitor Arman?

The chief Intel officer was watching the computer printouts. He was running down name searches and intelligence regarding Ukraine. He had to figure this out. The cyber unit was also trying to run the message back to the sender. They were quickly finding that the signal had been bounced from country to country, and perhaps from continent to continent.

Whoever had sent this message had covered their tracks very well. The search was continuing at a feverish pace.

Chapter 122

Back at Langley, Ali Assad had received a coded message from Darian informing him that he would be coming back on January 8. He was scheduled on Ukraine Air Flight 752 through Kyiv. They had figured that a route through a series of Russian carriers would be less suspect than through carriers from countries closely affiliated with the United States. He also stated in his message that he was traveling on alternate credentials. It indicated to Assad that the Babak Farhat passport needed to be valid and travel records relative to that passport prepared. It required the back entry through the State Department to all countries stamped in the passport. It would create a paper trail, putting Darian through the airports and cities that had been stamped in the passport. It was done.

Further, Assad had flagged the name Babak Farhat on Ukraine Flight 752 so that when his boarding pass was issued, a notice would be generated to the State Department. It would allow Assad to know that Darian had made his flight. He would then send an agent to assist him in Kyiv. In the background, network television was playing international coverage of the Qassem Soleimani funeral.

Chapter 123

Beau has been planning a trip back to Baton Rouge to tie up some loose ends. They had been nagging at him for a while. Imogene was feeling guilty for not having spent as much time with her parents as she thought she should. Beau and Imogene had planned a trip to see them but were planning on staying at the Benoit plantation. This decision was made because Beau and Imogene did not wish to make her parents uncomfortable about the seriousness of their relationship.

Mr. and Mrs. St. John were very conservative Christian people. They had raised Imogene in the church. They attended twice every Sunday, and on Wednesday evening. They had raised a daughter that had devoted her life to Christian Service. And they watched her go off to serve as a foreign missionary. They knew that Imogene had saved herself for marriage, as had they.

They were not aware that Beau and Imogene had fallen so deeply in love. Over the long period of time that they had communicated through the years, they had shared every secret in their lives. They were unaware that Beau and Imogene had both come to a mutual decision. It had happened independently and simultaneously. They suddenly knew that they wanted to spend the rest of their lives together. Mr. and Mrs. St. John would not understand that they lived together in Manhattan. Nor that they slept together in Evanston. They would not be happy with Beau and Imogene sleeping together in their home. So, Beau and Imogene visited for the day. Then, they would drive over to the Benoit home.

Both Beau and Imogene were keenly aware that the real reason for this trip was to meet Lilly and Virgil. They had a plan to be there at 9 a.m. sharp. This was precisely when visiting hours began. It was impossible to ascertain which of these two was more excited for tomorrow. Beau had been ready to meet his dad since he was seventeen years old. This had been his life-long mission. Imogene loved this man more than anything else. She was the sole person in Beau's life that shared his secret. She had sat there and heard Beau include her in the planned visit when he spoke to Lilly. There were no words to describe the joy and pride that she felt at that moment. Nine a.m. could not arrive quickly enough.

They pulled up to the Sunrise of Baton Rouge Alzheimer's Facility on 8502 Jefferson Highway at precisely 8:56 a.m. and parked in visitor parking. They paused to gain their composure and exited the car. They stepped up to the front desk and asked for directions to room 1219. They took off down the corridor. They were walking hand-in-hand. They arrived at the closed door at precisely 9:01 a.m. Beau looked down into Imogene's eyes, nervously smiled, and they knocked.

"Come in!" Lilly responded quickly. They walked in.

For the first time in Beau's life, he saw the face that he had wondered about over many years. He found himself looking for genetic similarities. Then, he veered to the right and hugged Lilly. He addressed her. "Thank you for having us, Lilly. I am Beau, and this is Imogene."

Lilly was crying and said, "Beau, your father and I have followed you throughout your life. We never wanted to interfere with your family. But this would have meant more to your father than anything else in the world. Thank you!"

Lilly took Beau's hand with her right hand, and Imogene's with her left, and they stepped to the edge of the hospital bed. Lilly spoke. "Virgil, I have someone here to introduce you to…"

Before she could say another word, a tear or recognition ran down Virgil's cheek. He smiled and said, "Beau!" They all cried with joy.

Chapter 124

The visit to the St. John's family home the next day was enjoyable. They knew Beau. They were thrilled that he and their daughter had found a way to be together. And they were delighted by their plan to get married. They were very concerned that they find a church to attend together. They were concerned that they continue their journey as man and wife with Christ in the center.

Mrs. St. John was mesmerized by the beauty of her daughter's engagement ring. She was happy to hear that the wedding would not be a prolonged wait. They enjoyed a meal together. Beau and Mr. St. John enjoyed a St. Louis Cardinal Baseball game on television. After the game, the two couples threw some hamburgers on the bar-b-que and had a family cookout. Imogene made her specialty, potato salad. Her mom made baked beans. They had a fun meal together, great conversation, and as the sun was going down, Beau and Imogene told her parents that they had to get on the road.

They did get on the road. They drove to the Benoit family home. So, technically they had not lied! Beau was also looking in his phone for Keith Soileau's number in Baton Rouge. One of the tasks he had to accomplish while he was in town was to get the master tape of The Driftwood cover of "Hound Dog" to Teddy Carroll. Teddy had come through big time for Beau. He certainly wanted to repay the kindness!

Another thing he wanted to accomplish was to retrieve the letters that Randy Bell had written to his mother. He wanted to know what he could learn about Virgil's history and about how she had kept track of him if Beau had encountered a medical need. Beau was a man of his word. He was also a man who appreciated his personal family history. They arrived at the Benoit farm. The crops were getting very close to harvest. The horses were out running in the field. It was almost as beautiful as a landscape painted by the Dutch masters.

Beau and Imogene headed up the stairway to the second floor of the Benoit family home. At the top of the steps, they walked directly to the closet, where Beau had found the photo. That photo had set him on his path of discovery. On this trip, he knew exactly where to look. He reached for a box labeled by Patsy "1965 PATSY;" Beau remembered setting it there. He opened the box and reached in. He picked up a bundle of eight letters with a string tied around them. The letters all had the return address of 101 Beauregard in Baton Rouge. They untied the parcel, opened them, and read them together.

The letters had short messages, indicating where Virgil was stationed and when he changed duty stations. There were also a couple of old addresses. It would not be a treasure trove of lost love letters. Instead, it was the dutiful fulfillment of a promise from one old friend to another. Beau and Imogene looked into each other's eyes, kissed, and returned the letters. Then, they went to Beau's old room to get some much-needed sleep.

Beau reached Keith on the first try. He was lying down on his old bed. He informed him that he had run down the master tape and had two copies dubbed. One was intended for Teddy, and one for himself. They agreed to meet for breakfast at a local restaurant near the Benoit farm.

On his way back to the farm after breakfast, he dropped into the local FedEx store. He addressed the label to Teddy Carroll in London. He bought a small roll of bubble wrap and rolled it around the six-inch reel of audiotape. He placed it into the self-sealing shipping package and paid the freight. The counter person took the box and dropped it into the pickup-cart. Beau had fulfilled his promise to both men who had helped him find the rest of Virgil's story. The closure had done wonders for Beau Benoit. The connection of Beau and Imogene to his other set of parents had further cemented the maturing relationship between them.

Chapter 125

The three-day period of mourning for Qassem Soleimani had run its course. The Iranian Quds Force and the Ayatollah felt a cultural pull to make some sort of a military response to the blatant daylight assassination. So, on January 8, Project Martyr Soleimani was executed by Major General Hossein Salami. Salami dispatched missile strikes on two military bases used by American troops. The Ayn al Assad airbase in western Iraq and an airbase in Erbil Kurdistan were struck. There were no American casualties. There were later reports of traumatic head injury incurred by numerous American troops. It was generally considered a feeble response.

Chapter 126

Brigadier General Nasirzdeh and the Quds Force intelligence directorate had been running computer scenarios for the words from the secure message. It was meant for the traitor, Colonel Arman. One security officer had been staring at the numbers and the two words. Why not try the name on the airlines flying to Ukraine?

He searched Farhat in the airlines flying to Ukraine. He found three Farhats with airline reservations traveling in the next month. One's first name was Babak Farhat.... The letter B! He was going today, January 8...1-8... UKRAINE Airlines. And he was booked on Flight 752... 752! This was it!

He had just seen something in a file on Colonel Arman's hard drive about a Darian using an alias Babak Farhat. Farhat is a common name in Iran. Darian was the wrong given name. He made a call to the IRGC Headquarters. The intelligence directorate ran the intelligence. They hastily concluded that Darian was the assassin. He was leaving Tehran tonight on Ukraine Flight 752! Why had they not seen it? It seemed right there in plain sight after the clue from Arman's hard drive. Let's just kill this dog!

Chapter 127

Darian had made his way into the Imam Khomeini International Airport at about noon that day. He had checked in for the flight very early to make sure that his handlers in Langley were alerted to his travel. There was a significant time difference between Tehran and Langley. He wanted to make sure the passport had been validated before he went through customs.

▭

JANUARY 8, 2020

Jackson Reynold's associate, Darian Amir, was seen getting out of a taxi in front of the Imam Khomeini International Airport, Tehran, Iran. He hopped out, looked down at his watch, and sprinted to catch his outbound flight. He only had a small carry-on bag. He stopped at the Ukraine International Air terminal to have his bag X-rayed and to get his boarding pass. Since he was booked on an international flight, he also had to go through a customs checkpoint. He was directed to take off his jacket and his cotton, button-up, collared shirt. He was patted down. He emptied his pockets into a plastic bin. He walked through the metal detector.

An IRGC guard was standing next to the table with a bomb-sniffing dog. He was dressed in a digital dessert camouflage-patterned uniform of tan and brown. Also hanging on his shoulder was an Iranian-made, KL-7.62 assault rifle. The uniform was topped off with a black beret. This indicated that he was a member of the elite Quds Force. Darian was an old hand at operating in high-pressure situations. He didn't even break a sweat during his screening. He put his shirt back on. He replaced the items into his pockets. He walked up to the counter, he had his boarding pass validated, and he walked into a waiting area. He was seated and waiting to board.

He was looking around. He was making observations regarding any details in his surroundings that were out of place. He was obviously anxious and ready to be out of Iran. His flight had arrived. He watched it taxi to the boarding ramp. The plane's door opened, and the arriving passengers deplaned. The air stewards followed the last passenger, pushing a cart. The cart was for removing trash and debris from the plane. It was exchanged for a cart containing fresh soft drinks, bottled water, and juice for the outbound international flight. After about a fifteen-minute wait, the air stewards returned with a replenished supply of beverages. The overhead speaker announced, *"Passengers boarding Iran Ukraine International Airlines Flight 752 may board at this time."* This announcement sounded oddly different in Persian. He boarded. The flight was exactly on schedule.

The plane began to push back from the terminal. The Rolls Royce engines of the Boeing 737 began to whine faster, as the plane was now under its own power. It crept to the designated runway for takeoff. The flight sped toward the end of the runway. Suddenly the tire noise stopped. The plane banked to the east. Darian loosened his tie and heaved a visible sigh of relief. He settled back and readied himself for a long flight. From his window seat, he looked out the window to see the shrinking city below.

And he immediately saw an Iranian cruise missile coming at the plane.

The plane exploded. Ukraine International Airlines Flight 752 was shot down. All 176 souls were dead.

Chapter 128

The Ayatollah had received the information at the last minute. It was believed that the assassin who had killed his friend, Qassem Soleimani, was on this flight. He knew that there would be plenty of international repercussions from shooting down a commercial airliner. He didn't have time to second-guess himself. He told Major General Hossein Salami to "*shoot that dog out of the air!*" In about four minutes, the plane was on the ground, in a field close to Tehran.

There were immediate reports that the plane had crashed. It had suddenly disappeared from radar. General Salami denied any involvement. Western news agencies questioned the reliability of the Iranian claims of innocence. Then, a video surfaced on the Internet of the doomed Ukrainian flight 752 being hit by a missile and gliding down shortly after takeoff.

They were busted, and they knew it. But they believed they could hide it. They finally had to face the fact that they could not conceal the deed. The following day they had to take the blame for the fallen plane. But they never admitted that it was a blatant strike at a commercial airliner to kill one man. They had sacrificed 175 innocent people to kill one person in anger. Instead, they told the world it was an errant Iranian missile. That the missile was fired accidentally and was a residual accident from having shot the two bases that housed American troops. Would the world buy this story? Only time would tell.

Chapter 129

At Langley, Ali Assad had picked up the early check-in by Darian and had done the necessary computer work to validate the passport. He had also tasked a CIA satellite to monitor activities at the Iranian International Airport. Assad wanted eyes on the flight from Tehran to Kyiv. Assad watched via satellite. Not only had Assad seen the shot by Iran that downed the Ukrainian airliner, he had recorded it as well. And, without anyone but Jacque Keller knowing, he had instructed Keller to install Freyredoon Adipour's final device in the computer system. It was now in Soleimani's command headquarters. It was hidden in the air-conditioned office in the hangar. Ali Assad walked over to another isolated network of computers. He began watching the operational details of the complete Iranian, Quds Force, IRGC, and IRIAF military movements.

There, in the operational details of that day, he saw the order to shoot a surface-to-air missile. It was shot at the exact coordinates of the Ukrainian plane. The Supreme Leader himself had given the kill order.

Assad notified Darian's next of kin. Further, since Darian had died in the service of the CIA, Assad wrote a request to the President of the United States. A request to have another star carved in the Wall of Honor at CIA Headquarters in Langley.

Then Ali Assad called the crow's nest at the MANOPOLY Project at Northwestern University, Evanston, Illinois. Jackson answered. The entire team was in a meeting. Ali Assad told them that Darian Amir had died finishing off the conspiracy that had started there on the gym floor. The room went stone cold silent. Then, Jackson wept at the loss of his friend.

⊏⊐

THE END

About the Author

Phil has a Bachelor degree in Computer Sciences and History and an MBA. He is a world class sculptor and has pieces from coast to coast, across America. He also teaches high school art. You can view his work at www.philjonessculptures.com. This is Phil's second book. In 2009, he published *Beneath the Meniscus*, a comprehensive history of keeping freshwater and saltwater aquaria. Additionally, Phil authored two issued United States Patents in water purification. He has been published numerous times in periodicals including *Tropical Fish Hobbyist*, *Taekwondo World*, and *Sports Illustrated*. Phil is also a World Record Holder and Black Belt in the ATA.

Phil grew up in Jefferson City, Missouri. He has two living children. His son Jeremy passed away in 2017. Phil and his wife Donna share twelve grandchildren whom they enjoy tremendously. Phil is active in the local arts scene and his work can be seen all over his hometown. Phil plays guitar and loves to draw, paint, and write.

CPSIA information can be obtained
at www.ICGtesting.com
Printed in the USA
BVHW061201270620
582418BV00012B/212/J

9 781734 928808